Multicultural Education Programmes and Methods

Multicultural Education Programmes and Methods

Edited by

Ronald J. Samuda
Professor
Faculty of Education
Queen's University

and

Shiu L. Kong
Professor
Faculty of Education
University of Toronto

Intercultural Social Sciences Publication, Inc.
Kingston/Toronto

ISBN 0-921113-00-5
    0-921113-00-3

© Intercultural Social Sciences Inc. 1986
All rights reserved.

Printed in Canada by
The University of Toronto Press

Canadian Cataloguing in Publication Data
Main entry under title:
Multicultural education: programmes and methods

Bibliography: p.
ISBN 0-921113-00-5 (bound) – ISBN 0-921113-01-3 (pbk.)
1. Intercultural education.   I. Samuda, Ronald J.
II. Kong, Shiu L., 1934 –

LC1099.M85 1986   370.19′6   C86-093349-0

Contents

vi

List of Contributors

1. Kogila Adam-Moodley is Associate Professor in the School of Education of the University of British Columbia, Vancouver.
2. Jean Augustine is Principal of an elementary school in Etobicoke with the Separate School Board of Metropolitan Toronto.
3. Helen Bochar is doctoral candidate at the Ontario Institute for Studies in Education, Toronto.
4. Richard Butt is Associate Professor in the Faculty of Education of the University of Lethbridge, Alberta and President of the C.S.C.S.
5. Ernest Cheng is Research Officer at the Scarborough Board of Education.
6. Raymond Chodzinski is Associate Professor in the field of Counselling at Brock University, St. Catharines, Ontario.
7. Inez Elliston is Counsellor and Consultant at the Scarborough Board of Education.
8. Robert Harrison is Consultant at the Ottawa Board of Education.
9. Yvonne Hebert is Associate Professor at the Faculty of Education, University of Regina, Saskatchewan.
10. Ahmed Ijaz is consultant with the Scarborough Board of Education.
11. Anthony Johnstone is Commissioner of Human Rights for the provincial government of Nova Scotia.
12. Gary Kellway is head of department of English in Frontenac Secondary School in Kingston, Ontario.
13. Shiu Kong is Professor in the department of Educational Psychology at the Faculty of Education, University of Toronto.
14. John Lewis is a teacher in the correctional schools with the Frontenac Board of Education and doctorate candidate at Syracuse University.
15. Trevor Ludski is consultant in the Values Department of the Scarborough Board of Education.
16. Ed May is Race Relations Officer with the British Columbia Teachers' Federation.
17. Peter McCreath is President of the Nova Scotia Teachers' Federation and President of the Canadian Council for Multicultural and Intercultural Education.
18. Daniel McDougall is Associate Professor of Educational Psychology in the Faculty of Education, University of Calgary.
19. Karen Mock is consultant in early childhood education with Intercultural Associates in Toronto, Ontario.
20. Beverley Nann is consultant in multiculturalism at the Burnaby School Board, British Columbia.
21. André Obadia is Associate Professor in the area of French at the Faculty of Education, Simon Fraser University, B.C.
22. Michael O'Sullivan is a teacher of French in the Regina Board of Education, Saskatchewan.
23. Fernand Ouellet is Professor at the Centre for Research in Intercultural Education at the University of Sherbrooke, P.Q.
24. Bridglal Pachai is Director of the Black Cultural Centre at Halifax, Nova Scotia.
25. Karen Parsonson is doctoral candidate in the department of psychology at Queen's University, Kingston.

26. Raymond Pavlove is a public school teacher with the West Parry Sound Board of Education.

27. Ronald Ripley is Associate Professor in the area of mathematics at the Faculty of Education, Queen's University.

28. Ronald Samuda is Professor in the area of psychology and philosophy at the Faculty of Education at Queen's University, Kingston.

29. Amargit Singh is Professor of Education at Memorial University, Newfoundland.

30. Esmeralda Thornhill is a Race Relations Officer with the Quebec Human Rights Commission, Montreal.

31. Dean Wood is a social studies specialist teacher at Keyano College, Fort MacMurray, Alberta.

32. Ouida Wright is Assistant Superintendent of Curriculum at the Toronto Board of Education.

PREFACE

This volume represents the culmination of an enterprise that began seven years ago with the publication of the Ontario Ministry of Education report on the *Testing, Assessment, Counselling and Placement of Ethnic Minority Students: Current Methods in Ontario* (Samuda and Crawford *et al.*, 1980) published by OISE Press. That study documented a lack of understanding among many of the teachers, administrators and counsellors concerning appropriate methods for coping with the burgeoning influx of ethnic minority students into Canadian schools. More particularly, the study demonstrated the need for the propagation of methods and materials for use in the training of teachers and in the in-service professional development of practising teachers if the ideals of the federal and provincial policies of multiculturalism were ever to be realized.

Over the past five years, we have been intimately involved with several professional organizations concerning multicultural education. We have provided keynote addresses and workshops for boards of education, including the Public and Separate School Boards of Greater Toronto, North York, Scarborough, the Alberta Teachers of English as a Second Language, the British Columbia Teachers of English as a Second Language, the Human Rights Commission of Ontario, Ottawa Separate School Board, and Frontenac Separate and Public School Boards. We have visited and spoken with colleagues at conferences in such cities as Fredericton, Montreal, Winnipeg, Calgary, Vancouver, and Ottawa. We have come to know firsthand many of the workers in the field of multicultural education. The information gleaned from our conversations and research confirm our conviction that one of the most significant deficits in the realization of the government's policy of multiculturalism lies in the area of professional development for teachers. But, many administrators have pointed to the scanty literature and the need for manuals, books and workshop materials on which to base courses at the faculty of education level and at the in-service level for practising teachers.

It was the recognition of those needs that prompted us to try to fill the perceived gap in Canadian books dealing with Canadian multicultural-ism. Our main goal has been to specify techniques for helping teachers meet the challenge of an ever increasing diversity of ethnocultural and linguistic students in our schools across the country. This book is there-fore one in a series of anthologies resulting from the proceedings of three symposia supported by funds from the Multiculturalism Director-ate of the Department of the Secretary of State.

The first conference was really a gathering of authors interacting at the Donald Gordon Centre at Queen's University in November, 1981. That first symposium dealt mainly with the philosophy and history of multiculturalism, attitudes towards multiculturalism, as well as such factors as language, adaptation and assessment. It was essentially a theoretical and conceptual overview that culminated in a volume published by Allyn and Bacon in 1984 entitled *Multiculturalism in Canada: Social and Educational Perspectives*.

A second four-day symposium was held at the same place – the Donald Gordon Centre at Queen's University – in October, 1983. The focus was specifically on a topic that had been identified as a priority – to publish materials geared for counsellor training with the emphasis on intercultural issues and strategies. The proceedings were edited and published in a volume entitled *Intercultural Counselling and Assess-ment: Global Perspectives* by C. J. Hogrefe in 1985. It comprised sections on the theoretical concepts, comparative models and perspec-tives from multicultural countries, techniques and trends in the assess-ment and placement of minorities, counselling of specific ethnic and cultural groups, and programs for training in intercultural counselling.

This present volume follows that same pattern as the two mentioned above. It is the result of the edited versions of papers presented at a symposium at the Donald Gordon Centre at Queen's University in May 2-5, 1985. Like the two preceding symposia, the event was supported by funds obtained from the Multiculturalism Directorate of the Department of the Secretary of State in Ottawa. As the topic of this volume indicates, it is focussed on *Methods for Teaching Multiculturalism in Canadian Schools*. Like those already mentioned, this book is the edited version of papers presented at the May 1985 symposium.

As can be seen from the list of contributors, we have tried to ensure a wide variety of perspectives, techniques, programs and approaches to the implementation of multicultural education in the classroom. We have made every effort to garner the widest possible range of talent. If we are accused of concentrating our endeavours on presenters from the Ontario region, we might have to plead guilty to such a charge. The fact is that we have recruited those people who we either know to be doing effective work in the field or those specialists who have been recommended by deans of education, program officers from a variety of boards across the country, program officers of the federal multiculturalism directorate, provincial ministry officials, and fellow teachers and professors in the field of multicultural education. Obviously, no one can be familiar with every individual doing creative work in multicultural education in all the municipal jurisdictions throughout Canada.

What we have tried to achieve is a balanced mix of individuals who can offer practical and proven methods of teaching multicultural education in all its various aspects. We have deliberately included young researchers and students as well as seasoned practising teachers, union representatives, principals, consultants, and representatives from the human rights commissions and the faculties of education from various provinces.

As the table of contents demonstrates, the book is divided into five parts, namely: a) a review of the issues; 2) professional roles; 3) curriculum development; 4) teaching methods; and 5) program guidelines.

Part 1 opens with Kogila Adam-Moodley's comparative analysis of multicultural policies in West Germany, South Africa and Canada. By the use of the comparative method, she really poses the important question that many have failed to answer – multiculturalism for what purpose? She proceeds to demonstrate the very tight link between multicultural education and the sociopolitical goals of the society.

Fernand Ouellet, from the University of Sherbrooke, emphasizes the Quebec perspective. He follows by postulating the notion that multicultural education is almost meaningless without attitude change on the part of teachers. He describes a program for cultural orientation that would have important experiential effects to help gear the teacher to cope with children from a culture other than his or her own.

Peter McCreath, as president of the Nova Scotia Teachers' Union and present president of the Canadian Council for Multicultural and Intercultural Education, has been one of the prime movers in the field of multicultural education. He deftly reviews the work and involvement of teachers' unions in the promulgation of multicultural education and calls for greater commitment to training and union activities in helping to make real the ideals of multiculturalism.

Karen Parsonson's contribution is focussed on the very important issues of learning style. She makes an eloquent plea for the introduction of learning style into the teacher training curriculum and outlines for us the impact that cognitive style, achievement motivation and perceived control exert on the academic achievement of minority students.

Part 2 is concerned with professional roles. Ronald Samuda's paper deals with an overview of the training of teachers and their resulting attitudes towards the selection, administration, use and interpretation of standardized psychological tests. He summarizes the invalidity of the indiscriminate use of tests, and the trends and directions being followed to achieve non-biased assessment for ethnic minorities.

Similarly, Ed May – a race relations officer of the B.C. Teachers' Federation – deals with the problems of racism among teachers and the dire need for teachers' unions to get more involved in professional training and in changing the pre-service programs for young teachers on the threshold of professional work.

Ouida Wright's paper is concerned with the role of the administrator. As a curriculum specialist with many years of experience, she indicates some of the ways in which school boards have tackled the problems of introducing multiculturalism into the schools.

Raymond Chodzinski's focus is on the training of counsellors. He calls for sweeping changes in the ways that counsellors are trained and he delineates ways in which counsellor attitudes can be modified. The paper provides some useful guidelines for making counselling more appropriate for the special needs of minorities.

Amargit Singh's paper demonstrates the ways in which teacher expectations affect and shape a child's self-concept and can encourage or discourage successful classroom performance. He then proceeds to show how insights derived from the research on teacher perception will have special implications for the organization of teaching and learning. He follows that with suggestions of strategies that would help promote multiculturalism in schools.

Part 3 is concerned with curriculum development. Ahmed Ijaz is a consultant who has successfully implemented audiovisual and experiential programs at the Scarborough Board of Education. In this paper, he calls on his wide experience in the field to provide us with the guidelines for developing curriculum materials presented in practical point form for easy reference and replication.

Bridglal Pachai, an experienced and senior member of the educational establishment of Nova Scotia, has similarly presented us with his insights into the integration of ethnic studies into the curriculum. As director of the Black Cultural Centre at Halifax, he brings to bear a unique perspective and the wisdom gleaned from vast experience in working in a multiethnic milieu in several African countries. His insistance that multiculturalism cannot and should not be compartmentalized again emphasizes the need for teacher understanding of the real purposes and goals of multicultural education.

Karen Mock, a specialist in early childhood education, underscores the point that multiculturalism must not be regarded as a fringe or separate topic in the education of young children. Instead, it should permeate the program of training so that healthy and humanistic attitudes may be inculcated at the critical preschool stages based on accepted theories of child development and learning. She, too, calls for change in teacher training and in the retraining of practising teachers if multiculturalism is to be effective in the long run.

Jean Augustine and Helen Bochar are the co-authors of the paper dealing specifically with multiculturalism in the elementary school. They are both experienced teachers and administrators and both writers bring to bear on the issues of elementary multicultural education their wealth of experience. They provide us with the key concepts to be considered in introducing multicultural education into the elementary school curriculum and they demonstrate how the principal can lead and orient her staff to carry out the program.

In a similar vein, Richard Butt presents a comprehensive set of guidelines for the secondary school and describes, as well, practical suggestions for implementing appropriate multicultural pedagogy at the high school level. He delineates training/learning strategies and clusters for sequencing the processes so as to facilitate his pedagogical methodology.

John Lewis is a teacher/counsellor at the maximum security Kingston Penitentiary and doctoral student in intercultural counselling at Syracuse University. It is not surprising that he brings to bear on the introduction of multicultural education in the correctional schools a point of view and a set of principles born of years of practical and experiential work in several correctional institutions. He points to the fact that a vast proportion of inmates are ethnic minorities and are being forced to survive in a system that is essentially geared for the Angloceltic individual. He makes some valuable recommendations for change and once again emphasizes the need for the restructuring of the cognitive processes of the inmates and stresses the need for educators to understand the cultural differences among prison inmates so that their needs can be met accordingly.

While the first three parts of the book deal with teaching methods in a conceptual manner, Part 4 is most specific in a practical sense. André Obadia, for example, takes us step by step through the issues and concerns in preparing teachers of French for multicultural schools. In particular, he touches on the results of research in teaching French immersion and compares the methods of teaching immersion classes with those for teaching the core French program. Finally, he outlines the model employed at Simon Fraser University which has proven to be highly effective and successful.

Yvonne Hebert and Michael O'Sullivan team up in co-authoring the paper on the implementation of French as a Second Language. Calling upon their experience in teacher training and in practical classroom practice in the schools of Regina, they have proposed a series of practical methodologies for introducing and establishing French as a second language with the emphasis on core French. But their proposals call for more than information and knowledge. The need for sensitization of teachers and students, and the experience of the French culture and psyche are key elements in their paper.

Dean Wood is well equipped to deal with models and guidelines in integrating multcultural education into the social studies curriculum. His emphasis is on instructional processes and his paper is very much geared for the "hands-on" approach. He describes sample lessons and a multiplicity of media potential for fostering multicultural education in the area of social studies.

Ronald Ripley presents us with the reasons why many minority students do not participate as well or as much as the mainstream students in the learning of mathematics. He then demonstrates the results of research and suggests intervention strategies along with novel activities and materials to enhance the interest of minority students in learning mathematics and the ways in which their understanding and motivation can be significantly improved.

Gary Kellway, an outstanding teacher of English with worldwide experience, speaks essentially from the practitioner's point of view. He emphasizes the dilemma of many practising teachers in Canadian schools who were trained by traditional means in normal colleges to teach regular and normal students, but who must now face a very different kind of student audience. Teachers must now cope with an ever increasing diversity of ethnic, linguistic and cultural groups from all walks of life in their day-to-day professional practice. He suggests techniques that can contribute to better understanding and enhance a more humane and accepting climate where mutual respect and warmth forms the basis for the teaching of English that stresses the experiential background of the individual student.

Beverley Nann's paper focusses on the support services for augmenting multicultural education in a school system. In particular, she draws on her experience as a consultant with the Burnaby School Board to delineate the issues and to show how a change agent can successfully make inroads into the school system. As a comparatively major centre of ethnic minority concentration, the Burnaby School Board is uniquely situated to serve as a model for this kind of intervention.

The fifth and final part of the volume concerns the principles and techniques for the development, implementation and evaluation of multicultural education programs on a system-wide level. Robert Harrison uses his experience as a consultant with the Ottawa School Board to describe the methods for establishing leadership camps. He lists the methods for facilitating communication skills, organizational methods, and the enhancement of self-confidence, cooperation and responsible attitudes among the students in the camp.

In a somewhat similar vein, the paper by Inez Elliston and Trevor Ludski, both with the Scarborough Board of Education, define for us the principles and purposes of leadership camps in fostering better race relations between students from diverse ethnocultural backgrounds. They, too, describe the program design that involved problem identification and analysis. They then proceed to synopsize the strategies for training facilitators, program implementation and the specific use of such techniques as films and participatory exercises that augment intercultural understanding.

Raymond Pavlove, a successful innovator in developing a student interchange model at a Parry Sound elementary school describes his project in a practical and comprehensive manner. He details the various steps that precede the establishment of interchange contact and gives practical suggestions that can be readily employed by the regular classroom teacher in other schools.

Daniel McDougall also focusses on the implementing of programs to reduce prejudice. He draws our attention to the Alberta scene where he is a professor of educational psychology at the University of Calgary. This paper specifically addresses the question of how to train administrators and teachers to foster a better intercultural climate in the classroom. He deals with methods of instruction as well as novel techniques for teaching empathic understanding.

Esmaralda Thornhill's paper is passionate in its denunciation of racism. She does not hesitate to mince her words in meeting the real issue which she has aptly labelled the "collective mindset" of a large proportion of the Canadian EuroCanadian majority towards visible minorities. As a race relations officer with the Quebec Human Rights Commission, she has incisively pinpointed the crux of the problem – the existence of structural, institutional and personal racism – which must first be addressed if multicultural education is to become anything more than windowdressing.

Ernest Cheng's paper is fittingly left to the last because his task is to summarize the need for evaluating educational provisions that purport to augment multicultural education. How will we ever know that our strategies and programs succeed without some form of overall evaluation? The paper differentiates between the appraisal of multicultural programs and that of the educational provisions of which the programs are a part. Ernest Cheng illustrates the confusion that could exist in dealing with culturally different children and the importance of evaluating what has actually taken place in the course of the pedagogical enterprise in terms of programs effects, many of which may very well be unanticipated.

All in all, we have tried to produce a book that can be used by faculties of education and by boards of education in their inservice professional development in multicultural education. We have also tried to be as practical as possible and we believe that the papers included in this volume provide the substance, principles and strategies that will help foster the cause of multiculturalism in the schools across Canada.

We have tried to ensure a reasonable degree of representation from all regions of the country, but it is obvious that there is a heavy concentration of writers from Ontario. Nevertheless, we are satisfied that we did bring together a group of specialists from various fields from Newfoundland to Vancouver. The network of concerned workers in the field of multicultural education met together, shared their insights and their knowledge, socialized together, and forged links that should persist. This volume is a testament to that ongoing relationship.

In conclusion, this book is unique in a special way because the editing and production are being shared by two friends who studied together in the years from 1958 to 1961 at the Department of Psychology at the University of Ottawa. We are both agreed that Canada needs the kind of enterprise which this book represents, namely, our own means of publishing materials for the fostering of multiculturalism in Canada. And, to that end, we have established a company entitled Intercultural Social Sciences Publications, Inc. This is the first venture under that joint umbrella and we hope and expect that there will be more to follow.

We are most grateful for the support of the Multiculturalism Directorate of the Department of the Secretary of State for the provision of funds to initiate the symposium and for their assistance in the production of the proceedings. We are grateful for the assistance of Lana Kong and Keith Lowe for undertaking much of the copyediting chores and we thank Betty Shaw for typing the manuscript onto the Micom disks. Thanks are also due to Ahmed Ijaz for advice. But, above all, we thank our contributors for their participation and for the good papers that we hope and expect to make a significant impact on the cause of multiculturalism in improving the teaching methods in the schools and fostering better programs in the school systems across the country. Finally, we hope our fellow professors, ministry and board administrators and teachers will find this book useful in enhancing teacher training in multicultural education.

R.J.S.
S.L.K.
1986

PART I

Reviewing The Issues

The Politics of Education in Three Multicultural Societies: Germany, South Africa and Canada

Kogila Adam-Moodley

In many plural or culturally heterogeneous societies, a multicultural education policy has been adopted to reconcile the divergent segments and to integrate the minorities into the larger society. The merit of multicultural education is taken to be self-evident, similar in content and intention in different political settings. This purely education-centred view of most pedagogues turns out to be a myth. Multicultural education not only means different things to different people in one society, but it is also profoundly shaped by the economic exigencies and distinct political ideologies of different societies. Comparative analysis can shed light on the crucial question of: "Multiculturalism for what reason?" By comparing multicultural education in West Germany, South Africa and Canada, the fallacy that the concept is apolitical can be demonstrated. A comparison can also increase the awareness of the practitioner in the classroom by including the socioeconomic origins and political implications through reflection on the optimal educational policy in a multicultural environment.

Comparative studies of culturally diverse societies have taken different forms. In the United Kingdom this area of study has its roots in the anthropological tradition of colonial research, especially during the 1930s and 1940s. In North America more recent comparative ethnic studies lie essentially in the domain of political science. Nation-building in the decolonized societies of the Third World became the focus of analysis in the tradition of modernization theories and development studies. A vast literature on ethnicity deals with issues of political power in divided societies (Horowitz, 1971; Enloe, 1973; Young, 1976; Jackson, 1977). With the modishness of ethnicity in the 1980s and the discovery of ethnic revival and persistence, studies in education reflect the current trends in the social sciences as a whole.

Analyses of multicultural education have been categorized in two ways (McLean, 1981): The first are those that attempt to comprehend particular educational policy responses to specific forms of culturally, linguistically and racially divergent populations. These policies range from assimilationist to pluralist orientations (Hans, 1949a, 1949b; Mumford, 1935). The second type of analyses are those that view the effects of (a) similar policies in different national contexts (Singleton, 1977; Wirt, 1979; LaBelle and White, 1980; Grant, 1977; Watson, 1979; Holmes, 1980), or (b) varying policies in apparently similar heterogeneous societies (Kirp, 1979).

It is along the latter lines that this paper compares state policies on the education of minorities in three societies: Canada, South Africa and West Germany.While the three settings differ considerably in their histories, political values, human rights records and educational policies, there are some commonalities. All three societies consider themselves Western-style liberal democracies, although in South Africa this applies to the dominant minority only.All three societies have experienced waves of immigration from culturally divergent societies. In South Africa, the longstanding conflict is not with newer immigrants but with the native inhabitants and a smaller Asian minority. Both Canada and South Africa share a multilingual population within an official bilingual order. Germany, on the other hand, is basically unilingual and does not consider itself an immigrant society. Its ten-percent population of "guest-workers" in the labour force remains an alien presence in a caste-like system. The similar economic needs in all three societies have, however, led to quite different educational policies, based on different political cultures and perceptions of identity of the dominant sector.

State policies concerning the education of minorities are firmly linked with political hegemony.While the idea of multiculturalism has been expressed elsewhere, it is only in Canada that it has been entrenched as official policy. In 1971, the policy was the Liberal Government's solution to the impasse that had developed in French-English relations, the constant tensions surrounding Native rights, and the pressure to recognize immigrant minorities. While acknowledging the special claims of the French Canadians and, to a lesser extent, of Native people, the policy neutralized all minorities under the status of "equal groups." By formally acknowledging the varieties of cultural adherence within the Canadian mosaic, the cultural hierarchy was in no way threatened, but rather, stabilized by the diffusion of claims of inferiority and superiority as a result of the concept of pluralism. Conservative and social democratic administrations alike have subsequently embraced the policy with enthusiasm. The Canadian mosaic was elevated to a national consensus.

In the case of Germany, the school system was totally unprepared for the influx of 4.5 million foreign immigrants and their children, starting in the late 1960s. The federal state does not recognize the permanency of this de facto immigration. By treating the migrants as sojourners, the government has adopted an educational laissez-faire policy. This lack of direction has been partially remedied by regional responses to minority integration in an obvious educational crisis in a staunchly monocultural society.

In South Africa, educational policy in the fifties and sixties was developed explicitly as a tool for implementing political apartheid. The country's four racial groups were expected to be proud of their imposed identity. Black education beyond a minimal level was considered dangerous to white dominance. However, with the breakdown of apartheid ideology under economic imperatives, the curriculum can no longer be racialized. The debate focusses not only on educational content but on the differential allocation of expenditure and the most appropriate organization of a segregated system for an integrated economy.

West Germany relies heavily on the labour of foreign workers. Most prominent among these are Turks, Yugoslavs and Greeks. They comprise 12 percent of the entire labour force. In some cities, such as Berlin and Frankfurt, the percentage of permanent foreign citizens approaches 25 percent. Although further recruitment was banned in 1973, the numbers continued to swell due to the entry of family members who were permissible immigrants. While their labour fills a need, the presence of these foreign workers is ambivalently received. Stringent criteria preclude most of them from qualifying for citizenship, although it is theoretically possible after ten years of uninterrupted residence. Most foreign migrants do not wish to give up their original citizenship or to return to their impoverished country of origin. This applies particularly to migrants from Turkey who comprise more than one-third of all foreign workers.

The German anxiety about not legalizing a de facto immigration society is based on two factors: (1) a commitment to a monocultural state which would require complete assimilation by the foreigner; and (2) a desire to avoid importing religious and ethnic turmoil from the periphery to the centre (Wilpert, 1983). For the most part, Turkish guest-workers living in West Germany are reluctant to shed their culture and continue to live as rightless, stigmatized foreigners, even though they have acquired permanent residence status and welfare benefits.

In contrast to the German situation, the Canadian policy is primarily one of immigration. Immigrants may acquire citizenship after two years of residence. Official policy values the retention of cultural heritages, and dual citizenship is permissable. At the same time integration into and political adaptation to one nation is stressed.

South Africa combines the coercive directness of the German policy with lip service to an official multicultural policy similar to Canada's. In the name of continued sound race relations, South Africa excludes the indigenous majority from political participation in the central parliament and gives only symbolic recognition in separate chambers to longstanding minorities of colour, such as Indians and so-called Coloureds. Hence, the numerical majority is reduced to the status of immigrants, eternally awaiting participation of any kind in the polity. The state, in its official rhetoric, values cultural diversity and self-determinism only along the lines it specifies and controls, while it fragments the numerically stronger majority.

Unlike the situation at the beginning of the century, Canadian immigrants now emanate from both rural and urban backgrounds. They are distributed throughout the occupational strata, are generally economically upwardly mobile and are achievement-oriented. While European minorities have greater success in attaining positions of status and power, visible minorities, despite their ongoing battle with subtle racism, also strive for white-collar and professional occupations. Consequently, they are found throughout the social structure, save in the top echelons of the power elite.

In contrast, immigrants in Germany come mostly from working-class and peasant backgrounds. Their educational level is accordingly low. In their new society they continue almost exclusively in menial jobs or low-status positions in the service sector.

The South African situation is more complex. Black South Africans are largely in the same position as guest-workers in Germany. Caste barriers have been slow to shift. Indians and, to a lesser extent, Coloureds occupy the "middle-man" minority role as small traders and middle-management civil servants and workers. As is to be expected, they have their own bourgeois and white-collar middle classes, in contrast to the African majority which mostly belongs to a ghettoized urban proletariat.

In all three societies, the economic roles fulfilled by the "minorities" (so-called in South Africa) are vital in the overall division of labour.

Their level of education, literacy and skill is crucial to their productivity. A more detailed description of the educational policies in the three countries follows, which points out their differing definitions of multiculturalism in the context of different economic and political exigencies.

West Germany

Given the decentralization of education in Germany and the autonomy of the different states or *Länder*, no one policy applies to all of the states. What consensus does exist is that: (1) compulsory education should be extended to include all children, including those of foreign workers; and (2) pre-school and preparatory education should provide assistance to foreign children making the transition into German society. The recommended practice was to continue mother-tongue instruction and subsequently move into German. There was widespread recognition of the right of foreign children to be educated in their own language. Whether this should be done by teachers from the home country or by German teachers trained in those languages is still contended. The preference seems to lie heavily in favour of the former.

Less consensus prevails on the issue of whether the children of guest-workers should be integrated into the regular school system or educated in separate schools. Those provinces in favour of incorporating the minorities into German society are supportive of integrated education as well. The aim is to accept their presence officially and pursue a policy that neither assimilates them nor segregates them into impenetrable ethnic ghettos (Rist, 1979:350).

The success of educational integration has been substantial. In the most populous German province, Nordrhein-Westfalen, 95 percent of all foreign children are now taught in the same classes as Germans, whereas in 1980 almost two-thirds were instructed separately. The failure rate of foreign children has declined from 60 percent in 1980 to 30 percent in 1985. In this relatively progressive province with 220,000 foreign children (140,000 of whom are of Turkish origin), the percentage of foreign students in the various types of German high schools has also doubled since 1980, with the result that three percent of the students at the most demanding and prestigious gymnasiums are non-Germans.

By contrast, conservative strongholds like Bavaria have pursued separate educational arrangements on the grounds that they facilitate identity maintenance and the return to the homeland. Very little is said on whether or how guest-worker children should be integrated into the school system. This perhaps reflects the ambivalence felt by the majority concerning their presence. They are expected to work and function in the economy like competent Germans, yet are supposed to never lose sight of their roots in their country of origin, to which they are eventually expected to return. The problem extends even further in that the roots of many involve Islamic principles. Given the revival of strict Islamic orthodoxy, there is a dread that the Koran schools currently involved in the maintenance of guest-worker culture may well be antithetical to the German ethos of sexual emancipation and civil secularization.

Under conditions of increased unemployment, guest-workers are often prime targets of hostility. Newcomers are sometimes seen as the cause of unemployment for native Germans and a drain on limited resources. This social insecurity spills over into a competitive educational system. Ursula Boos-Nunning (1981) cites the antagonism of a German father who fears a lowering of standards.

> In recent years it has been shown that the other schools with lower concentrations of foreign students have a noticeably higher level of educational performance. The few German children, who are still being born, should be given the optimal attention (*Schulreport* 3/1979:18).

Immigrant children in Germany face some of the problems of immigrant working-class children everywhere. They lack the material and financial resources to succeed in the way that their German counterparts do. Due to their parents' limited education and their lack of fluency in the German language, they are also unable to draw upon the parental resources that the German children have. This is especially evident in the area of homework which is heavily emphasized in German schools (Rist, 1979:366-367). Moreover, they are raised in a marginal way, neither knowing the land of their so-called roots nor accepted in the only society they do know. The school curriculum tacitly emphasizes that they do not and will not count. This situation of structural segregation is especially poignant for second-generation immigrant children.

South Africa

As is well known, South Africa uses segregated educational institutions at all levels for its four racial groups, regardless of linguistic and cultural commonalities between them. This practice enforces the separation of different segments of society in residential areas and political rights. The intellectual underpinnings of apartheid in the school curriculum, particularly in history textbooks, has been amply documented. The texts are mainly devoted to events in Afrikaaner history with little reference to pre-colonial Africa. The colonial and Eurocentric bias sees history mainly in terms of competing nationalities. Blacks are portrayed as posing problems for the whites. Black poverty is assumed to be a natural state. The apartheid doctrine, however, is not based specifically on the teachings of racism, but on the more insidious myth that whites occupied an empty land, that black underdevelopment is self-imposed, and that the conquerors amply deserve their spoils.

The gross inequality in education merely reflects the larger inequality in life opportunities. In addition to facing many legal barriers, black students coming from materially impoverished backgrounds are severely handicapped in competing with their white counterparts. The vastly higher drop-out rates for black students are merely one indicator of this problem. The educational system does little to compensate the societal inequality but, in fact, reinforces it by a differential allocation of resources along racial lines. The expenditure per capita for a black student is one-tenth of that for his or her pampered white counterpart. As a consequence, teacher-student ratios are much higher in the poorly equipped black schools, in comparison with the much better facilities of the other groups.

However, the different racial groups are no longer taught according to different curriculum norms and standards. At the end of the secondary school phase, black school-leaving students write an examination similar to that of white students. Black students are required to meet the same requirements for matriculation exemption as any other candidates. They also have to write these tests in their second language, English. The language of instruction for the first four years is one of the black languages, after which English, almost without exception, is adopted as the medium. This is done at the behest of the black communities themselves.

Both the inferior resource allocation and the second-language instruction combine to ensure a much higher failure rate for blacks than for whites, despite similar syllabi. However, better education ranks at the top of all black aspirations. Good educational credentials are seen as the only feasible route to a better life and at least minimal status in a society where most other normal routes for advancement are blocked.

The state has had to respond both to the political frustrations expressed in black educational institutions and to the shifting economic imperatives of a more skilled work force.

Beginning in the early seventies, and accelerated by the Soweto uprising in 1976 and the rise of the Botha administration, a new ideological discourse was developed and adopted by the South African state. "Separate development" was no longer a goal worthy of being pursued because of its intrinsic value. Rather, it became an ad hoc policy to be applied, modified, or even discarded according to other imperatives. This instrumental legislation allowed state planners to be pragmatic. No longer bound by a sacred ideology or principle, they could show flexibility and compromise in accordance with changing pressures and exigencies. In short, the dominant group increasingly embraced a technocratic perception of its political environment.

The new alliance between government and big business, together with the split in the ruling party, helped to push economic needs onto the agenda and ideological concern in the background. The need for manpower in the economy now dominated the educational debate. It was no longer possible to restrict blacks to being hewers of wood and drawers of water, as in the old "Bantu" education policy. The developing need for a skilled work force, trained in vocational and technical skills that the white sector alone could no longer supply, altered educational priorities. In addition, the new strategy of co-opting the relatively privileged black urban sector into the system opened up the prospect of higher education for future black middle classes. The policy was envisaged as a bulwark against the rural underdogs and as a stabilizing force for free enterprise.

Thus far, both of these expectations have failed to materialize. The anticipated depoliticization and defence of the status quo by relatively privileged black students have instead turned into the most politicized and longlasting school unrest the society has ever experienced. Petty grievances about learning conditions were combined with the much deeper resentment blacks felt of being second-class citizens and of having no future in the new constitutional design and rather stagnant economy. The prime targets of co-optation – the urban, educated black sectors with the much sought-after residence and work rights – have turned out to be the most militant rejectors of the new policy, voicing grievances about the imposed racial order. Simple material promises have not succeeded so far in diffusing the feelings of deprivation and injustice.

The dissent continues, despite increased expenditures on black education. Although the overall unit costs (excluding capital expenditure) in 1984-85 of R 156 per black student, R 498 per Coloured, R 711 per Indian and R 1211 per white, still reflect vast discrepancies, the educational budget has superseded military expenditures. Much of this budget is, of course, spent on needless duplication of segregated facilities. However, salaries of teachers with the same qualifications have been equalized, although only 24 percent of the 120,650 black teachers in 1982 had the minimum requirement of senior certificate plus professional training. Most black teachers were severely underqualified, or had no professional training at all.

The dilemma of the educational system lies in the economic need to train people, which undermines the restrictive intentions and purposes of the education policy. Whereas the number of white students has basically remained the same, in line with the declining white population, the number of black students at the various educational institutions has increased rapidly. Between 1978 and 1983, the number of black students at secondary level educational institutions increased from 467,000 to 678,500, and from 19,000 to 44,300 at the tertiary level. The appearance of sizeable numbers of black university graduates on the job market is a recent phenomenon and distinguishes the South African economy from its African counterparts elsewhere.

An educated class of this size can no longer content itself with political rightlessness, even if substantial payoffs are offered. It is precisely the fulfillment of material equality that has enabled black groups to tackle the political and social inequalities. The South African educational system has yet to find an answer to this predicament.

The establishment has diagnosed a crisis of education in South Africa. Various commission reports, notably that of the de Lange Commission, no longer discuss the crisis in terms of ideological content or curriculum, but in terms of organization. What now dominates the debate is how scarce resources should be allocated among the racial groups, and how educational administration should be effectively organized.

There is a tendency by the establishment to ignore the political underpinnings of the racial conflict in education and the society at large, by treating the antagonisms as a management problem. By contrast, the political perspective of most black activists is directly focussed on conflicting interests. They probe how competing claims can be reconciled through institutionalized bargaining. They explore how different parties can be empowered to participate meaningfully in the bargaining process, according to mutually acceptable procedures that bestow legitimacy to the process.

The government, in its management approach, adopts manipulation as its principal technique. It is one-sided, imposing solutions on the weaker party in the hope that it will succumb to the stronger. It denies that there are conflicting interests. It assumes that the interest of the dominant party also benefits the others. The question becomes one of removing obstacles (i.e., "agitators") from an assumed consensus on the part of all concerned. At the same time, the educational policy aims to fragment resistance and co-opt useful allies. The slightest provocation, however, triggers coercion. While a manipulative management of conflict may succeed in the short run on the basis of superior resources, it lacks social legitimacy and carries with it the increasing costs of enforced domination, as compared with the political incorporation of universal franchise and equal citizenship.

Canada

Multicultural education in Canada reflects much of the ambiguity that the government policy itself embodies. The policy has had a mixed reception, ranging from ignorance of what it means to fear that it may Balkanize the nation. Essentially, however, multicultural education takes place as something superimposed upon an Anglo-Saxon mainstream curriculum. Arguments in favour of this approach are varied. Multicultural education emphasizes the equal value of all cultures and attempts to redress the diminished image of non-white backgrounds (Wilson, 1984). It has been seen as a way in which the self-concepts of minority children are boosted by including their heritages and presence in the curriculum (Bagley, 1981). However, others see current multicultural education as a superficial palliative, which does little to combat the problems of language education, inequality of access and the covert racism that differentiates between physically assimilable minorities and visible ones. Hence, the praxis of multicultural education is very varied. This is compounded by the fact that there is no national policy on multicultural education. Each province assigns its own priority to different agendas. Some provinces, such as Ontario, Alberta and Saskatchewan, have firmly committed themselves to the goal of multicultural education. Other provinces pursue very focussed attempts at local levels, such as the Vancouver School Board, which has confronted the issue of race relations in conjunction with representatives of local communities.

Underlying the mixed reception of multicultural education is the fact that a pluralistic view of Canadian society is only nominally accepted. More rhetoric than practice is evident in the attempt to recognize a pluralistic society. The celebration of cultural differences at the educational and ideological level has not been carried through to the high-level social and political positions, which generally remain solidly closed to ethnics, especially visible minorities in Canadian society.

As long as multicultural education continues in this vein, de-emphasizing access to real power, multicultural education can continue to have a peaceful existence.In this respect, it is not controversial in the same sense that minority education is in South Africa or Germany.

Conclusion

The German and South African case studies indicate that education of subordinate groups cannot succeed in any meaningful way unless the political question of "Education for what reason?" is first solved, satisfactorily. Curriculum experiments, administrative reorganization and shifting of educational expenditures are not substitutes for unre-solved political contradictions. Successful education of minorities hinges on a political consensus between the dominant and subordinate groups. Canada's multicultural policy, despite its ideological overtones and obvious political motivations, comes closest of the three to satisfying the educational aspirations of both the majority and minority in an ethnically divided society, and should continue to do so as long as it can avoid the political consequences of its logic.

References

Boos-Nunning, U. (1981). Muttersprachliche Klassen für auslandische kinder: Eine kritische Diskussion des bayerischen Offenen modells. *Deutsch Lerner, Zeitschrift für den Sprach unterricht mit auslandischen Arbeitnehmer, 21*, 40-70.

Enloe, C.H. (1973). *Ethnic conflict and political developments*. Boston: Little Brown.

Grant, N. (1977). Educational policy and cultural pluralism. *Comparative Education, 13*(2).

Hans, N. (1949). *Comparative education*. London: Routledge and Kegan Paul.

Hans, N. and Lauwerys, J. (1949). The problems of independence. *Yearbook of Education*.

Holmes, B. (Ed.) (1980). *Diversity and unity in education*. Allen and Unwin.

Horowitz, D (1971). Multiracial politics in the new states: Toward a theory of

14

conflict. In R.T. Jackson and M.B. Stein (Eds.). *Issues in comparative politics* (pp.164-180). New York: St. Martin's Press.

Jackson, R. (1977). *Plural societies and new states.* Berkeley: University Press.

Kallaway, P. (Ed.). (1984).*Apartheid and education.* Johannesburg: Raven Press.

Kirp, D.(1979). *Doing good by doing little.* Berkeley: University of California Press.

La Belle, T.J. and White, P.S. (1980). Education and multiethnic integration. *Comparative Education Review, 24*(2).

Marcum, J.A. (1982). *Education, race and social change in South Africa.* Berkeley: University of California Press.

McLean, M. (1981). Comparative approaches to multiculturalism and education in Britain. Occasional Paper No. 33. London: University of London Institute of Education.

Mumford, W.B. and Orde-Brown, G.S. (1935). *Africans learn to be French.* Evans.

Rist, R. (1980). *Die ungewisse Zukunft der Gastarbeiter, eingewanderte bevolkerungsgruppen verandern Wirtschaft and Gesellschaft.* Stuttgart.

Rist, R. (1979). On guest-worker children in Germany. *Comparative Education Review, 23*(3), 355-369.

Samuda, R., Berry, J. and Laferriere, M. (Eds.). (1984). *Multiculturalism in Canada.* Toronto: Allyn and Bacon.

Singleton, J. (1977). Education and ethnicity. *Comparative Education Review, 21*(2/3).

Watson, K. (1979). Educational policies in multicultural societies. *Comparative Education, 15*(1).

Wilpert, C. (1983). From guestworkers to immigrants: Migrant workers and their families in the FRG. *New Community, 1*(1/2). 137-142.

Wirt, F.M. (1979). The stranger within my gate: Ethnic minorities and school policy in Europe. *Comparative Education, 23*(1).

Young, C. (1976). *The policies of pluralism.* Madison: University of Wisconsin Press.

Teachers' Preparation for Intercultural Education

Fernand Ouellet

I n the last few years, intercultural education has appeared on the agenda of many Canadian educators. There is growing awareness of the responsibility of schools and colleges for the promotion of a better understanding of cultural diversity in Canadian society; of more positive attitudes toward the various cultural groups; and of a greater recognition of their contribution to Canadian life. However, if this awareness is to result in a coherent strategy for the development of intercultural education in our schools, it is essential that educators should reach at least a minimal consensus on the general objectives of intercultural education. And, since school and college teachers are likely to play a crucial role in the implementation of a policy on intercultural education, I will concentrate here on the general objectives for the training of teachers, focussing on three main problems:

1) Is intercultural education mainly concerned with students from minority cultural groups or with all students in a school?
2) What is intercultural education? What would be the main ingredients of an ideal training program for teachers?
3) How would it be possible to generate among school and college teachers enough interest in intercultural education to get them involved in such a program?

There is a general tendency among educators to define intercultural education in relation to "problems" experienced by teachers and counsellors dealing with substantial groups of students who belong to cultural minorities. Even if it is recognized that multi-ethnic schools represent a unique situation and that special attention must be given to providing help and guidance to teachers and counsellors working in these schools, it is important to resist the tendency of defining intercultural education as a "special" service offered only to minority group students. Such an approach could leave the monocultural character of the school system intact and, by implication, teach majority students that pluralism is not a problem for them but only for minority students who must integrate into a new society.

If the school is to contribute significantly to the promotion of collaboration and better relations between members of the various cultural groups in the country, intercultural education must become a priority not only in multi-ethnic schools but in all schools. Its objectives must be defined in such a way that it might be shown to all students, whether they are members of a minority or majority group, that their education is incomplete if they have not learned to deal with the problems of cultural diversity.

Even if the institutional logic of the school system tends to promote the restrictive view of intercultural education as a special service offered to a special group of "clients" – namely, minority students experiencing learning difficulties and problems of adjustment to their adopted society – we must still look for a broader definition of intercultural education, a definition that would apply to *all* students and not only a minority. This leads us to the second of our three problems: "What is intercultural education?"

For the members of the *Collectif de recherches interculturelles de l'université de Sherbrooke*, intercultural education is defined as the systematic effort towards the development, among members of majority groups as well as minority groups, of:

1) a better *understanding* of the various cultures;
2) a greater capacity to *communicate* with persons of other cultures;
3) more *positive attitudes* towards the various cultural groups of society.

Our knowledge of the means of promoting such noble values is still very scanty. The concepts of intercultural understanding and intercultural communication are themselves very complex, and it is often difficult to know if those who use the terms speak of the same thing.

With the help of research assistants, I have tried to explore some of the cognitive operations involved when high school students try to understand a foreign culture. The theoretical framework of this research has been centred around an "ideal" form of these cognitive operations. In order to get a clearer picture of the contribution that educators could make to intercultural education, I will give here a brief outline of this theoretical framework.

Our research has led us to distinguish three distinct groups of cognitive operations involved when a person tries to understand a foreign culture.

1) A strategy of *insiders' understanding*, where one tries to give an interpretation of the various manifestations of a culture through the "auto-interpretations" provided by members of that culture.
2) A strategy of *scientific hetero-interpretation*, where one tries to give rational explanations of the various manifestations of a culture from the transcultural point of view of a scientific discipline.
3) A strategy of *critical relativisation*, where one tries to identify the various factors that give their partial and provisional character to the understanding of other cultures obtained through the first two strategies, and where one may acknowledge that all cultural productions are essentially relative and conditioned.

At the present time, we have been able to distinguish eight cognitive operations related to one or another of these three strategies.

1) *To try to give interpretations of the various aspects of a culture of a given group through an explication of their relations to the total system of representations of the group.* (Strategy a) If there is a lesson that is clear in the classical and recent developments of anthropology, it is that a given cultural product cannot be understood correctly if its relation to the total cultural system in which it belongs is not brought into the picture. This supposes a longterm study, in which one tries systematically to see things from the perspective of members of the culture under study.
2) *To try to indicate the situation of the various auto-interpretations that have been gathered among the different ideological tendencies of the group.* (Strategy a) Modern anthropology and sociology have insisted on the necessity of recognizing the plurality of conflicting ideologies within a given social group. The concept of intercultural understanding must be formulated in such a way that it would take this plurality into account and not give a privileged status to a given ideology.
3) *To try to find some explanations other than those provided by the members of a culture when one tries to understand an aspect of it.* (Strategy b)

4) *To describe with precision the cultural manifestations that are under study.* (Strategy b)

5) *To provide an explanation for the specific characteristics of a given cultural manifestation through the use of the concepts and the ways of scientific thinking.* (Strategy b) However important, the participant's point of view, with all its ideological stances, is not the only one that has to be considered in a definition of intercultural understanding. Science is now an integral part of the common cultural heritage of humanity, and members of all cultures must learn to deal with the transcultural point of view of scientific rationality. There is a wide range of positions here. Some researchers tend to reject scientific rationality in the face of a cultural entity whose sacred foundations they consider beyond the reach of scientific enquiry. Others tend to reject the irrationality of culture in the name of a scientific humanism which has a mission to eliminate those aberrations.

6) *To try to clarify the nature and scope of ideological and scientific discourse.* (Strategy c) We have now reached the third group in our model of cognitive operations: the strategy of critical relativisation. The participant's ideological stance and the observer's scientific analysis must not be considered as dogma that must be accepted according to the prestige or authority of the person who presents it. Such an attitude would accentuate intercultural misunderstanding rather than understanding. It is only through a critical effort to clarify the nature of ideological and scientific discourses and to see the specificity and limits of these discourses, that it is possible to go beyond the fruitless confrontations between different dogmatic stances and to seriously start on the difficult road to understanding.

7) *To be constantly vigilant in order to identify one's own cultural bias in one's interpretations of another culture.* (Strategy c) This second aspect of the strategy of critical relativism implies that one becomes conscious of a fundamental difficulty that can never be completely overcome: the impossibility of developing the interpretation models needed to understand a foreign culture without being influenced by one's own culture. A strategy of critical relativisation aims precisely at minimizing as much as possible this influence in our interpretations of foreign cultures. This necessitates a constant effort to identify the hidden postulates of one's own culture and subculture. That is why it is right to say that training for intercultural understanding requires as much attention to the exploration of one's own culture as to that of others.

8) *To define one's position towards the theories of cultural relativism, which tend to postulate the diversity of cultures and the essentially relative and conditioned character of all cultures.* A definition of intercultural understanding that tries to take into account the viewpoints of the participants and the scientific observers cannot ignore the debate between the proponents of a theory of "cultural pluralism" and the proponents of a theory of "levelling." The theory of cucltural pluralism is based on a double presupposition. It postulates the possibility for each culture to develop visions of mankind and systems of values and beliefs whose characteristics make them incomprehensible to another culture. But this postulate is not possible unless the person who adopts it recognizes that her own world view, values and beliefs are also the product of a culture, and unless she is ready to redefine her relations to her own cultural model while exploring foreign cultures. The ideology of cultural pluralism, then, seems impossible to dissociate from cultural relativism.

At the other extreme are those who have put forward the theory of "levelling" and who postulate the disappearance of distinct cultural entities and the development of a single world society. We do not have to decide between these two extreme theses, but since this debate is part of the ideological context in which the problem of intercultural understanding is being raised, our concept has to permit a critical discussion of the theories of cultural relativism.

From the outline presented here it is clear that education for intercultural understanding means more than simply giving factual information about exotic aspects of other cultures, or delivering exhortations on the values of pluralism. It assumes a serious attempt to gain understanding into at least one other culture and to define one's position in relation to it. This is not an easy task, and in this field as in any other, good intentions are not enough. Specific educational strategies will have to be developed if schools genuinely want to provide students with the intellectual equipment they need to deal with the reality of cultural pluralism, both at the national and international levels.

However, if the cognitive strategy of intercultural understanding did not lead to better communication between individuals belonging to different cultures, it would have only a theoretical value and would be difficult to use to give a more definite content to the concept of intercultural education. Intercultural communication has become a recognized field of study in the last ten years, especially in the United States. It represents a special form of communication where the "producer" of a message belongs to one culture while the "receiver" belongs to another. According to Samovar and his collaborators, the researchers of intercultural communication have focussed on three main problems: perception, language and non-verbal processes. One of the main objectives of these researchers has been to find the best ways of developing "skills" likely to contribute to the improvement of intercultural communication.

Educators wishing to promote intercultural education have much to learn from these studies, but they must be aware that it is possible to develop intercultural communication skills while at the same time holding uncriticized monocultural or assimilative assumptions.

In light of this brief presentation of our conception of intercultural education in terms of intercultural understanding and communication, it appears that very serious and complex issues are involved. In order to be able to face these issues in a critical and pedagogically creative way, it is clear that the educator needs a solid and systematic training program and not only a few isolated sensitization sessions. This belief underlies the teacher training sessions of the *Collectif de recherches interculturelles de l'universite de Sherbrooke* in the field of intercultural education. We believe that a program of in-service teacher training has a better chance of success if the initiative comes from the teachers themselves and if it is centred on projects that are pertinent to them. But the complexity of the problems calls for close collaboration with specialists in the field for the planning, realization and evaluation of such training projects in intercultural education.

In light of the previous discussion, it is now possible to outline the main ingredients that, ideally, should be included in any systematic program of teacher training in intercultural education. We have distinguished twelve main subjects to which a competent teacher should be introduced. These subjects can be classified under three main themes: culture and cultural pluralism; communication and cultural barriers; and psycho-social identity and inter-ethnic relations.

Culture and pluralism
1) The reality of culture.
2) The diversity and particularity of cultures.
3) The relativity of cultures.
4) The dynamics of culture (cultural change, acculturation).

Communication and cultural barriers
1) Theories of communication.

2) Culture and diversity of mode of perception.
3) Body language and non-verbal communication.
4) Languages and diversity of ways of thinking according to cultures.

Psycho-social identity and inter-ethnic relations
1) Cultural differences and gestation of psycho-social identity; nega-tion of differences (assimilation); affirmation of differences (segre-gation).
2) Ethnocentrism, racism, discrimination.
3) Stereotypes.
4) Intercultural understanding, bureaucracy and minority situations, sociopolitical aspects.

There might be discussions about the relative importance of one or another of these ingredients of a program for teacher training in intercultural education. But what concerns us here is not so much the details of the program but its general framework. If the schematic outline presented above is not completely off the mark, one fact becomes obvious: an intercultural perspective in education cannot be wished into existence. If the provincial educational authorities are serious in their desire to introduce such a perspective into the schools, they must take concrete steps to stimulate the creation of research and training centres for intercultural education. There must also be incentives to attract teachers to this new educational field.

However, the present economic context makes it very unlikely that the provincial government will be ready, in the foreseeable future, to invest the resources needed to create suitable conditions for attracting a substantial number of teachers to coherent training programs in intercultural education. This situation will probably have very serious consequences for its future. There will probably be a very strong tendency to reject, or rather, to ignore, the broader concept of intercultural education for all students that has been discussed here. As long as the intercultural "trend" in education lasts, there will be various "initiatives" towards intercultural education in multiethnic schools; but the educational system will not have been modified in its essentially monocultural thrust.

This view of the structural resistance to the introduction of a broader intercultural perspective might seem rather sobering. But it is better to be aware of the obstacles that will have to be overcome if we want our efforts in this field to have some lasting results. And since it is impossible to introduce any important change in education without the enthusiastic participation of competent and dedicated teachers, it is important to be conscious of the pressures that afflict them and that may affect their perception of intercultural education and their willingness to get involved in a training program, however serious and well-balanced it might be. According to my perception of teachers' present attitudes towards educational innovation and in-service training programs, it would be utopian to anticipate a massive participation on their part in training programs for intercultural education. But I believe that it is possible to find at least a small group of teachers who would be ready to participate in a systematic training program, even though the present working conditions do not favour such involvement. Having been in charge of such a training program since 1972, I would like to present an outline of a training formula which has received a favourable response from teachers.

The Study Tour Formula

The training formula that will be briefly discussed here includes three main components:
1) Courses on a foreign culture and on the problems of intercultural education;
2) A study tour in a country or area where the culture under study is prevalent;
3) Preparation of didactic material for an exploration of the culture with school or college students.

After a brief description of each of these components, I will present some of the main principles underlying such a training formula and discuss their relevance to the development of intercultural education.

1) *Courses on foreign cultures and on the problems of intercultural communication.* We have selected three cultural areas as focal points of the intercultural exploration that teachers are invited to undertake: South Asia, the Muslim world and Northern Quebec natives. The courses provide teachers with a systematic presentation of the main features of the cultures under study, with a special emphasis on the elements that are relevant for an ethno-sociological understanding of the contemporary life in a country or region where the cultures are prevalent. The courses are offered by specialists of these cultures during summer sessions. The courses respond to an immediate

concern of the participants who want to be as well-prepared as possible in order to understand what they will see and hear during the study tour. But we do our utmost to go beyond this immediate interest and to invite teachers to explore the various problems faced by those who want to introduce an intercultural perspective in education.

It is very difficult, in the space of a few weeks, to be seriously initiated into the main aspects of a foreign culture and into the key problems of intercultural education. This is why we prepare textbooks for the participants to study at home before they come in contact with the specialists during the summer sessions.

2) *Study tour*. This element constituted the main attraction of the training program and is an extremely important motivation factor. Six study tours, each generally lasting four weeks, have been organized in the last seven years. These tours have brought the participants into direct contact with the life and culture of people in India, Nepal, Sri Lanka, Egypt, Israel and Northern Quebec. During their brief stay, the participants are able to observe manifestations of the cultural systems they have studied and to communicate with representatives of those cultures. When ever possible, they spend some time with families so that this communication can become intimate and more personal.

3) *Preparation of didactic material for intercultural education*. If teachers are to play an active role in introducing an intercultural perspective in education, the preparation of didactic material offers a golden opportunity. This brings us to the third component of our training formula: how to stimulate interest in intercultural education among teachers. During the two-year preparation period and on the study tour, teachers are actively involved in gathering visual and written material that will be used to prepare a "didactic tool" for intercultural education. This didactic tool includes both a teacher's guide and a slide presentation or video. We spend a considerable amount of time during the summer sessions and afterwards, helping teachers to select a theme that will enable their school and/or college students to understand some important aspects of the culture under study and of Western and Canadian cultures. We insist that the didactic tools be prepared with the view of being used to introduce an intercultural perspective in one or more school programs.

In conclusion, it might be useful to summarize the general principles underlying the formula for intercultural education that has been briefly described here.

1) The introduction of an intercultural perspective in education should not be restricted to a special discipline. This perspective should be integrated into all school programs. Even if its presence will naturally be more visible in some disciplines than in others, training in intercultural understanding and communication should in principle be offered to all school and college teachers.
2) The efforts of those trying to develop an intercultural perspective in schools and colleges should not be isolated from those who insist on the importance of international education and development education.
3) A realistic policy for the promotion of intercultural education must concentrate on teacher training. If there are not at least a few teachers in every school interested in this discipline and willing to be initiated into the complex problems of introducing such an awareness, there is little hope that the monocultural orientation of the school system will be overthrown.
4) A serious initiation into intercultural education should include communication with members of at least one other culture.
5) In order to communicate with members of a foreign culture, the teacher should explore the system of representation and values that prevails in that culture, as well as the historical and sociological conditions in which it developed and maintained its validity.
6) In many cases, a brief stay in a country where the culture under study exists will contribute an experiential element in the training for intercultural understanding. Moreover, the perspective of a study tour in a foreign country creates a very strong motivation factor in teachers who are not yet aware of the necessity to explore the various problems of intercultural education.
7) The participation of teachers in the creation of didactic materials represents an excellent opportunity for them to apply their knowledge in this field and to contribute to the promotion of intercultural education among other teachers, school administrators and professionals.

The Multicultural Policies of Teacher Organizations in Canada

Peter McCreath

Teacher organizations exist to enhance the cause of the teaching profession and to safeguard the best interests of their members. Public interest, including media attention, most commonly focusses on the role of teacher organizations in collective bargaining, whether it be for higher salaries or for greater job security.

Much less visible from a public standpoint has been the role and impact of teacher organizations on education. Often, the public forgets that the organizations are not just unions, but are also associations of professionals. As such, they are as concerned as any other group in society with both the quality of education and the effectiveness of teachers.

In this context, teacher organizations develop through their democratic processes extensive policies covering a wide variety of educational concerns. Of course, policies can serve more than one purpose. A statement of policy is, in one sense, a statement of intent or purpose, an ethic believed, a goal to be pursued. Sometimes it is merely a politically expedient position taken in a given context at a given time. Policies can also be justifications for action, or guidelines for program development or for future action.

During the last decade and a half, an increasing number of Canadians have become aware of multiculturalism and its implications for life in Canadian society. This growing awareness has affected teachers and their organizations as well as others in the country.

Multiculturalism as a subject for teacher organization policy can manifest itself in a variety of ways. Policies can articulate the ethical niceties associated with the recognition of multiculturalism and the observance of human rights. Policies may define a position relative to a specific issue in multicultural education, such as heritage language education. Policies relating to multiculturalism, or the lack of it, may represent a statement with respect to some other aspect of Canadian reality, such as our historic tradition of linguistic dualism and the adoption of official languages.

Depending on how they are counted, there are 19 teacher organizations in Canada, plus the umbrella organization, the Canadian Teachers' Federation. The CTF is a federation, not of teachers, but of teacher organizations. Unfortunately, the single largest teachers' union in the country, the Central des Enseignants de Quebec, declines to join CTF. As a result, while the CTF is able, with some degree of validity, to speak for Anglophone teachers in Canada and for Francophones outside the province of Quebec, it does not reflect the views and opinions of Francophone teachers in Quebec. Ironically, the result has not been under-representation of the Quebec Francophone perspective on issues of culture and language but, in fact, a substantial effort on the part of the CTF to woo the CEQ by taking positions designed to appeal to that missing element.

For example, whereas the policy on multiculturalism was proclaimed by Prime Minister Trudeau in 1971 and effectively recognized by the Charter of Rights and Freedoms in 1982, the annual general meeting of the CTF in July, 1984, turned down a proposal to recognize the multicultural reality of Canada instead of the antiquated (in a Canadian context) concept of biculturalism.

Nowhere in Canada is an aversion to or paranoia of the concept of multiculturalism more evident than in the declarations and policy positions of Francophone teacher organizations. The often stated reason for this is that Francophones see multiculturalism as a threat to the position and status of the French language and culture in Canada. The research conducted on three organizations in preparation for this paper yielded the following results:

1) The Central des Enseignants de Quebec (CEQ) stated that it has no policies or programs on the subject.
2) The Association des Enseignantes et des Enseignants de Franco Ontariens (AEFO) stated that it has no policy nor is considering any.
3) The Association des Enseignantes et des Enseignants Francophone du Neuve Brunswick (AEFNB) did not respond at all. The author has, however, personally heard presidents of this organization speak against the concept of multiculturalism in the Canadian context on more than one occasion.

This Francophone attitude is undoubtedly the greatest single challenge to the concept of multiculturalism as a national policy, if not as a definition of Canadian society.

Many Anglophone Canadians are slow to accept the concept of multiculturalism, particularly those of British and Irish ethnic origin. However, the supremacy and survival of their language is in no way imperilled by multiculturalism. The preeminence of the English language, if only in a North American context, ensures that.

Many Francophone Canadians fear that growing acceptance of multiculturalism will in due course lead to official recognition of the concept and, ultimately, to the diminution in the use and importance of the French language in Canada. Perhaps their fears are well-founded – especially if one listens to the anti-French rhetoric of some leaders of non-visible ethnocultural groups, or to the anti-Quebec rhetoric that has been known to flow from the lips of more than one Western or rural Eastern member of parliament.

A review of the policy treatment of multiculturalism among the Anglophone teacher organizations of Canada essentially reveals one of three results:

1) no policy at all;
2) policies borne out of specific issues; or
3) what could be described as comprehensive policies.

The teachers' associations of the Northwestern Territories, Prince Edward Island, New Brunswick, and three of the four Anglophone ones in Ontario (the Ontario Secondary School Teachers' Federation, the Ontario Public School Teachers' Federation and the Ontario English Catholic Teachers' Association) have no policy nor positions relative to multiculturalism. The umbrella organization of the five Ontario teacher organizations, the Ontario Teachers' Federation, while having no policy on multiculturalism *per se*, does have a statement proscribing discrimination and strongly supporting the concept of equality. Although the only references to equality are to issues of sex, the language of the policy is sufficiently general to apply also to discrimination on the basis of ethnicity or race.

Within some teacher organizations, it is clear that policies have been developed in response to specific issues or longstanding problems. For example, the British Columbia Teachers' Federation has, for over a decade, been actively involved in various programs and policies designed to combat racism within the profession, the schools and the province. Indeed, BCTF has had a professional staff member working full time in this field for over four years – making it the only teacher organization in the country that has one. The result has been a variety of projects and countless in-service sessions aimed at overcoming the sorts of problems multicultural policies have to deal with. Representatives of the BCTF would probably consider that their commitment to multiculturalism and racial equality has been demonstrated not so much by policies as by actions – although the organization did establish an action-oriented policy on multiculturalism in 1984. As well, the BCTF in 1985 became the first teacher organization in Canada to adopt a policy of affirmative action in its own employment practices.

In Alberta, the Keegstra affair gave rise, one suspects, to a series of resolutions at the 1984 Annual General Meeting of the Alberta Teachers' Association. These resolutions seemed to be targeted at preventing a recurrence of similar abhorrent and, to the ATA, embarrassing incidents. Two of the ATA's resolutions called for teacher-training institutions to include sensitivity and awareness training in their programs, as well as bias evaluation. A third resolution called for the provincial Department of Education to provide "appropriate materials to promote cultural, ethnic, racial and religious understanding." A special interest council called the Multicultural Education Council has also been established under the umbrella of the ATA. This well-established organization includes a detailed statement of purpose in its constitution, setting forth the objectives of the educational system with respect to multiculturalism, as well as the specific means and goals by which the council hopes to see these objectives fulfilled. Although these are certainly positive steps, one still wonders if the Keegstra affair would have been possible if the council's statement of purpose had been more prominently ensconced in the policies of the ATA.

One dimension of multicultural education which has far-reaching implications for the teaching profession as well as for the school system is the matter of heritage language education. It can be found, in one form or another, in every province and territory of Canada. Especially in the prairie provinces and in cities like Toronto and Montreal, the demand for heritage language education has implications for Anglophone teachers which are similar to those for French immersion education in most parts of Canada.

Some teacher organizations have established language policies, including the subject of heritage language. The Saskatchewan Teachers' Federation and the Manitoba Teachers' Association have been leaders in this field. In Ontario, heritage language is an issue crying out for recognition by the teacher organizations; but to date, it seems to be treated as a threat by the established organizations of that province.

Interestingly enough, one of the few initiatives by teacher organizations in this area was the symposium organized by the Nova Scotia Teachers' Union in March, 1982. This symposium brought the union, the provincial Department of Education and the school boards together with the leaders of the heritage language schools in the province. The result was the establishment of a heritage language association in Nova Scotia and of a language policy by the NSTU. This policy endeavours to assess the compatibility between a multicultural society and an official bilingual policy, and at the same time recognizes the rights of Canadians to retain use of their ancestral languages. Because the number of ethnic minority groups is relatively small in Nova Scotia, the significance and impact of this policy initiative has been limited.Nevertheless, it serves as a useful and valid model for other provinces.

Three organizations mentioned above, the NSTU, the STF and the MTA, have what could be considered comprehensive policies on multiculturalism and its implications and expectations for teachers and schools. The NSTU established its policy in March, 1981, becoming the first teacher organization in Canada to do so.Its policy consists of a statement of beliefs and assumptions, and a set of goals and guidelines. Consistent with its goals, the NSTU has undertaken a number of projects and in-service sessions. It has also cooperated actively and fully with other organizations working in the field of multicultural education. While the NSTU does not have a professional staff person working full time in this area, considerable staff resources have been devoted to appropriate activities.

The STF and the MTA each have policies that articulate a concept of a multicultural Canada and that make strong commitments to multicultural education and second-language education. Both organizations have devoted considerable staff and committee time and resources to the development of these policies.

The STF has been particularly active. Through its professional staff as well as its members, the organization plays an active role in the recently formed Saskatchewan Association for Multicultural Education. This development is perhaps not unexpected in what was, after all, the first province of Canada to have its own Multiculturalism Act. As in the case of the NSTU, BCTF and ATA policies, there is a strong emphasis on developing intercultural understanding, equality of opportunity, and appropriate and unbiased materials.

The policies of both the STF and the MTA include a strong

commitment to the right to heritage language education within the context of public education, and to the use of non-official languages of instruction where numbers warrant. In the societal context of these provinces, these policies constitute significant commitments, all the more impressive since such positions probably represent a limited threat to the job security of at least some of the current members of the profession in these provinces.

While the provinces of Atlantic Canada are certainly multicultural in terms of the number of distinct ethnocultural groups that can be identified in their populations, the number of individuals relative to the major Anglo-Celtic and Acadian populations is quite small. There is, nevertheless, a growing interest in multiculturalism in all four provinces. In Nova Scotia and, to a lesser extent, in Newfoundland, the teacher organizations and members have played major roles in creating awareness and initiating the process of developing intercultural and cross-cultural understanding throughout the public schools. Neither the PEITF nor the NBTA have been particularly active in establishing policies on multiculturalism. But nor have they been averse to it. Both have indicated that they support initiatives by the CTF in this area. Thus, their lack of policies seems to reflect more a lack of demand rather than a lack of interest.

True to its independent character, Newfoundland has developed an interesting and unique policy on multiculturalism. Using the NSTU model, the NTA policy reflects the uniqueness of Newfoundland and Labrador society and was formally adopted in the spring of 1984. It endorses all the federal goals concerning multiculturalism while at the same time taking into consideration the province's special developments in culture and education. Newfoundlanders, after all, are the one group of Canadians who joined the country as an already established social entity.

Finally, a word on the Canadian Teachers' Federation. Owing to the English-French politics in the organization and its relative dominance by the Ontario teacher organizations, the CTF has been relatively slow to respond to multiculturalism in Canada from a policy point of view. The CTF did take an initiative in the field as early as 1981, conducting a national symposium on the subject. However, it is arguably a fact of Canadian history that Ontario has tended to be more responsive to the concerns of its neighbouring province of Quebec than to the concerns of western Canada and the Atlantic provinces. This perhaps explains the CTF's apparent greater interest to date in the linguistic dualism of Canada rather than in the implications of multiculturalism.

A heated policy debate took place at the 1984 annual general meeting over replacing the concept of "biculturalism" by "multiculturalism" in the CTF policy on official languages. In the end, the proposal was not defeated but shelved on procedural grounds. It is interesting to note that a policy statement on multicultural education stating a strong commitment to the program is now before the 1985 AGM. This policy proposal, developed after lengthy and heated debate, is being presented by the CTF Board of Directors. So it would seem that the leaders are finally catching up to the pack.

In conclusion, it is clear that teacher organizations across Canada have become very conscious, particularly during the last two years, of multiculturalism as a dimension of Canadian society, one that has significant implications for teachers and schools.One would expect to see increasing interest, program activity and, indeed, policy creation in this area in the next few years, notwithstanding the fact that the primary focus of teacher organizations will continue to be job security and the financing of public education.

This brief survey does leave open two questions to consider. Do teacher organizations work to reinforce established views, or can they claim to provide educational leadership? And how significant are policy statements as indicators of the *bona fide* priorities of teacher organizations? The answers to these questions I shall leave to the reader.

Review of the Effects of Learning Styles on Achievement

Karen Parsonson

In examining the classroom, it is important to understand student differences which may affect their academic achievement, and ultimately, their success in later life. Within a multicultural context such as Canada, the effect of ethnicity upon the ways students learn must be taken into consideration in order that all children have an equal opportunity to achieve academic success. We will focus specifically upon differences in learning styles that can have immediate implications for how students can be successfully taught. Three theoretical perspectives that have been shown to affect achievement, cognitive style, achievement motivation and perceived control, will be reviewed in their relation to learning styles and academic achievement. We will see how all three have been found to differ by ethnicity, which suggests important implications for a multicultural educational system.

Cognitive Style

The concept of cognitive style was developed by Witkin (Witkin, Dyk, Faterson, Goodenough and Karp, 1962) in his theory of psychological differentiation. Cognitive style involves the manner in which people perceive and interpret their environment. This factor was first defined and studied using the concept of field dependence/independence, a perceptual indicator which determines whether people rely upon their external environment or are able to dissociate their perceptions from it. Typically, people who are field dependent tend to use external referents from their environment, whereas those who are field independent are more able to take the elements from their respective field and use them separately from their context. They are more able to perceive complex shapes in a complex background and are less likely to be confused by disorienting stimuli in the environment.

Field independence/dependence has been used as an indicator of psychological differentiation, which Witkin and Berry (1975) characterize along a developmental continuum. People who are field independent exhibit greater psychological differentiation which affects the complexity and effectiveness of how their cognitions are integrated. The authors note, however, that differentiation involves the *structural* properties of a person's cognitions, *not* the content. It thus affects the way we process the environment, not the amount processed.

In a later work, Witkin, Goodenough and Oltman (1979) further expand upon differentiation as what they call an "organism-wide process", a major property that distinguishes more articulated cognitive functioning and a greater sense of a separate identity from others. In this respect, greater differentiation allows a person to operate without the need of support and guidance from others, thus affecting interpersonal behaviours also. Those who are field dependent develop in different domains from those who are field independent, as the former, in their greater identity with others, foster better interpersonal relations with other people. Conversely, field independent, or more differentiated people, are more impersonal in relation to others. Thus, the two develop different patterns of abilities and no judgement is made of which abilities are better.

When we turn to the question of how these differences arise, Witkin and Berry point to socialization practices. As Berry (1971) found, societies in which independence, achievement and self-reliance are fostered, tend to exhibit more field independence, whereas those which emphasize obedience and responsibility exhibit more field dependence. Field dependent people are more likely to adhere to authority in parents and society. Another factor shown to influence cognitive style is the school, as Serpell (1976) and Wasner (1978) suggest that some types of schooling can produce greater field independence. In his study of school children in Morocco, Wasner found that with a greater amount of education, children become more field independent. Witkin and Berry also suggest that maturation has an effect upon differentiation as children become more differentiated as they develop.

Thus, cognitive style or psychological differentiation involves an interaction of social and psychological variability in cognitions. As Berry and Dasen (1974) stress, however, we are not looking at quantitative differences but qualitative differences in how people perceive. Up to this point, we have established that people differ in how they process the world, and now we will focus upon how these differences can effect learning styles, which has relevance for the educational system.

Cognitive Styles and Learning Styles

Since people process the world in different ways depending upon their cognitive style, or level of psychological differentiation, it is possible that they also develop different styles of learning. Research has consistently shown this to be the case. Cohen (1969) dichotomized field independence as an analytical style and field dependence as a relational style. He found that those who utilized the analytical style were better at abstraction, had a longer attention span, were more articulated and tended to use the teacher as a resource. Conversely, those with the relational style were more easily distracted, used a more global view of the world and saw the teacher as someone with whom to interact socially. The importance of this distinction is seen as Wasner (1978) describes schools as more analytical in their requirements.

Witkin (1978) characterized cognitive style as influencing the learning of social material, the effect of reinforcement, the use of mediators in learning, cue salience, student and teacher interaction, career choice and specialization in school. Specifically examining the role of field dependence upon learning, Goodenough (1976) found field independent students use a more "participant" approach to learning, are able to sample more fully from salient cues and perform better with intrinsic motivation. Conversely, those who are field dependent use a more "spectator" approach to learning, are less attentive to salient cues, perform more poorly under conditions of intrinsic motivation and are more affected on learning by stress.

The effects of these differences were shown in that in order to understand concepts, people should be able to remove the salient cues and restructure the field, a task which shows field independent students to be better at concept attainment. Goodenough characterized much of school learning as reliant upon concept attainment. He stressed that the greater structuring ability of field independent students was due to their more active organization of material and hypothesis-testing. Further, field dependent students are more affected by negative social reinforcement and punishment. All in all, Goodenough contends that cognitive styles affect how learning occurs, not how effectively.

In summarizing the effects of cognitive style upon learning style,

Berry (1983) advocates that teachers be aware of students' cognitive styles in order to maximize student learning. Now that we see how cognitive style can affect learning style, it is important to determine whether cognitive style can affect academic achievement, as this would further prove the necessity for a full understanding of students' cognitive styles.

Cognitive Styles and Academic Achievement

Research evidence shows differences do exist in academic achievement by cognitive style. Cohen (1969), in differentiating between the analytic and relational styles of field independent and dependent students, found those who were field independent did better academically. In a review of the effects of field dependence upon intellectual functioning, Goodenough and Karp (1961) showed field independents performed better than field dependents on intelligence tests, since most intellectual tasks tap the independents' abilities.

Whereas previously it was noted that there was only a qualitative difference between cognitive styles, based on this limited amount of research it appears that schools require the cognitive abilities which field independents perform better, as Goodenough had stated. Hence, cognitive styles do appear to affect academic achievement.

Ethnicity and Cognitive Style

We have now established that individual differences exist in cognitive styles which can affect learning styles and achievement. Research has also shown that group differences exist in terms of cognitive style. Witkin's and Berry's (1975) review of the cross-cultural research on psychological differentiation traces a developmental sequence of differentiation in other cultures similar to that in the Western world. The difference is that differentiation occurs earlier in Western cultures. The authors contend that differentiation is due to socialization practices that are culturally universal and hence cross-culturally, there exists the same pattern of development. However, in Berry's (1966, 1976) ecocultural adaptation model of psychological differentiation, he contends that depending upon the demands of the environment, the cognitive style of the culture will adapt to its requirements. Thus, if the ecological constraints of a culture's environment demand a particular psychological differentiation, it is likely that a culture from a different environment will have different requirements.

In a more recent review, Berry (1983) acknowledges both ecocultural and acculturational influences on cognitive style, which are appropriate for consideration in multicultural environments. Bagley and Young (1983) examined the effects of acculturation in comparing Jamaican children in Jamaica, Jamaican children in schools in England and English students. They found effects of socialization, social class and ethnicity upon cognitive style. Whereas Jamaican children in Jamaica tended to be more field dependent, those in England were comparable to English children in their greater field independence. The authors note the comparability of English school children to those in the U.S. in their relative psychological differentiation. Whereas Witkin and Berry (1975) characterize the United States as encouraging more separate, autonomous functioning which is associated with greater differentiation, this may prove to be a difficulty for groups from environments outside of the U.S. which have adapted to environments with less differentiation and must function in this new domain. Thus, we see both ethnic differences in cognitive style but also the adaptability and acculturational influences which can affect cognitive style.

Closer to home, in examining cultural differences in Canadian schools, Fellers, Kleinplatz and Lorte-Lussier (1978) found Anglophone, Francophone and Italian-Canadian children approached problem-solving differently. Anglophones were more autonomous, Francophones more interpersonal and Italian-Canadian children were between the two. These results, along with the other evidence on ethnic groups, should suggest important implications for teaching in the multicultural educational system. If ethnic groups with different cultures and cognitive styles are in the Canadian school system, cross-cultural research suggests it is of paramount importance that these differences be recognized in order that learning and academic achievement can be maximized for all school children. Further recommendations for dealing with varying cognitive styles will be examined after we review the other perspectives on learning: achievement motivation and perceived control.

Achievement Motivation and Perceived Control

The work on achievement motivation is discussed in conjunction with perceived control as it is presented from the perspective of attribution theory, a theory of perceived control. Weiner, Frieze, Kukla, Reed, Rest and Rosenbaum (1971) first articulated attribution theory which proposes that people try to explain events that occur in their lives. An attribution is a cause that a person uses to explain why an outcome has occurred. Two dimensions of attributions are classified in order to identify underlying causes. A locus of causality dimension directs the cause as either internal to the person or due to an external factor. A stability dimension (variable/stable) determines the expectation of control over future expectations, with a variable expectation less likely to affect future expectations than a stable attribution which would predict similar expectations for the future. According to attribution theory, a person would experience an outcome as either a success or a failure and attempt to determine the cause, characterized as either within one's control (internal) or not (external), and either expected to recur (stable) or not (variable). An example of an internal stable attribution is an attribution to ability, whereas an external variable attribution would be an attribution to luck.

Weiner views attributions as affecting achievement motivation. If an outcome is perceived as uncontrollable, a person will be less motivated to try, whereas if the outcome is perceived as within one's control, a person will be motivated to try and achieve the outcome.In a reformulation (1979), Weiner applies an attributional analysis to classroom achievement and concludes that achievement-related behaviours (the motivation to try) are mediated by higher-order cognitions, attributions. Similarly, Kukla (1972) addressed achievement motivation as determined by attributions in studying students measured as having either high or low achievement motivation. He found high motivators tended to attribute their outcomes to ability and effort while low motivators attributed their outcomes to ability alone. These results have important implications, as an attribution to ability, though internal, is not controllable because we either have ability or we do not. Conversely, an attribution to effort is also internal but is subject to one's control as it is possible to put more effort into a task. Kukla concludes that the behavioural differences exhibited by those with high and low achievement motivation are due to their differing cognitions about the causes of outcomes.

In an extension of perceived control theory, Dweck and Licht (1980) dichotomized children as either mastery-oriented or learned helpless on the basis of their reactions to failure outcomes. Mastery-oriented children tended to persist in the face of failure as if still motivated, whereas helpless children tended to give up, as if they had lost their motivation. Characteristics of mastery children was their attribution to effort, a controllable cause, whereas the helpless children tended to attribute their failures to a lack of ability and did not increase their effort. Despite the fact that these two groups of children had comparable levels of intelligence, their cognitions about success and failure influenced their motivation to achieve. Helpless children did not perceive themselves as successful when they succeeded and mastery children did not consider it a failure when they failed.

Thus, in examining achievement motivation and the concomitant cognitions about achievement outcomes, we see that differences exist in how children perceive their controllability of academic achievement. Perceived control is intimately related to achievement motivation. As we have seen, individual differences exist in attributions of causality and achievement motivation, and we will now examine their effects upon learning style.

Achievement Motivation, Perceived Control and Learning Style

The effect of the learned helpless/mastery orientation was shown to affect learning styles. Dweck and Licht found that mastery children responded with greater effort, more concentration and persistence, and greater sophistication in the strategies they employed. Helpless children showed decreased effort and deterioration in their approach to problem-solving. Not only did cognitions differ between the two, but also their achievement-related behaviours. The helpless children became more withdrawn and avoided tasks that posed a challenge, but mastery children persisted as they were more task-oriented and showed greater desire for challenges. A sex difference was also demonstrated as females tended to be more helpless and males more mastery-oriented in their approach.

We have seen that achievement motivation and attributions for achievement can have a direct effect upon both students' learning style and preferences. If the style of learning is affected, it is also possible that these varying styles can determine students' academic achievement.

Achievement Motivation, Perceived Control and Academic Achievement

The research on perceived control and achievement motivation suggests decisive effects upon academic achievement. Crandall, Katkovsky and

Crandall (1965) found children who felt less in control performed more poorly in school. Lessing (1969) actually found that for a grade eight student sample, 12 percent of students' GPA could be explained by their perceived control orientation. These results are interpreted by Wolk and Ducette (1973) as demonstrating that perceived control mediates the relationship between achievement motivation and academic performance.

Studies manipulating perceived control have also found an effect upon achievement. In an examination of learned helplessness in the college classroom, Perry and Dickens (1984) review a series of studies that directly manipulated students' perceived control. Students who were made to feel out of control exhibited poorer performance than students who were made to feel in control.

Thus, we can see how perceived control and achievement motivation are linked in their effect upon academic achievement. It appears necessary to examine students' perceived control and achievement motivation in order to better understand the reasons for their academic achievement. Though we have seen individual differences in perceived control and achievement motivation, group differences have also been shown on these dimensions.

Achievement Motivation, Perceived Control and Ethnicity

Distinct differences in achievement motivation, values and academic aspirations were found by Rosen (1959) in a study of children in the United States. Maehr (1974) and Murray and Mednick (1975) also discuss differences in achievement motivation, values and expectations by ethnicity. If differences exist in achievement motivation by ethnicity, then it follows there should also be differences in perceived control. This proves to be the case as Parsons and Schneider (1974) found strong differences in perceived control in a wide cross-cultural sample. Japanese were found to perceive less control while East Indians indicated feeling the greatest control over outcomes. For academic outcomes in particular, Israeli, Canadian and East Indian students indicated feeling most in control and Italian students felt least in control. Meredith (1976), studying perceived control in Hawaii, found that even third-generation Japanese-Americans felt less control than Anglo-Americans.

Socialization has been implicated as a mediator of ethnic differences in controllability. Porter's (1965) analysis of ethnic stratification in

Canadian society describes a vertical mosaic whereby a hierarchy determines ethnic groups' differential levels. Each ethnic group has its own "control potential" (Porter, p. 73) or control over selection and socialization of its members, depending upon where it stands in the hierarchy. Groups lower in the mosaic would experience less control and through socialization would come to expect less control. Thus, family socialization combined with societal factors link ethnicity and perceived control in Canada.

Porter conceptualizes the educational system as the mechanism through which vertical mobility and opportunities can be attained. Thus, children's experiences in school may be particularly important for an ethnic group's mobility. In a study of the vertical mosaic in a Canadian university, Parsonson (1984) found ethnicity to significantly influence attributions to ability and effort, feelings of success, and achievement results as a function of varying levels of perceived control. The results suggested that ethnic groups may have differential perceptions of controllability, which in turn affect their responses to various teaching behaviours.

This review of the effects of perceived control upon academic achievement and differences in perceived control by ethnicity leads to one conclusion: ethnicity may affect children's academic achievement as a result of their sense of control. Differences in achievement motivation, coupled with variability in perceived control, suggest ethnic children may be at a distinct disadvantage in the academic environment.

Implications for the Educational System

A synthesis of the results on cognitive style, achievement motivation and perceived control suggests individual differences exist in learning styles and academic achievement. More importantly for the Canadian educational system, it appears that ethnic group differences exist in all three respective formulations. This has a direct bearing upon the learning styles and academic achievement of children from different ethnic groups. We must be extremely careful in our treatment of these differences, however.

Cole and Bruner (1971) stress that different styles of viewing the world should be seen as "equally logical ways of cutting up the world experience," and competence should not be inferred from performance. They advocate that educational difficulties be viewed as a difference rather than as an intellectual "disease" by the teacher, who should not try to create, but merely to transfer new skills. Similarly, Berry (1983) advocates that cognitive styles should be taken into account as *differences*, not *deficits*.

In an examination of the implications for teachers in multicultural schools, Perry and Clifton (1983) argue that different belief patterns, cognitive styles and coping styles must be recognized for the effective teaching in multiethnic classrooms. We have recognized that differences exist between students of varying ethnic groups and it is necessary to understand these differences. If all children are treated alike, however, we may be abdicating our responsibility to better understand these differences in an attempt to create a homogeneous group. Teaching styles must take into account differences in learning styles. Berry (1983) contends that knowing students' cognitive styles and resultant learning styles should change teaching strategies. Witkin and Goodenough (1981) even suggest that teachers should be aware of their own cognitive styles in order that learning be maximized as they interact with students' cognitive styles.

In terms of perceived control in particular, the review by Dweck and Licht demonstrates the importance of teachers' feedback practices upon children's interpretations of their failures. Teachers' behaviours have consistently been shown to interact with students' perceived control (Perry and Dickens, 1984).

Thus, we have reviewed the effects of learning styles on achievement, which make it clear that teachers must consider and understand these differences between their students. The responsibility for dealing with these differences remains with the educational system as it must focus upon how to maximize achievement for all children. Variety as introduced by ethnicity in the classroom should not be viewed as a liability, but rather, as a challenge to find the appropriate teaching styles to match with students' cognitive styles.

References

Bagley, C. and Young, L. (1983). Class, socialization and cultural change: Antecedents of cognitive style in Jamaica and England. In C. Basley and G. Verma (Eds.), *Multicultural childhood*. Hampshire, England: Gower.

Berry, J. (1983). Comparative studies of cognitive styles. In R. Samuda and S. Woods (Eds.), *Perspectives in immigrant and minority education*. New York: University Press of America.

Berry, J. (1976). *Human ecology and cognitive style: Comparative studies of cultural and psychological adaptation*. New York: Sage-Halsted.

Berry, J. (1971). Ecological and cultural factors in spatial-perceptual development. *Canadian Journal of Behavioural Sciences, 3*, 324-336.

Berry, J. (1966). Temne and Eskimo perceptual skills. *International Journal of Psychology, 1*, 207-229.

Berry, J. and Dasen, P. (Eds.). (1974). *Culture and cognition: Readings in cross-cultural psychology*. London: Methuen.

Cohen, R. (1969). Conceptual styles, culture conflict and nonverbal tests of intelligence. *American Anthropologist, 71*, 828-856.

Cole, M. and Bruner, J. (1971). Cultural differences and inferences about psychological processes. *American Psychologist, 26*, 867-876.

Crandall, V., Katkovsky, W. and Crandall, V. (1965). Children's beliefs in their own control of reinforcement in intellectual-academic achievement situations. *Child Development, 36*, 91-109.

Dweck, C. and Licht, B. (1980). Learned helplessness and intellectual achievement. In J. Garber and M. Selisman (Eds.), *Learned helplessness: Theory and applications*. New York: Academic Press.

Fellers, G., Kleinplatz, P. and Lortie-Lussier, M. (1981). *Cognitive style and cultural values:A study of Francophone, Anglophone and Italian-Canadian children*. Presented at the Canadian Psychological Association annual convention, Toronto, 1981.

Goodenough, D. (1976). The role of individual differences in field dependence as a factor in learning and memory. *Psychological Bulletin, 83*(4), 675-694.

Goodenough, D. and Karp, S. (1961). Field dependence and intellectual functioning. *Journal of Abnormal and Social Psychology, 63*(2), 241-246.

Kukla, A. (1972). Attributional determinants of achievement-related behaviour. *Journal of Personality and Social Psychology, 21*, 166-174.

Lessing, E. (1969). Racial differences in indeces of ego functioning relevant to academic achievement. *Journal of Genetic Psychology, 65*, 153-167.

Maehr, M. (1974). Culture and achievement motivation. *American Psychologist, 29*, 887-896.

Meredith, G. (1976). Interpersonal needs of Japanese-American and Caucasian-American college students in Hawaii. *Journal of Social Psychology, 99*(2), 157-161.

Murray, S. and Mednick, M. (1975). Perceiving the causes of success and failure in achievement: Sex, race and motivational comparisons. *Journal of Clinical and Consulting Psychogosts, 43*, 331-385.

Parsons, A. and Schneider, J. (1974). Locus of control in university students from eastern and western societies. *Journal of Consulting and Clinical Psychology, 42*, 456-461.

Parsonson, K. (1984). Ethnicity and perceived control: Implications for the college classroom. Unpublished Master's Thesis. University of Manitoba.

Perry, R. and Clifton, R. (1983). Counselling in multicultural schools: Implications for teachers and students. Paper presented at a conference on Intercultural Counselling, Queen's University, Kingston, October, 1983.

Perry, R. and Dickens, W. (1984). Perceived control in the college classroom: The effect of response-outcome contingency training and instructor expressiveness on student achievement and attributions. *Journal of Educational Psychology*, 76(6), 966-981.

Porter, J. (1965). *The vertical mosaic*. Toronto: University of Toronto Press.

Rosen, B. (1959). Race, ethnicity and the achievement syndrome. *American Sociological Review*, 24, 417-460.

Serpell, R. (1976). *Culture's influence on behaviour*. London: Methuen.

Wasner, D. (1978). The effects of formal schooling on cognitive style. *Journal of Social Psychology*, 106, 145-151.

Weiner, B., Frieze, I., Kukla, A., Reed, L., Rest, S. and Rosenbaum, P. (1971). Perceiving the causes of success and failure. In E. Jones, D. Kanouse, H. Kelley, R. Nisbett, S. Valines and B. Weiner (Eds.), *Attrition: Perceiving the causes of achievement*. Morristown, N.J.: General Learning Press.

Weiner, B. (1979). A theory of motivation for some classroom experiences. *Journal of Educational Psychology*, 71, 3-29.

Witkin, H.S. (1978). *Cognitive styles in personal and cultural adaptation*. Worcester, Mass.: Clark University Press.

Witkin, H. and Berry, J. (1975). Psychological differentiation in cross-cultural perspective. *Journal of Cross-Cultural Psychology*, 61(1), 4-87.

Witkin, H., Dyk, R., Faterson, H., Goodenough, D. and Karp, S. (1962). *Psychological differentiation*. New York: John Wiley.

Witkin, H. and Goodenough, D. (1981). *Cognitive styles: Essence and origins*. New York: International Universities Press.

Witkin, H., Goodenough, D. and Oltman, P. (1979). Psychological differentiation: Current status. *Journal of Personality and Social Psychology*, 37(7), 1127-1145.

Wolk, S. and Ducette, J. (1973). The moderating effect of locus of control in relation to achievement-motivational variables. *Journal of Personality*, 41, 59-70.

PART II

Professional Roles

The Role of Psychometry in Multicultural Education: Implications and Consequences

Ronald J. Samuda

T he word psychometry in the title of this paper was selected to apply in its broadest context. It is intended to include the selection, use and administration of tests as well as the interpretation of test scores to justify the placement of students in regular or special curriculum programs. More particularly, the paper will focus on the efficacy of the theory and practice of the testing of aptitudes, mental ability, achievement and learning potential of students who are culturally or socioeconomically different from the Angloceltic mainstream of Canadian society.

Those of us who were trained in the late fifties and in the sixties can look back on almost three decades of changing programs and attitudes towards standardized psychological tests. In those days, no student at institutions like Ottawa University dared question the reality of the IQ or the scientific basis of Spearman's "G" factor. Yet, today there are many respected social scientists who speak of normative assessment and the placement of minorities as being tantamount to the perpetuation of a racist philosophy. In 1960, such a viewpoint would have been regarded by the established authorities in psychometrics as sheer heresy.

The validity and reliability of tests of aptitude were proven by their ability to predict levels of achievement and it was even claimed that, rather than discriminating against minorities, the Scholastic Aptitude Tests tended to overpredict. On numerous studies, the differential pattern of results between the white mainstream American students and the black and hispanic minorities remained consistently at one standard deviation. It was an unfortunate fact but that was that and the difference was interpreted to mean that minorities were inherently inferior in intellect and should be taught by different means or that they should be provided with special education programs to help them cope with the standard curriculum of the schools.

The massive volume of assessment instruments comprised tests of learning ability, mechanical reasoning, spatial ability, clerical speed and accuracy, individual and group tests, the Wechsler, the Stanford-Binet, the Slosson, the Lorge-Thorndike, to name but a few.

The testing of students had grown to become an industry in itself – a mammoth and lucrative enterprise. And the power of the testing industry lay in the fact that the results could and did determine educational, social and economic opportunity. There are those who might think that such conditions were more typically American and did not necessarily apply to Canadian schools. Nevertheless, our research into the assessment, testing, counselling and placement of students in Ontario schools has attested to the fact that testing did, and still does, play a very important role in the placement of students. In fact, the educational programs in every province in Canada are permeated by American norms, instruments and methods of assessment.

As a case in point, most practising teachers in Ontario will remember the Robarts Plan and the division of schools into the academic, technical, vocational and occupational programs. At institutions like Lisgar Collegiate in Ottawa, students were tested by the instruments like the Dominion or the Differential Aptitude Tests and then placed in one of the programs that seemed most appropriate on the basis of the test results – in the academic, technical, vocational or occupational program. Many a minority student was steered into a terminal program with limited potential for further education because of his or her inability to handle the multiple-choice variety of tests or because he understood very little about the consequences, or lacked the motivation, the competitiveness, the notions of speed or the information to perform normally. Very often, minority students were beset by anxiety in a threatening and alien situation. In the sixties, we took for granted the immutability of the IQ and the inevitable reality that a low score meant inferior potential to learn.

I can remember some very tricky and hostile situations in 1978 and 1979 when Professor Douglas Crawford and I were doing research into the methods of assessment, testing, placement and counselling of students in Ontario Schools. When, for instance, we asked a group of teachers and administrators in one Ontario school how they dealt with incoming minority students, the response was indignant. "We treat them all alike," one teacher said with obvious impatience. And we understood from that remark that she believed that regardless of the ethnic, linguistic or cultural background of the individual students, they should all go through the same intake procedures and they should be sorted according to the resulting test scores. A student from the Azores or Bangladesh should take the same tests and the results could then be used to establish placement in regular or special classes.

It is precisely that kind of thinking that led one of the most eminent psychologists of this century to make the following comments when confronted with the test performance of a pair of Mexican-American and Indian children:

> Their dullness seems to be racial [said Lewis Terman, the originator of the Stanford-Binet) or at least inherent in the family stocks from which they come . . . there will be discovered enormous significant racial differences which cannot be wiped out by any scheme of mental culture. Children of this group should be segregated in special classes. There is no possibility at present of convincing society that they should not be allowed to reproduce.

That quotation epitomizes the three aspects of racism – structural, technical and scientific. Structural racism could be more blandly described as ethnocentrism or a sort of collective mindset which requires that each individual be judged according to the same standards, procedures and values, regardless of cultural or class differences.

Technical racism refers to the simplistic and sometimes unwitting use of correlations and the glib citations of construct, content and concurrent validity as statistical evidence to justify the labelling of minorities and the placement consequences of test results. Scientific racism resides in the implication of Professor Terman's theory of the racial inheritance of inferior mental stock by those who are not of Northwestern European lineage.

It is that collective mindset which permitted the California school system to test black and Mexican-American children with the Stanford-Binet and to place them on the basis of their test results in classes for the mentally retarded. It is that collective mindset which pervades the ways that teachers are trained in many of our own Canadian faculties of education. For, although there exists in Canada an official policy of multiculturalism, at the federal and some provincial government levels there still persists a predominant WASP value system that insiduously seeps into the hidden curriculum and remains embedded in the methods of teacher training and in the concomitant ways in which those teachers approach the job of teaching in the schools.

That collective WASP and middle-class mindset forms part of the pattern by which the norms are set, teachers are employed and becomes the implicit prototype of what constitutes proper standards of behaviour. In the final analysis, it establishes the very notion of what it is to be a worthwhile human being.

In spite of what has been said above, it is important to emphasize that there is nothing inherently wrong with standardized tests themselves. Norm-referenced tests are relatively valid and reliable. They provide useful information about most children and there does exist a significant correlation between the scores of intellectual potential and performance in the schools as tested by measures of achievement. It is no wonder that this would be so since both the tests of intellectual aptitude and those of achievement are permeated with the values, experiences, language, and skills of the Anglo-Saxon mainstream curriculum. They were, after all, designed by white urban Anglo-Saxon middle-class psychologists from the mainstream of American society and comprise the typical skills and information embodied in the experience of the average Euro-American middle-class individual. They are essentially culturally loaded and the students who get the best results will naturally be those who have imbibed the values, skills, and motivational patterns from their middle-class homes and neighbourhood environment.

Where, then, is the problem? Why has there been the recent outcry against the injustice of testing? Those answers lie in the assumptions underlying the use of tests and in the interpretation and consequences that flow from the use of test scores, especially for those minorities whose cultural orientation is different and for those students who are economically and socially disadvantaged or culturally deprived. But, more importantly, the problems of testing lie in the interpretations of inherent intellectual inferiority ascribed by some social scientists to explain, for example, the relatively lower scores of blacks and Mexican Americans in the United States.

The most pernicious form of racist consequence rests in the use of tests to label and place minority students in classes for the subnormal and to justify the failure of our educational system to cope with those who are culturally different and those from the mainstream who are economically and culturally deprived. The assumptions underlying the use of tests are:

1) that there exists a commonality of experiences shared by those who take the test;
2) that the educational opportunities in the home and neighbourhood are comparable across groups;
3) that all test takers have equal facility with the language of instruction;
4) that the syntax and word usage are familiar to those who take the test and that sociocultural, economic and linguistic differences can be ignored.

The most significant change in the attitudes towards the assessment of minorities occurred in the United States. Perhaps the turning point might be identified as the case of Larry P versus Wilson Riles in the State of California. It was in the city of San Francisco at the beginning of the seventies that a group of concerned psychologists decided to tackle the status quo by selecting six black children from the classes for the mentally retarded. Upon retesting by registered psychologists, it was discovered that none of the children were retarded and that they had been robbed of their civil rights on the basis of test results that did not reflect their true potential. Indeed, they had been labelled and placed in classes for the mentally retarded because of the inadequacy of the testing procedures.

The changes in attitudes towards the testing of minorities can also be traced to pioneer endeavours of men like Robert Williams (the originator of the BITCH test), Edward Barnes, Frank Wilderson, Reginald Jones, Harold Dent and Asa Hilliard who, as members of the Association of Black Psychologists, dared to question the very foundations of norm-referenced testing and to point to the fact that men like Sir Francis Galton, Lewis Terman and Carl Brigham had blatantly used testing to expound their racist interpretations of the hereditary nature of intelligence and the alleged inferiority of people who were of non-European origin. There were those social scientists from the mainstream of American society who also challenged the overwhelming proportions of ethnic minority children who were being labelled as intellectually subnormal and placed in special programs with no hope of receiving a normal education. Unquestionably, the research of Professor Jane Mercer (the originator of the SOMPA) at the University of California at Riverside was very important to the movement and to the enlightenment that followed in the seventies.

For those of us who have been working in the field for the past sixteen years, it seems trite to repeat what might seem to some as truisms. Yet, there are still teachers practising in the field who need to be reminded that norm-referenced assessment is not very useful for minorities because tests of aptitude, intelligence and achievement comprise attitudes and patterns of behaviour more typical of the mainstream Anglo- or Euro-Canadian middle-class groups and do not necessarily reflect the cultural pattern of ethnic minorities; and that standardized tests are for the most part normed on middle-class children and even when they include minorities they do not properly represent the spectrum. Tests of ability are heavily loaded culturally and typify the performance of the mainstream pupil while discriminating against minorities.

52

But, more significantly, the linkage between the results of norm-referenced testing and the system of ability grouping existing in many schools forms the ultimate cycle that guarantees that many minorities will never get a just share of the educational and, by extension, the social, economic and political privileges of our society. For, despite the predilection of most teachers for homogenous groups, the research has demonstrated that such practices benefit the higher achievers mainly.

Moreover, ability grouping goes hand in glove with testing to complete the cycle leading to ethnic and socioeconomic separation or segregation and racial imbalance in the classrooms to the detriment of lower achieving groups. Ability grouping plays an important role in determining the labelling, lowered self-concept, lowered teacher expectations and perceptions, and leads inevitably to poor teaching conditions and the inferior performance of minorities. Streaming leads to vocational and terminal placements for minorities and a lowered number of minorities entering the fields of higher education.

From an educational point of view, norm-referenced testing can deal only with product, not with process; they do not help us restructure our teaching so that we can optimize the individual needs of individual students. They indicate to us that the pupil is deficient in relation to the typical performance of typical students but they do not tell us why; they give no clues as to the strengths of the individual, his individual cognitive deficits, or his methods of coping with problems presented in the testing situation.

In a multicultural society like Canada it is encumbent on the school to determine accurately what a student is really capable of accomplishing, to find what Vygotsky has called the *zone of proximal (potential) development*. We need to find out what the student does know, what his lacks consist of and how to optimize the mechanisms and rate of learning. In short, norm-referenced testing does not help us as teachers to improve the learning situation because they are based on norms that are alien to the minority student.

Tests of ability that purport to predict the potential of minorities merely serve to shelve the problem. The key issue and the essential purpose for testing should be to match instruction to learning needs. To do so, we need much more information than a single score can provide. We need the kind of comprehensive background data which can give us a more complete picture of the individual within the context of his cultural, familial, linguistic, socioeconomic and environmental circumstances.

But, more than that, if our teaching of minorities is to be effective, we will need to move away from the collective mindset to adopt the theories and methods of such innovators as Vygotsky, Budoff, Sternberg, Detterman and especially, Reuven Feuerstein. That signifies the need for teacher retraining and new methods of teacher education in the faculties of education.

We have come a far way since the seventies. The IQ is no longer the holy grail. Social scientists are beginning, more and more, to recognize the injustice in a set of assessment systems which would categorize individuals for all time as mentally retarded or as learning disabled without a proper understanding of the etiology or the facilities for mediation. Teachers are demanding better methods of diagnosis. There is now a rejection of Spearman's G factor as the determinant of intelligence and in its place we are moving closer to the more adequate theory of Cattell's notions of fluid and crystallized intelligence. And the notions initiated by the Soviet scientist Vygotsky are now being linked with Piagetian procedures and methods for studying the developmental processes of learning.

In the place of the IQ as the immutable cause of deficiency, and instead of viewing learning deficits from a pathological stance, the dynamic assessment of Reuven Feuerstein is primarily geared towards the assessment of the student's potential for modifying basic cognitive structures by apprehending the gaps in his developmental learning pattern and enhancing the effectiveness and efficiency of learning, thinking and problem-solving through accurate and individualized programs of mediation.

In the place of the single score, we are moving towards a more precise examination of the individual's ways of perceiving and problem-solving by actually teaching cognitive principles and strategies through a test-train-test methodology that Feuerstein has demonstrated to be effective in helping Israeli youngsters overcome their cognitive deficits and remediating their ineffective learning patterns resulting from their cultural deprivation.

Much of our psychometric technology and practice is still imported from the United States. The tests we use are mainly American and the attitudes of teachers and social scientists have been influenced by events like the case of Larry P versus Wilson Riles. The militant and vocal social scientists have managed to underscore the fundamental injustice of using tests to label children on the basis of inappropriate results which are not merely useless but very damaging in terms of the self-concept and teacher expectation. Such court cases have culminated in special legislation to guard the civil rights of children in the case of Public Law

94-142 enacted in the United States in 1975. That law guarantees to all handicapped children the right to a free public education, to an individualized education program, to due process, and to the least segregated environment. But, more importantly, it proscribes the use of culturally discriminatory assessment and advocates a system of relevant and multi-dimensional assessment (Jones, 1985).

Such legislative acts have drastically altered the process and shape of psychometry in the U.S. There are very real and beneficial consequences for ethnic minorities who were the main victims of the former system. Even such tested and tried psychometric instruments like the WISC-R have not escaped the critical scrutiny of the new movement. Similarly, in the Canadian context, there have been serious attempts to respond to the cultural and linguistic diversity in the schools of such urban centres as metropolitan Toronto where more than fifty percent of the students come from homes where a language other than English is spoken. In Vancouver, the comparable figure is forty percent (Yeung, 1982). As early as 1970, the Dante Society (an Italian-Canadian cultural organization) confronted the educational establishment because of the disproportionate numbers of immigrant students in vocational rather than academic programs. They criticized the school for the use of culturally and linguistically biased procedures (Costa and di Santo, 1973).

The demand for better methods of assessment and more appropriate programs have led to the formulation of policies in certain school boards of delaying the testing of ethnic minorities for two years when it is anticipated that acculturation will occur. The unfortunate fact is, however, that such policies are not based on a proper understanding of the problems of assessing and educating minorities. They merely reflect the same collective mindset whereby the attempt is made to fit the student to a system of norms that are not only alien to the ethnic minority student but are useless as pedagogical tools. In Ontario, the passage of Bill 82 in December 1980, signified an important change in the responsibility of teachers to take into account the learning needs of *all* students. For this piece of legislation mandates that school boards will identify all exceptional students (e.g. learning disabled, gifted) and devise programs suited to their needs and abilities. Moreover, decisions for individual students must be based, not only on initial screening tests, but also on a more detailed assessment by a psychoeducational consultant to advise the Identification, Placement and Review Committee.

These are laudatory developments in our recognition of the cultural diversity of students in our schools and the need to change the system to meet student needs. But these legislative measures cannot succeed without a concomitant program of training and retraining for teachers. Our research (Samuda and Crawford, 1980) has demonstrated the wide gap between policy and practice. We have witnessed and documented the abysmal ignorance of many practising teachers who still cling to the notions gleaned from their "normal school" training. We have seen evidence of resistance by many teachers to the notions of multicultural education. And, we are painfully aware of the need for school boards to institute professional development for the in-service practising teachers. It should never be forgotten that the classroom teacher is the key element in the assessment process. It makes no sense to limit re-education to the school psychologists or to relegate the problems of educating ethnic minority students to the domain of the special education branch.

Teachers and counsellors need to be retrained; but they also need to be sensitized to the special needs of minorities. They need more than technical knowledge. In other words, it must be a change in the heart and in the head.

As educators, we need to remember that the primary justification for the use of an assessment technique is its contribution to educational practice. Measurement instruments should assess a child's functional needs and be evaluated on the basis of relevance to educational decisions.

The paradox of multicultural education is that, in some situations, it is necessary to treat students differently in order to ensure equality of educational opportunity. The real challenge lies in the difficulty of matching instruction to the results of assessment; for, without that link the entire psychometric paraphernalia becomes futile. As Reschly (1980) has advocated,

> Illumination of improved practices in psychology and education, especially procedures that would expand opportunities and improve competencies of children, have been conspicuously absent. [quoted in Jones, 1985.]

Reschly has further emphasized that the debates concerning non-biased assessment derive from a focus on the wrong problems and questions. It is true that the major concern in non-biased assessment has been the identification of learning potential in minorities. But assessment is not the main issue. The real challenge is whether we can design pedagogical programs that maximize the competences and opportunities for minority students. Moreover, we need to attend to all facets of bias – the educational validity of procedures and techniques as well as the teaching-learning theories.

The present trend in the assessment of minorities is towards a more comprehensive appraisal of several facets of experience. The advocates of such comprehensive programs stress the need for

1) a broad base of information on which any diagnostic decision, program change or revised placement should occur;
2) the utilization of a team of assessors who access information pertaining to acculturation, language, behaviour, socioeconomic background and ethnocultural history;
3) identification of needs, strengths, weaknesses and current level of functioning appraised in the light of background data;
4) the definition and design of a program profile which would best assist the child to profit from the school system;
5) the profile to be managed by a team and monitored regularly.

The system presupposes parental involvement and the elimination of IQ testing unless conducted by a professional sensitive to the pitfalls and with a definite purpose in mind (such as, estimating the sociocultural distance of the student from the mainstream).

Such changes in the role of psychometry can turn the school into a place where the child from the Azores or Bangladesh might have the same chance to learn as the child from Britain or Sweden. In that kind of pedagogical enterprise, we can help to make the official Canadian government policies of multiculturalism a reality in our educational systems across this great land of ours.

References

Barnes, E. *IQ testing and minority school children: Imperatives for change*. Storrs, Conn.: National Leadership Institute Teacher Education/Early Childhood, N.D.: University of Connecticut, p. 8.

Budoff, M. (1972). Measuring learning potential: An alternative to the tradition intelligence test. *Studies in learning potential*, *3*, No. 39.

Dent, H. (1976). Assessing black children for mainstream placement. In R. L. Jones (Ed.), *Mainstreaming and the minority child*. Reston, VA.: Council for Exceptional Children, pp. 77-92.

Feuerstein, R. (1979). *The dynamic assessment of retarded performers*. Baltimore: University Park Press.

Findlay, W. and Bryan M. (1971). *Ability grouping; 1970. Status, impact and alternatives*. Athens, Ga.: Center for Educational Improvement.

Haywood, H. (1985). Dynamic assessment: The learning potential assessment device. In R. Jones (Ed.), *Non-discriminatory (high validity) assessment of minority group children: A casebook*. Berkeley: University of California, pp. 35-72.

Hilliard, A. Cultural diversity and special education. In *Exceptional children*, *46*,584-588.

Jones, R. and Wilderson, F. (1976) Mainstreaming and the minority child: An overview of the issues and a perspective. In R. L. Jones (Ed.). *Mainstreaming and the minority child*. Reston, VA.: The Council for Exceptional Children, pp. 1-14.

Jones, R. (Ed.). (1985). *Non-discriminatory (high validity) assessment of minority group children: A casebook (volume I)*. Berkeley, CA.: University of California.

Kamin, L. (1974) *The science and politics of IQ*. New York: Wiley.

Larry P. et al versus Wilson Riles, superintendent of public instruction for the state of California et al, (1979). No. C-71-2270. N.D. Cal, Oct. 11, 1979.

Mercer, J. & Lewis, J. (1978). *System of multicultural pluralistic assessment*. New York: Psychological Corporation.

MacIntyre, R. (1985). Techniques for identifying learning-impaired minority students. In R. Samuda and A. Wolfgang (Eds.). *Intercultural counselling and assessment; global perspectives*. Toronto: Hogrefe, pp. 155-164.

Reschly, D. (1981). Psychological testing in educational classification and placement. *American Psychologist*, *36*,1094-1102.

Salvia, J. and Ysseldyke, J. (1978). *Assessment in special and remedial education*. Boston: Houghton Mifflin.

Samuda, R. (1975). *Psychological testing of American minorities: Issues and consequences*. New York: Harper.

Samuda, R. (1976). Problems and issues in the assessment of minority group children. In R. L. Jones (Ed.), *Mainstreaming and the minority child*. Reston, VA.: The Council for Exceptional Children, pp. 65-76.

Samuda, R. & Crawford, D. (1980). *Testing, assessment, counselling and placement of ethnic minority students: Current methods in Ontario*. Toronto: Ontario Ministry of Education Contract No. 213, OISE Press.

Samuda, R. & Woods, S. (1983). (Eds.) *Perspectives in immigrant and minority education*. Washington, D.C. University Press of America.

Samuda, R. (1983). Testing within a multicultural society. In S. Irvine and J. Berry (Eds.), *Human assessment and cultural factors*. New York: Plenum, pp. 591-605.

Samuda, R., Berry, J. & Laferriere, M. (Eds.). (1984). *Multiculturalism in Canada: Social and educational perspectives*. Toronto: Allyn and Bacon.

Samuda, R. & Wolfgang, A. (Eds.). (1985). *Intercultural counselling and assessment: Global perspectives*. Toronto: Hogrefe.

Scarr, S. (1977). Testing minority children: Why, how, and with what effects? In R. Bossone and M. Weiner (Eds.), *Proceedings of the national conference on testing*. New York: City University, pp. 71-101.

Sternberg, R. (1981). Testing and cognitive psychology. *American Psychologist*, *36*, 1181-1189.

Williams, R. (1971). Abuses and misuses in testing black children. *The Counselling Psychologist*. *2*, 62-73.

Multiculturalism and Race Relations: The Role of Teacher Organizations

Ed May

As Canadians gradually recognize the extent to which racism permeates their country, the cast of players in the effort to press for a more tolerant society continues to grow. Among the bit players is the teacher organization, a reluctant group forced by demands from its members to do something about "problems" that relate to schools. Most teacher organizations straddling a wide range of political persuasions among their fee-paying members, have opted to play safe. They have either yielded to the argument that their energies should be devoted to bread-and-butter matters, such as pensions, salaries and learning conditions, or they have avoided possible controversy by using the term "multiculturalism" and have been content to issue mild statements against racism. Only one teacher organization, the British Columbia Teachers' Federation (hereafter referred to as the BCTF) has funded and developed a program specifically geared to combating racism in schools. (BCTF *Members' Guide*, 1984-85.)

This report will first review the activities of a sample of teacher organizations in Canada. Then, in the second half, it will deal with the BCTF program against racism more fully. The lessons learned by this group, its errors and successes, might assist other teacher organizations in their effort to meet the challenges of our rapidly changing society. Now that Section 15 of the Charter of Rights and Freedoms has been proclaimed, teacher groups will be among many agencies that will face growing demands from minority communities to bring about changes in our education system.

Responding to these demands will not be easy. Faced with declining membership, increased calls for member services, and a conviction by many teachers that social problems are the responsibility of governments and service agencies, teacher organizations have little incentive to become involved in multicultural and race relations programs. In addition, teachers from ethnic minority communities have not been vocal in matters of racism and intercultural relations.Finding themselves part of a small and often scattered sub-group, minority teachers have preferred to keep a low profile. For them, the more prudent course has been to accept the lack of opportunity for advancement in the school system and the implication that somehow they are not quite equal to their white colleagues. Minority teachers do not care to be known as ethnics with chips on their shoulders. But the biggest drawback that teacher groups must face in their participation in race relations programs is the apathy of their own members. The fact is that those people who are not pained by racism are not likely to involve themselves in a problem which is not their own.

Typical of the role played by most teacher organizations is that of the Canadian Teachers' Federation. This group has issued a few statements on the need to oppose racism. Bit it has not played an active role in promoting such things as non-racist teaching materials, teacher education for a multiracial society, and the inclusion of minorities in the power structure that controls public education. Despite calls from delegates at a conference on multicultural education held in March 1984, the CTF has not provided leadership in the struggle against racism. One apparent explanation for this reluctance to act might be found in the composition of the CTF's board of directors and its administrative staff. They are all white.

Of those teacher organizations which we surveyed for their involvement in multiculturalism and race relations activities, the Nova Scotia Teachers' Union appears to have the most aggressive system. Thanks largely to the drive and vision of one staff member, the NSTU can claim credit in having initiated the following:

- an in-service project, started in 1981, which produced a book for teachers who wish to implement multicultural practices in their classrooms;
- a Heritage Language Symposium which promoted the idea of expanded programs in the province;
- a human rights project to increase awareness of the more covert forms of discrimination in the school system;
- intervention in certain hiring policies of the Greater Halifax Board of Education;
- activities related to Section 15 of the Charter of Rights and Freedoms,

such as a conference on "Obstacles and Opportunities in the Charter," and in-service programs on the obligations of administrators;
- development of a Nova Scotia Multicultural Education Committee, with a staff person assigned to this committee;
- a multicultural/race relations policy for the NSTU. (Peter McCreath, Nova Scotia Teachers' Union)

These steps represent the beginning of an ongoing effort to persuade teachers in that province that multicultural education and improved race relations will enhance their teaching.

The Alberta Teachers' Association has not developed a race relations policy but has issued some statements outlining the Association's position on racism and multiculturalism. At present, a review of a disciplinary process to be applied to teachers who practise racism in their classrooms is in progress. The ATA, like Alberta's provincial government, strongly supports multiculturalism through a multicultural council based on a comprehensive policy. As in the case with most other teacher organizations, the ATA does not have an affirmative action policy. (David Flower, Alberta Teachers' Association)

The Saskatchewan Teachers' Federation has a "policy on language, culture, discrimination and education" which is consistent with similar policies of the Canadian Teachers' Federation. The STF has also developed a mechanism for dealing with violations of this policy. A review of the need for affirmative action, in keeping with policies of both provincial and Canadian human rights codes, has been undertaken. The STF also reports a close liaison with the province's universities in promoting native education. (Terry McKague, Saskatchewan Teachers' Federation)

In Manitoba, the Manitoba Teachers' Society was the first provincial teacher group to formulate a multicultural policy. A paper on racism in schools, including textbook contents, stereotyping and other manifestations of racism, is pending. The MTS also works closely with the Department of Education's multicultural officer in promoting education that seeks to meet the needs of a diverse society. (Walter Pindera, Manitoba Teachers' Society)

These examples indicate the penchant of teacher organizations' activities for what they term "multiculturalism." The examples also invite some questions. What do these teacher organizations mean by "multiculturalism"? Is "multiculturalism" meeting the needs of a multiracial society, or is it a smokescreen for the lack of substantive action against institutional racism?

British Columbia has always been regarded as one of Canada's more volatile provinces, and the brand of racism which surfaced there in the early seventies was in keeping with the province's reputation. At that time, immigrants from the Indian subcontinent were targets of racist behaviour which quickly spilled over into the school system. Faced with calls from concerned teachers to "do something", the British Coumbia Teachers' Federation called for volunteers to serve on a Task Force on Racism in 1975. The nine neophytes who made up this task force met in September 1975 and were charged with "identifying the nature and causes of racism in the schools, and with formulating strategies to combat racism." The choice of the use of military terms – task force, strategies, combat – to describe the objectives was not without its irony. Within a few weeks of coming into existence, the fledgling group found itself in the midst of what seemed to be a war of words (Joyce Upex, Simon Fraser University graduate student).

Because there were no known precedents for a teacher-sponsored study of racism in schools, arguments against such an activity took the task force by surprise. So did the degree of resistance from many quarters. There were those who bridled at any suggestion of racism in Canada. Other critics of the task force felt that the current wave of bigotry was a passing fad which, if ignored, would eventually disappear. Yet another camp saw racism as a "topic" that could become a self-fulfilling prophecy: the more attention it received, the more likely it was to manifest itself. Perhaps the most widely-held argument against a discussion of racism was that the topic was "negative". If we could only approach racism in a "positive", constructive manner, then perhaps people would not find the topic intimidating!

There was also the view held by some that "attitudinal engineering" was the desirable goal, and until it had been achieved, any hope of behavioural change was premature. Exponents of this view glibly put together slide shows which depicted prejudicial behaviour on school playgrounds. They also produced a number of attitudinal tests on racial prejudice. Opposed to this position were socially disadvantaged groups which pressed for behavioural change through government policy and other forms of legislation. They believe that racially related offences should be duly punished.

Within the ranks of the BCTF there were wide divisions which the task force had to straddle. At one end of the spectrum were teachers who opposed any involvement in social issues. According to this group, peace education, anti-racism, the rights of children, the status of women and similar issues should be the concern of government service agencies. For years, every annual general meeting of the BCTF saw an attempt by this group to reduce or eliminate the program against racism. At the other end of the spectrum were teachers who were known as "activists". They are teachers committed to generating social and political change. Between the two extremes was the great majority of teachers who, because they lacked an awareness of the pervasiveness of racism, were not interested in the debate.

It was to this large group that the task force directed much of its efforts: workshops to "sensitize" teachers to the reality of racism; simple tracts with titles like "What is Racism?"; lists of resources for teachers to refer to when dealing with what the task force felt would be a many-pronged attack of racial slurs, ethnic jokes, name-calling, stereotyping and racist graffiti. There were also attempts at advocacy and intervention, including an appeal to the University of British Columbia to train more native teachers, a plea to the Ministry of Education to produce textbooks which more accurately reflected our diverse society, and crisis resolution operations.

After three years the task force felt that it has not reached its goal of sensitizing teachers to the dangers of racism in schools. At this point, it was time to evaluate what had or had not been accomplished. The sensitization program and its objectives were seen to have been based on intuition and perceived needs, rather than on what was demonstrably effective. Some program activities were also seen as of dubious value. For example, the program was mostly directed at teachers. Little attention was paid to help prevent children, especially younger ones, from acquiring prejudiced views of people who are merely different. Almost all programs initiated by the task force were short-term or "one-shot" efforts. A typical activity would be a short workshop which formed part of a district's professional day. Competing with a motley of other offerings, including many highly entertaining ones, such a workshop would likely reach only a few teachers, thus lessening its impact.

In dealing with students, the task force placed a high value on frontal attacks against racism. This method was known to backfire, sometimes actually reinforcing rather than diminishing the prejudiced views of some students. Far too much effort went into attempts at attitudinal change and far too little into modifying values.

Perhaps the greatest challenge the task force faced was seeking change in an environment that resisted it. The education system in British Columbia and, indeed, in all of Canada is controlled by a network of old Anglo-Saxon Protestant boys who have demonstrated an amazing capacity for excluding women and minorities from positions of power. This exclusivity is most frequently achieved through what Bartol (1978) calls the "filtering process," in which the senior positions in the educational hierarchy are filled almost exclusively by white males who, of course, must keep the status quo in order to maintain their privileged status. Even new positions created by multicultural programs, major research grants, and lucrative consulting contracts with various government agencies supposedly promoting minority rights are largely given to the white male candidates. In its efforts to lobby school boards, faculties of education and the ministry, the task force met with a standard response: "We have no problems here!" "Racism" was perceived as overt acts of the kind that attract media attention. Institutional racism and systematic discrimination problems were simply dismissed by those who disregard demographic changes which have transformed entire school districts.

As the membership of the task force changed, a new debate threatened to divide it: multiculturalism versus racism? Neither of these terms had been defined, but a group within the task force felt that "multiculturalism" was a more acceptable term than "racism": its use would open more doors and the task force would gain more supporters if it were known as a multicultural group. Opposing this view were those members, including BCTF's leaders, who felt that there were already enough multicultural groups, so why add to their numbers? The problem, they argued, was not multiculture, but racism. By the beginning of 1980, the task force had torn itself apart. With a single BCTF staff person playing a part-time caretaker role and one or two persistent task force members trying to meet requests for workshops, the program against racism all but disappeared.

However, the need for such a program was underscored by two subsequent sets of circumstances. First, the British Columbia provincial government began a series of attacks on its Human Rights Branch which heralded the eventual disbanding of the branch. Second, the Ku Klux Klan staged one of its periodic revivals in the province. As a result, the BCTF had a new Committee Against Racism by the end of 1980, led by a full-time staff person and supported by an operating budget of about $45,000. With racist incidents receiving comprehensive media coverage in both Canada and the United States, and with revitalized community groups like the British Columbia Organization to Fight Racism demanding action against bigotry, the committee could broaden the base created by the old task force.

Racism in the school system was now perceived as much more than the usual litany of overt actions, such as name-calling. Using such data as the Toronto School Board's 1979 report on racism, the British Columbia committee identified institutional racism as its main target. Other areas of concern were: textbooks and other materials which show undue ethnic bias; the need for effective pre-service and in-service teacher training programs in plural education; race relations policies that would commit local school boards to developing and implementing strategies for dealing with racist behaviour in their schools; and an overhaul of hiring and promotional policies to ensure positions for minorities at all levels of the educational hierarchy.

The committee also recognized the importance of multicultural programs directed at students, especially elementary students, and trained a cadre of resource teachers who could work in collaboration with classroom teachers to develop teaching methods and materials aimed at meeting the needs of a multicultural school population. The importance of ethnic communities in their effort to increase tolerance between racial groups was also recognized and promoted by the committee.

Recognizing that racism in our schools must be resisted by a broadly-based coalition of agencies, community groups and teacher organizations, the committee set out to develop two networks: 1) an internal network of BCTF agencies and contact teachers in each of the province's seventy-five school districts; and 2) an external network of community groups, ethnic societies and service agencies, each dedicated to the ideal of racial tolerance in Canada. At present, all but seven of the school districts in British Columbia have representatives in the BCTF's program against racism as consultants. The network of community groups continues to expand, often taking actions such as lobbying school boards for race relation and multicultural policies. The BCTF has also developed a comprehensive race relations policy for its members, referred to at the beginning of this paper. (BCTF *Members' Guide, 1984-85*)

After ten years of promoting anti-racist education, the BCTF's program has achieved a degree of success in demonstrating the need for education to play a role in creating a more tolerant society. However, the constraints on a professional body such as a teachers' federation mean that its contribution to the fight against racism can only be limited. Until all levels of government collaborate with teachers and ethnic communities, efforts such as those of the BCTF are at best palliatives. At present, because of the political and financial realities in the province, the demands on the BCTF's program against racism are beyond its capacity. Yet, attempting to meet the needs of its members is a political necessity. Sometimes this leads to some poorly-conceived and ineffective activities. For example, despite evidence that merely talking to one group about another group does not necessarily change attitudes, the BCTF's program must answer many calls of the show-and-tell variety. It still arranges for members of various ethnic minorities to "perform" in schools and tell about their cultures.Usually, this means emphasis on what is exotic and hence, the reinforcing of stereotypes. Worse still, there is seldom any assessment of the effect of such presentations. Do they in fact increase tolerance of the group presented? Do they perhaps damage the self-concept of children from that particular ethnic group?

As part of its resources package, the BCTF's program has acquired or developed some audiovisual ideas which promote the concept of acceptance of human differences and help students to explore their own attitudes toward members of minority groups. When presented by a trained facilitator, such material can lead to an increase in racial tolerance. As yet, however, many teachers use these audiovisual programs merely as a means of filling time.

While the grindingly slow process of developing curriculum material that reflects the diversity of Canada's population continues, the BCTF has sponsored the development of supplementary items designed to offset some of the more blatantly biased and inaccurate portrayals of ethnic minorities. But unless such supplementary material is reinforced with adequate in-service training, it too often ends up unused on the shelf. Nor is there any incentive for hard-pressed teachers to develop their own resource materials. Based on the experience of the BCTF, we can identify a few areas where teacher organizations could be effective in promoting non-racist education.

1) In lobbying for teacher preparation, which will require more practitioners of cross-cultural counselling and communication as resource persons. Because present-day realities dictate that most effort should be directed at the retraining of in-service teachers, training programs are best organized for minimum disruption of teachers' duties. A generic in-service program, with enough flexibility to be adapted to local conditions, would be most practical.
2) In establishing a system of interprovincial contacts for the development, evaluation and sharing of non-racist resources, and for the exchange of resource people who have demonstrated their ability to assist colleagues in using multicultural classroom techniques.

3) In monitoring the textbook industry, identifying ethically unsatisfactory mataerial, and providing guidelines to publishers concerning the portrayal of minority groups.
4) In becoming more involved in the development of curriculum to promote a greater awareness of and sensitivity towards multicultural issues.
5) In taking a lead in community projects which encourage minorities to participate in the democratic process and which promote the ballot box as an effective device for bringing about needed changes that will lead to a more democratic syste of education.

The temptation for teacher organizations to do nothing about race relations and multiculturalism is great. The opportunities for action are even greater. Because teacher organizations must rely on persuasion, they should not expect their efforts to produce dramatic results. However, until schools, boards of education and other levels of government recognize the need for broadly focused ongoing programs, teacher groups can keep alive the ideal of an education system that is free of racism.

References

Bartol, K. (1978). The sex structuring of organizations: A search for possible causes. *Academy of Management Review, 3*(4), 805-815.
Martin, J. (1982). Excluding women from the educational realm. *Educational Digest, 48*(4), 43-46.
Morland, J. (1963). The development of racial bias in young children. *Theory into Practice*, 120-127.
Musgrove, F. (1982). *Education and anthropology, other cultures and the teacher*. Toronto: John Wiley.
Overing, R. (1977). Teacher education and multi-ethnicity. In V. D'Oyley (Ed.), *The impact of multi-ethnicity on Canadian education (2nd edition)*. Toronto: Urban Alliance on Race Relations, 73-78.

The Role of the Administrator in Multicultural Education

Ouida Wright

Perceptions of multiculturalism are as varied as those of beauty. Faced with the reality of a multicultural Canada, everyone supports the idea of multiculturalism with varying degrees of enthusiasm. Opinion runs the gamut from mutual accommodation of minority cultures with the dominant cultures to the view that ethnic cultures are acceptable only insofar as they do not change (or challenge) the status quo.

That Canada is a country of cultural diversity, of pluralism within a democratic society, is clear. What is less generally acknowledged is that the concept of multiculturalism varies with the degree to which the several cultures are present within a particular context or locale. Where the latter is the case, as in increasing numbers of educational jurisdictions across the country, there is some attempt to restructure the total educational environment to meet the educational, social and cultural needs of all the students. Such restructuring and maintenance not only make unexpected demands on the conceptual framework and the ingenuity of administrators in education but also generate heightened awareness of themselves as well as of the cultural groups which they serve.

The role of educational administrators has changed enormously over the last two decades. Gone is the affluence of the burgeoning sixties. Gone as well are precise, clearly defined curricula. Indeed, the Ontario Ministry of Education now provides numerous curriculum guidelines and resource documents which boards are expected to follow and to adapt to local conditions. Today educators are faced with an increasing array of issues, of which multiculturalism is only one, while financial resources shrink and dwindle like a snowman at the onset of warm weather. Notwithstanding the demands which a growing awareness of multiculturalism places on administrators, they must be recognized to be legitimate and appropriate considerations in planning a total program of education.

The role of the administrator has as its goal a process of change for which the product is an enhancement of one's own culture as one moves towards an increased appreciation of cultures other than one's own.

Language, the essence of culture, becomes the cutting edge of multiculturalism. It is the Great Divide which separates the extremes of opinion on multiculturalism and, to a lesser, extent the various shades of thinking between them. Immigrants whose native tongues are other than English or French, for the most part and at the present time, tend to concur with the following point of view:

> It [multiculturalism] means actively supporting their languages and cultures. All jurisdictions should support the concept of the maintenance of one's linguistic and cultural heritage, but this should not be done to the detriment of acquiring English, if in Ontario, and French, if in Quebec (Ferguson, 1976).

There is also agreement with this statement from the First Annual Report of the Canadian Consultative Council on Multiculturalism:

> Multiculturalism may be viewed as the development of a consciousness of our ancestral roots or ethnicity for creative purposes in the hope that a distinctive Canadian identity will emerge – language is important – the better one understands the ancestral language, the deeper will be the understanding of a group's culture, and the stronger will be the creative base for the talent that exists (Canadian Consultative Council on Multiculturalism, 1975).

This point of view was placed in an even more fundamental position by the Toronto Board of Education's Work Group on Third Language Instruction which observed in 1982:

> A firm sense of identity and self-respect requires roots and appreciation of one's heritage. And such self-respect is a necessary condition to promote genuine respect for others different from oneself. Programs which enhance students' languages throughout their school careers are those which actively demonstrate a school's forthright recognition, endorsement, acceptance and support of their identity. This learning places the student in a strong psychological position to take full advantage of all the educational opportunities available in the school. For that reason alone, the provision of programs which enhance a student's own language is simply good educational policy.

Clearly, then, a dynamic concept of multiculturalism which implies acceptance, appreciation and understanding of the cultures which make up society rejects the idea of a "mosaic" which implies a patchwork of cultures, static in isolation, co-existing but rarely interacting. Such a concept fosters divisiveness, ghettoization, even racism. Each culture retreats into itself and throws up protective barriers against assimilation into the dominant cultures which in turn strive to retain supremacy and their own distinct identity.

Multiculturalism as it is emerging in Canada today implies not mere tolerance but acceptance of each culture by others, a willingness to reveal itself to others, and, in turn, a reaching out to others. It is sharing based on mutual understanding and respect.

Multiculturalism bespeaks an attitude which enhances the human spirit, which promotes harmonious relations among the members of the cultural communities, which unites them all and diminishes none. This is what it means to be Canadian.

From time to time the words "integration" and "acculturation" are used to describe this process. Even when defined, these terms tend closely to resemble or inevitably lead to the "melting pot" which we in Canada have come to reject. The process of choice reflects the aspirations of individuals who, through their own cultural roots, speak their home language as well as one or both of Canada's two official languages, are informed of the culture of other cultural groups and may acquire one or more other languages.

It is this attitude which best defines the role of administrators in education and which informs their primary function as leader. Nowhere will this attitude be in greater evidence than in the environment in which students find themselves.

When students of various cultural groups find that there is no evidence anywhere of the heritage in which their own identity or personal history is rooted, they also find the source of alienation and loss of personal identity. The resulting struggle to rediscover a new identity in the new and alien environment produces anxieties and conflicts which no one should be expected to endure.

> For a growing child the question of personal identity is fragile under the best circumstances. To expect that child to resolve the conflict as a result of his/her own deliberate decision, is to desert the meaning of healthy growth and development. Resolving the conflict usurps the energy, attention and commitment of the child which she/he would normally utilize in pursuit of his/her school career to say nothing of the psychological impact which affects his/her academic life when she/he discovers him/herself alien to his/her own education in the first place (Board of Education for the City of Toronto, 1975).

An environment which promotes positive cross-cultural interactions enhances the self-esteem of students of all cultures and its effects are typically evidenced by improved academic performance. There are, of course, a myriad of contributors to academic excellence of which self-esteem, though powerful, is only one.

In recent years increasing attention has been directed towards various theories of cognitive development and the learning styles of students. It is being asserted that one of the reasons for the failure of some students is that they are unable to respond effectively to the manner in which information is presented, that their learning style is in conflict with the style of teaching.

Learning style as defined by Rita Dunn,

> ... is the way individuals concentrate on, absorb, and retain new or difficult information or skills. It is not the materials, methods, or strategies that people use to learn; those are the resources that complement each person's style. Style comprises a combination of environmental, emotional, sociological, physical, and psychological elements that permit individuals to receive, store and use knowledge or abilities (Dunn, 1983).

Learning style may also refer to the way in which people "identify, judge, substantiate, confirm and validate truth. To some people seeing is believing. To others truth comes through feeling it in one's bones, through chills, or through gut reaction" (Gregorc, 1982).

While learning styles are specific to individuals, theories of cognitive development, as for example those of Jean Piaget, seek to characterize learners in general and provide guidelines for the instruction of all pupils. Piaget points out that while human beings generally pass through four major stages of cognitive development – sensorimotor, preoperational, concrete and formal thought – they do so at their own rate and the onset of these stages varies from culture to culture the world over. The last stage, that of formal thought, may not be achieved unless appropriate educational opportunities are provided.

The provision of educational support will therefore require responsiveness to both group and individual needs. Where students vary not only in their developmental stages but in their cultural backgrounds as well, the demands on the system of educational delivery becomes dramatically more complex. This, in turn, requires that the scope of professional training must be broadened both in pre-service and in-service situations to include modifications to content, methodology and the environment to ensure curriculum delivery which is relevant, responsive and nurturing to all students. The administrator's awareness of, and sensitivity to, these issues must be translated into practical support systems for both staff and students.

Administrators in education are expected to be not merely managers and supervisors, but most essentially, leaders. Administrators in multicultural education will lead in a variety of ways. They will be knowledgeable about the cultures of the students in the schools which they administer. This knowledge will be reflected in personnel practices which demonstrate respect and appreciation for people of all cultures. Staff members will be representative of their institution's cultural mixture.

The curriculum in the institutions they administer will be rich in the heritage of all the cultural groups which work in them: the environment will reflect their language and culture; activities based on various cultural traditions will be integral points of the curriculum, not merely add-ons for "show-time"; their festivals and holy days will be remembered and celebrated.

Textbooks and other learning materials will reflect the cultural diversity of Canada not by tokenism – a picture here, a name there – but multiculturalism will be incorporated into the texture and fabric of the text.

Artwork displayed will reflect the many cultures in Canadian society; music will be evocative of our many heritages; and literature will be enriched by that of many cultures, in translation, where necessary.

In recognition of the increasingly supportive research in language learning, children will be taught initially in the home language, and careful transition made to one of the two official languages while at the same time preserving the home language. All children will be proficient in at least one of Canada's official languages. All children will be encouraged and facilitated in experiencing or acquiring proficiency in more than one language as well as in respect for other languages.

Educational institutions will be characterized by outreach into the community to ensure that all pupils participate fully in the school environment. Parents of all cultures will find a warm welcome and experience ready access to all services and activities. Parents' organizations will reflect the cultural diversity of the community and administrators will take care to ensure the participation and involvement of all parents. The approach will be evident in all school-community relations and may be evidenced not only by meaningful relationships between staff and parents but also by staff specially hired and trained to develop informed school-community interaction.

In order for this to happen, teaching and support staff must receive the professional training which encourages attitudes and instructional practices which are appropriate to all pupils and students. Special courses, workshops and conferences are valuable but more significantly the concept of multiculturalism will permeate *all* teacher training and staff development. Such training goes beyond cultural activities to the basic instructional methodology which affects cognitive development and promotes self-esteem. It includes recognition of, and attention to, varied home experiences and learning styles and is predicated on the knowledge that each person is unique, valuable in himself/herself and is capable of providing something worthy for himself/ herself and for society.

Such a concept of multiculturalism was enunciated by the Ontario Ministry of Education in 1977:

> Multiculturalism is a philosophy based upon the belief that each of the diverse cultures now present in our country has something of value to share with others and something of value to learn from others as together we strive to build a new and better way of living together – a more ideal society. (T. Ramautarsingh, M. Calisto, and E. May, 1977).

To lead in this ideal society administrators must be open, tough yet flexible – like steel! While keeping this ideal view before them they must have the courage and flexibility to co-opt others in this endeavor, to be responsive to their fears, objections and limitations and yet be capable of encouraging each small tentative step forward with tenacity and singleminded purpose.

Such purpose will be evident in every policy the administrator proposes or promotes, in every interaction with colleagues, in every aspect of his/her endeavours. The essential determinant of his/her effectiveness will be an increasingly relevant curriculum and the enhancement of collegial respect and appreciation throughout the system.

References

Baker, G.C. (1983). *Planning and organizing for multicultural instruction*. Menlo Park, California: Addison-Wesley.

Baptiste, H., Baptiste, M. and Gollnick, D. (1980). *Multicultural teacher education: preparing educators to provide educational equity*. Washington: Commission on Multicultural Education, American Association of Colleges for Teacher Education.

Board of Education for the City of Toronto. Work Group on Multicultural Programs. (1975). *Draft Report*. Toronto.

Board of Education for the City of Toronto. (1982). *Towards a comprehensive language policy: the final report of the work group on third language instruction*. Toronto.

Canadian Consultative Council on Multiculturalism. (1975). *First Annual Report*. Ottawa: Canadian Consultative Council on Multiculturalism.

Dubois, S. (Ed.). (1977). *Conference on Multiculturalism in Education*. Toronto: Ontario Association for Curriculum Development.

Dunn, R. and Dunn, K. *Teaching students through their individual learning styles: a practical approach*. Reston, Virginia: Reston Publishing.

Dunton, A. and Laurendeau, A. (Co-Chairmen). (1968). *Report of the Royal Commission on Bilingualism and Biculturalism: Book 11 – Education*. Ottawa: The Queen's Printer.

Dunton, D. and Laurendeau, A. (Co-Chairmen). (1968). *Report of the Royal Commission on Bilingualism and Biculturalism: Book 1V – The cultural contribution of the other ethnic groups*. Ottawa: The Queen's Printer.

Ferguson, R. (Ed.). (1976). *We are all immigrants to this place*. Toronto: Board of Education for the City of Toronto.

Ginsburg, H. and Opper, S. (1979). *Piaget's theory of intellectual development*. Englewood Cliffs, N. J.: Prentice-Hall.

Keefe, J. (Ed.). (1982). *Student styles and brain behaviour*. Reston, Virginia: National Association of Secondary School Principals.

Samuda, R., Berry, J. and Laferriere, M. (Eds.). (1984). *Multiculturalism in Canada: social and educational perspectives*. Toronto: Allyn and Bacon.

The Role of the School Counsellor in Multicultural Education

Ray Chodzinski

T he role of the school guidance counsellor has been defined in a variety of ways. In Canada, specific job functions vary from one province to another. However, in the main, we can argue that the primary responsibility of the school counsellor is to ensure that students are provided with opportunities which will assist them in understanding their environment, themselves and others. The counsellor also helps students make use of opportunities which will assist them in maximizing their potential toward personal self-actualization.

Counsellors have been and continue to be trained to deliver services within the context of a predominantly Anglo-French cultural context. However, the population mix of schools, particularly those in the major urban areas of Canada has changed significantly. Immigration from the Caribbean, the Middle East, the Far East and South America, as well as from traditional sources, has provided us with an enriched pluralistic cultural mosaic.

It is in this context that we must review the role of the school counsellor and delineate some of the issues, concerns and responsibilities to which the counsellor must respond if effectiveness is to be increased.

It is an understatement to claim that this is a rapidly changing world, even more so to suggest that counsellors must address change. However, the evidence shows that counsellor services tend to be offered from a traditional perspective and that counsellor role descriptions have not changed dramatically. This is particularly true with respect to providing services that meet the needs of a multicultural student population. As Samuda and Crawford (1980) have pointed out:

> Guidance procedures seem to be very little in evidence when the reception and placement of new Canadian minorities are examined.... Of all the 128 documents analyzed, only 10 of the total had any direct or specific reference to guidance and

counselling. ... In other words, there seems to be an attitude among a large proportion of counsellors that the problems related to new Canadian minority students fall outside their province (pp. 242-243).

Startling as this is, when we realize how little has been accomplished by counsellor educators to provide training in the area of multicultural education, we see that the fault cannot be attributed solely to the practitioners alone. As Wolfgang (1984) and others have pointed out, too few programs provide training in the areas crucial to effective intercultural counselling. This is particularly true with respect to school counsellor training.

This paper should not be construed as an attempt to blame counsellors for their lack of attention to yet another demand on their time and energy, nor does it suggest that all counsellors refrain from providing services in this vital area. Rather, it simply identifies that a problem exists and that there is a need for vigilance on the part of counsellors to recognize that counselling within a multicultural milieu demands that attention be paid to special needs and special concerns. This paper focusses on how the practising counsellor can increase the effectiveness of the delivery of counsellor services to a multicultural student population.

Policies and Regulations

First, it is important to review some of the policies which provide a basis for establishing delivery models of counselling services within a multicultural context. The Human Rights Code of Ontario states that: "Every person has a right to equal treatment with respect to services, goods and facilities, without discrimination because of race, ancestry, place of origin, colour, ethnic origin, citizenship, creed, sex, age, marital status, family status or handicap" (p. 1). Certainly, the implications for delivery of services are clear, concise and leave no room for interpretation.

The Ontario Ministry of Education Guidelines on Guidance advance this credo with specific direction to school guidance personnel. The new Ontario School: Intermediate Divisions Program and Diploma requirement guide (OSIS, 1984) speaks to all teachers with respect to their responsibility for promoting multicultural educational experiences. This document requires that schools help prepare all students to live in a multicultural society and underscores that "it is essential that every individual, of whatever colour, race, religion, age or sex, have the right to be treated with respect" (p. 8). The document specifically identifies how Ontario's multicultural policies can be advanced through school goals.

Schools will provide students with assistance and encouragement to:

1) develop and maintain confidence and a sense of self worth;
2) develop a sense of continuity with the past;
3) begin to understand and appreciate the points of view of ethnic and cultural groups other than their own;
4) develop an understanding of such concepts as community; conflict; culture; and interdependence;
5) learn the social skills and attitudes on which effective and responsible cooperation and participation depend (p. 8).

The report continues:

> that the policy of multiculturalism should permeate the school curriculum, policies, teaching methods, course of study and assessment and testing procedures as well as the attitudes and expectations of its staff and all of its interactions with students, parents and the community.

Other aspects of the guide focus on the need for teachers, principals and administrators to provide students with opportunities whereby they might develop positive attitudes towards the rights of others and project respect for other races, cultures, languages and religions, through educational experiences.

The Ontario Guidance document, Curriculum Guidelines for the Intermediate and Senior Division (1984) specifically speaks of multiculturalism:

> Guidance counsellors share with other staff the responsibility for helping all students to become aware of their own individual identity and heritage and to understand and respect the heritage of others. Students should understand that our national heritage is constantly evolving as new ethnic groups contribute ideas and experiences to our multicultural society (p.17).

This philosophical premise is supported by specific goals, aims and learning objectives for student teachers and counsellors. The school shall provide students with opportunities to acquire the skills, knowledge and attitudes necessary to:

1) appreciate themselves;
2) relate effectively to others;

3) develop appropriate educational plans;
4) explore career alternatives.

Clearly, we have a message to school boards to provide a milieu whereby the policies of the Canadian government, both federal and provincial, regarding multiculturalism must be advanced through educational goals, objectives and experiences. To this end, school counsellors must be committed to their responsibility for delivering services which reflect such policies. No longer can school boards be allowed to ignore this vital area of need as they did when Samuda and Crawford investigated the assessment, counselling and placement of minorities in Ontario schools.

The school counsellor, then, must review traditional delivery systems and modify and create a delivery model which will increase the effectiveness of a guidance service within the global community which is Canadian society.

As I have stated elsewhere (Chodzinski, 1981; 1984), school counsellors must confront themselves with fundamental questions pertaining to how they as individuals perceive the multicultural mosaic. Furthermore, they must address to what extent internalized biases and prejudices hinder their acceptance of multiculturalism as a policy and affect the delivery of services to minority group students. In addition, school counsellors must identify and become sensitive to the differences which must be addressed when providing services to a multicultural student population.

Considerations

Although school counsellor roles and responsibilities often differ from province to province, in the main, duties are defined in terms of elementary, junior, intermediate and senior school models. Counsellors are expected to have acquired skills in the following areas: (1) counselling skills; (2) assessment and placement skills; (3) career development and vocational awareness skills; (4) consultative and administrative skills; and (5) values, education and human resources management skills. Implementation of these skills within a pluralistic environment requires that the counsellors become sensitive to the plethora of barriers which might hinder their effectiveness and to learn techniques and strategies which will increase effectiveness.

Counselling Skills

It is important to recognize that while different needs require different strategies, all students, regardless of status, should be provided with counselling opportunities which help them to maximize their potential and develop self-worth. Therefore, guidance counsellors can apply their counselling skills in many of the traditional formats. However, the key is to adjust the delivery model to reflect an awareness of the cultural blending of the school population. This awareness can be demonstrated in individual and group counselling sessions, guidance classes and civics programs, vocational and career development explorations, work study skills and personal development seminars, conflict resolution formats, academic counselling, peer counselling and leadership programs, and information management activities.

With respect to the application of counsellor skills, research shows that school counsellors must learn to differentiate and understand differences in verbal and non-verbal behaviours of different minority groups. It has been shown, for instance, that majority group counsellors often promote inappropriate or ineffective message statements to clients because of a lack of understanding with respect to language or custom (Sue, 1981; Waxer, 1984). Counsellors may inappropriately infringe upon personal space, or unconsciously intimidate students by requiring them to reveal or express feelings when it is culturally inappropriate for them to do so (Sue, 1981). School counsellors must recognize that behaviour such as maintaining social distance, eye contact, recognition gestures, body language and self-disclosure commitments are not only revealed differently by different minority groups but are interpreted differently by different groups (Wolfgang, 1981; 1984).

Therefore, it is possible for well-intentioned counsellors to inadvertently confuse and offend student clients simply by inviting them to participate in activities such as personal or group counselling which, although familiar to students acculturated to Western concepts of communication, may be totally foreign to new Canadian students. Thus, while the school counsellor, who in most cases will be a member of one of the majority groups, believes that empathy, respect, positive regard and effective listening, questioning and responding skills are adequate tools to facilitate the counselling role in school environments, to be effective, they must be employed with sensitivity and care. Despite the fact that research shows that clients select and prefer counsellors cross-culturally on the basis of similarity of race, sex, style and personality (Waxer, 1984), it is my belief that minority group clients recognize that sensitive, caring individuals who demonstrate tolerance, acceptance and recognition of differences, can provide counselling services which are helpful and effective. Therefore, they will utilize the services available to them if given the opportunity to do so.

Assessment and Placement

School counsellors employ a variety of tests within a context of an educational setting. It is imperative that they exercise vigilance with respect to the inappropriate use of tests with minority group students. Unfortunately, despite the many references in the literature to concerns regarding reliability and validity issues, inadequate norming samples, cultural bias and loading of questions, ineffective scoring methods and general misuse issues (Samuda, 1975; 1984) derived data continues to be used inappropriately, and judgment placements and programming based on erroneous information continues.

Cummins (1984) writes that in a recent analysis of psychological assessments of new Canadian students, it was shown that when no account was taken of English as a second language, placement based on obtained test scores were substantially lower than when primary language was accommodated in the interpretation of test scores. The literature documents many similar abuses with respect to academic and vocational placements, special education placements, standardized achievement testing programs, attitude surveys, language ability testing, and pre-school screening programs.

It is imperative that school counsellors recognize that new Canadian students, particularly those who have little or no facility in English or French or who have not had time to become at least minimally acculturated should not be permitted to take tests which represent a WASP perspective and reflect standardizations which cannot be interpreted in terms of other cultures. This restriction applies to almost all achievment, ability, vocational and attitudinal protocols currently being used by school counsellors. As Samuda (1984) has suggested, counsellors must actively seek out ways of avoiding the perpetuation of racist ethnocentricism which these tests promote. Counsellors must restructure the delivery of services to avoid institutional, structural, technical and psychometric attitudes which contribute to inequities in schools and society in general.

Assessment procedures must be redefined and specific policies set in place. Assessments must always emphasize meeting the needs of the student as a learner. Learning style, language, background and past school experiences, identified program needs, and appropriate placement strategies are important considerations for assessing the abilities or interests of minority group students (Chodzinski, 1984).

Vocational assessment techniques must be of special concern for school counsellors since so many variables contribute to the accurate interpretation of test scores. Attention to the implications of vocational decisions cannot be overstated. Vocational assessments must respect differences in cultural background, values, traditions, language, customs, family pressures, perceived opportunities, economic realities and career goal aspirations.

It must be remembered always that many new Canadian students have not been exposed to the freedom of choice which so often is taken for granted in this country. Therefore, career aspirations of some new Canadian students may need to be nurtured insofar as equal opportunity for crystallization and realization of career path goals are realized.

Essentially, then, when counsellors employ tests, they must examine the instrument for biases, cultural loading, reliability and validity data, the appropriateness of questions, and the applicability of the norming sample with respect to interpretation of test scores. If the instrument does not satisfy basic requirements for safe-guarding human rights, it is incumbent upon the counsellor to refrain from using the test. Furthermore, it is my belief that the inequalities of utilizing such material should be made known to school board administrators and officials.

Educators must utilize alternate approaches to gain access to achievement information. For instance, criterion tests rather than norm-referenced tests allow more personal insights into skill development. Diagnostic batteries which incorporate various observational methods have proven to be useful. Dynamic assessment strategies such as those developed by Feruestein (1969) and Vygostsky (1978) provide insightful data on learner style and strategies. Mercer's (1979) pluralistic assessment program (SOMPA) offers counsellors opportunities to decrease the incidence of test discrimination. For more information on alternative methods consult two recent works: *Multiculturalism in Canada* by Samuda and Berry (1984) and *Intercultural Counselling and Assessment* by Samuda and Wolfgang (1984).

Community Involvement and Human Resources Management Skills

Counsellors must learn to recognize that differences exist within a cultural mix and, accordingly, must address the demands and needs of culturally different children (Samuda and Crawford, 1980). Specifically, these authors challenge school counsellors to recognize the Canadian mosaic as a cultural mix and to develop guidance programs and counselling techniques which reflect adoption of the multicultural policies of Canada.

Counsellors can demonstrate acceptance of policies in a variety of ways. Guidance classes should stress a values education program which highlights understanding the importance of responding positively to needs and feelings of others in the community. Programs should reflect the daily interaction of people from different cultures, races, religious groups and other affiliations. Community leaders can be invited to attend classes and participate in inter-ethnic activities. While multicultural days are an asset, caution must be taken to ensure that activities reflect a Canadian perspective rather than a "we and them" carnival approach which so often permeates multicultural events. Immigrant services programs can be developed and encouraged.

Peer counsellors, other staff members, cultural leaders and community resource personnel can be encouraged to participate in counselling functions. Students should be encouraged to attend multicultural leadership programs. Citizenship mini-courses can be developed and presented. Upgrading and work study skill programs can be provided to assist new Canadians. Report cards, information bulletins, memos, career information, community resources, employment assistance, emergency data and other useful information can be translated for parents and students. Meetings can be arranged, with interpreters on hand, to relay and discuss important information. Heritage language programs should be encouraged, and cultural customs and traditions of different groups can be highlighted through theme days, art work, cultural expositions, vocational expositions, and so on.

Information about legal rights and government policies affecting status and opportunities and civic responsibilities should be made available. Life coping skills, medical assistance, information and social assistance programs should be available to minority group students through school guidance offices.

Guidance counsellors can play an important role in helping new Canadians, visible minorities, and other groups outside the majority to feel important within the mosaic of Canadian life. As helpers and facilitators, counsellors must play an active role in ensuring that school officials recognize the need for funding and implementing guidance services which not only serve the needs of minority students but serve the community as a whole.

Summary

This paper has developed the theme that school counsellors must respond to a changing world by adjusting the perspective from which they deliver services.

Despite the plethora of barriers which inhibit the effectiveness of school counselling within a multicultural society and despite the existence of conditions which serve to support structural, institutional and personal racist attitudes, school guidance counsellors can and are obliged to provide services which facilitate the eradication of injustices not only within the context of the school community but also within the community at large. The following is a paraphrased summary of some suggestions offered by Westwood (1984) as guidelines for counsellors working within a multicultural environment:

1) Cross-cultural counselling theory and practice must be incorporated in all counsellor training and practice environments.
2) Acculturation of counsellors to minority clients' needs customs, cultures and tradition is essential.
3) Involvement with community and cultural institutions should be encouraged.
4) Counsellors should actively seek out experiences whereby they can experience different cultures and customs.
5) Counsellors should become sensitive to cultural variations in personal style, values, manners, verbal and non-verbal behaviours, emotional behaviour and learning style.
6) Recognize that barriers exist with respect to attainment of career goals for minorities and that vocational aspirations must be explored adequately.
7) Recognize the limitation imposed by counselling theories founded on traditional Western values.
8) Focus on prevention as well as remediation.
9) Encourage training of persons from specific cultural groups to become counsellors.

As a postscript, I suggest that school counsellors are charged with modelling the attributes of persons committed to the eradication of racial discrimination and cultural biases. Counsellors must become sensitive to the effects of racial tension on a student's personality, achievement and motivation as well as the realization of goals. Minority rights are guaranteed under the Human Rights Code, and therefore it is the responsibility of school counsellors to foster experiences which uphold values integral to this policy. I believe that Canadian school counsellors must meet the challenges of providing guidance and counselling services within a multicultural society, must recognize the diversity of human values and traditions, and must respond creatively and passionately to the challenge of helping all students to achieve a responsible attitude toward a changing society in a changing world.

To this end, counsellor educators and practitioners must re-design traditional training programs and courses to accommodate multicultural concerns and issues. In-service training, workshops and seminars must be provided for practising school counsellors in order to assist them in increasing their effectiveness. If we are at all serious about implementing the Charter of Rights, we must act immediately. It is time for all educators to change within a changing world.

References

Chodzinski, R. and Samuda, J. (1984).A training model for implementing non-biased assessment procedures. In R. Samuda and A. Wolfgang (Eds.), *Intercultural counselling and assessment: Global perspectives*. Toronto: C.J. Hogrefe, Inc.

Chodzinski, R. (1984). Counselling ethnic minorities. In R. Samuda, J. Berry and M. Laferrière (Eds.), *Multiculturalism in Canada: Social and educational implications*. Toronto: Allyn and Bacon.

Cummins, J. (1984). Psychological assessment of minority language students. In R. Samuda, J. Berry and M. Laferriere (Eds.), *Multiculturalism in Canada: Social and educational implications*. Toronto: Allyn and Bacon.

Feruestein, R. (1969). The instrumental enrichment method: An outline of theory and technique. Jerusalem: Hadessah-Wizo Canada Research Institute.

Mercer, J. (1979). In defense of racially and culturally non-discriminatory assessment. *School Psychologist Digest, 8,* 89-115.

Samuda, R. (1975). *Psychological testing of American minorities: Issues and consequences.*New York: Harper and Row.

Samuda, R. and Crawford, D. (1980). *Testing, assessment, counselling and placement of ethnic minority students: Current methods in Ontario*. Toronto: Ontario Ministry of Education.

Samuda, R., Berry, J. and Laferrière, M. (Ed.). (1984). *Multiculturalism in Canada: Social and educational implications*. Toronto: Allyn and Bacon.

Samuda, R. and Wolfgang, A. (Eds.). (1984). *Intercultural counselling and assessment: Global perspectives*. Toronto: C.J. Hogrefe, Inc.

Sue, D.W. and Sue, D. (1977). Barriers to effective cross-cultural counselling. *Journal of Counselling Psychology, 24*(5), 420-429.

Sue, D.W. (1981). *Counselling and the culturally different*. New York: John Wiley.

Vygostsky, L. (1978). *Mind in society: The development of higher psychological processes*. (M. Cole, V. Steiner, S. Scribner and E. Soberman, Eds. and Trans.). Cambridge, Mass.: Harvard University Press.

Waxer, P. (1984). Non-verbal aspects of intercultural counselling: Interpersonal issues. In R. Samuda and A. Wolfgang (Eds.), *Intercultural counselling and assessment: Global perspectives*. Toronto: C.J. Hogrefe, Inc.

Westwood, M. (1983). Cross-cultural counselling: Some special problems and recommendations for the Canadian counsellor. *Canadian Counsellor, 17*(2), 62-66.

Wolfgang, A. (1984). Intercultural counselling and non-verbal behaviour. In R. Samuda and A. Wolfgang (Eds.), *Intercultural counselling and assessment: Global perspectives*. Toronto: C.J. Hogrefe, Inc.

Effects of Teacher Perception on Achievement

Amargit Singh

Introduction

Teachers' expectations shape a child's self-concept and can encourage or discourage successful classroom performance. This general idea has been supported by a long tradition of research in the sociology and social psychology of education that has come to acquire at least two labels: 1) the self-concept of ability approach to classroom learning, teaching and school achievement, and 2) the expectation communication process research. In this paper I intend to review selected aspects of research done in these two areas, discuss some related issues, and suggest how several insights derived from this set of research have implications for the organization of teaching and learning for various purposes, both at the macro (the societal) and the micro (the school) levels, not only in Canadian society which now officially subscribes to the policy of multiculturalism, but also in other societies – the Western and non-Western – as well. Finally, based on the review of research, the reader's attention is drawn to a few strategies he/she might find helpful in implementing multiculturalism in our schools.

Briefly, the self-concept of ability approach capitalizes on a few basic tenets of the Meadian school of social psychology (Mead, 1934): that we develop ourselves, our identities and our feelings of self-worth through our interaction with others, and that the most important ideas which affect people's behaviour are those they have about themselves (Brookover and Erickson, 1969, 1975; Singh, 1977, 1984). The second approach focusses on the classroom expectations of teachers, teacher behaviour, student self-concept and student achievement by integrating "the teacher expectation literature with several social psychological theories, including the notion of causal attribution, learned helplessness, and self-efficacy" (Cooper and Good, 1983). Both approaches draw our attention to the fact that achievement expectations in various schools demonstrate quite clearly that school teachers, administrators and students hold differing expectations of student performance in various schools. The first approach in education recognizes the fact that in school there is a whole system of variables which will affect the students; that students behave in terms of others' expectations; and that teachers' expectations are relevant to elementary and high school age students in regard to their self-concept of ability and achievement in the school. Research in both approaches suggest that the school climate is an important variable in the organization of learning and teaching; that it can be changed to ensure success for all children; that schools can make a difference in the achievement outcomes; and that one major barrier to the development of a positive self-concept of ability is the existence of certain patterns of differential expectations for different groups of students. Thus, these approaches to research in education complement each other and have implications for the organization of teaching and learning activities at the macro and micro levels of society.

At the macro level we should be concerned with increasing the "collective level of ability" (Faris, 1961; Botkin, 1979) of Canadian society, while at the same time creating equal educational opportunity for an individual to enhance his/her social mobility by increasing the level of individual achievement in the school structure. Such a focus on education and society seems appropriate in order to overcome the "vertical mosaic" nature of Canadian society (Porter, 1965), and also in view of the fact that Canada is a pluralistic society in which schools have become multicultural, at least in many urban centers like Toronto; that there is a dwindling supply of unskilled jobs; and that school dropouts are not qualified for most available jobs. Further, in the context of existing economic, political and social world order, it is imperative for Canada, like any other nation in the world, to continue to upgrade its human resources. Excellence in education and equal opportunity for social mobility through education are the twin goals that Canadian society cannot afford to ignore. There is some reason to doubt that schooling alone has much impact on social mobility (Berg, 1970; Bowles and Gintis, 19976; Collins, 1979; and Jenks, 1979). However, education and occupation in societies like ours remain intimately associated and the interplay between them begins early in life. Thus, although education may not be a sufficient condition for success, it is usually a necessary one. Without it, many opportunities are closed for people, especially for those who come from poor families (Duncan,

1967). The implications of the self-concept of ability approach and the expectation communication process research for organizing learning and teaching at the micro level, i.e., at the level of the school, are usually related to macro level concerns being discussed here. In a nutshell, the micro level issues are: how can we structure our schools so that they provide equal opportunity to all students, and also increase their overall achievements and attainment of excellence in education. However, before discussing these ideas further, there are some related issues that I propose to discuss here.

Related Issues

These related issues are: sensitivity to the context of research; making sense of knowledge being produced by the research and publications industry; the contexts of self-concept of ability and expectation research in education; characteristics of teachers and schools; the role of outside involvement – i.e., other than teachers – in achieving successful outcomes in schools and in increasing individual abilities; and the meaning of multiculturalism, multicultural education and cultural differences.

It has been argued by many (Karabel and Halsey, 1979; Friedricks, 1970) that research in education and social science always reflects the changing social, political, economic and ideological contexts in any society. Thus production of knowledge through research is seldom "neutral", and knowledge is often used in the political arena to sustain and legitimize the status quo or to change it through critical dialogue and reflection. Different groups of researchers commit themselves to doing research built around certain interests, and similarly, funding agencies tend to allocate funds to those researchers whose research approximate their organizational interests and goals. Further, in any research undertaking, several ethical and moral issues are involved. Sometimes, researchers, intentionally or unintentionally, violate basic ethical and moral standards that are critical to educational and social science research (Sjoberg, 1967; Beauchamp, et al., 1982). Project Camelot in the social sciences, and education research done by Cyril Burt in England, are two cases in point.

Thus, making sense out of the enormous number of studies that are being produced by the research and publications industry should be the priority concern for any reader. Research sould be evaluated, not only on the basis of scientific methodology, but also on the basis of accountability (Brookover, *et al.*, 1974); benefit to the people studied (Hamnett, Singh, *et al.*, 1984); and whether or not it encourages justice, equality of opportunity, participation, self-respect, human rights and dignity in the community and the society at large. It is even more important that these criteria are recalled by the reader when reading studies done in the area of multiculturalism, because the knowledge being produced in this area has potential to affect the lives of millions of children in schools.

If research reflects the on-going concern of society with its political, social, economic, prevailing and shifting ideologies, as is being suggested above, what then has been the main interests of researchers in the self-concept of ability and expectation communication research areas? Cooper and Good (1983) point out that "teacher expectations and their possible effects upon student behavior and achievement have been salient research ideas for the past two decades." They also comment that

> expectation research seems certain to be of active interest in the 1980s as well. The importance of issues such as the mainstreaming of handicapped students and the desegregation of minority students guarantees a continuing analysis of the relations between teacher beliefs and differential instruction. In addition, there is concern at present about teacher efficacy beliefs, or how teachers evaluate themselves and the conditions under which they teach. Finally, the issue of teacher "burnout" has recently become a pertinent issue to educators. The study of teacher expectations is central to each of these societal concerns (p. 4).

Concern with issues such as grouping, tracking, testing, racism, and mainstreaming of minority students has also emphasized the research on teachers' perception and differential interaction. Reginald (1976) points out that

> from the perspective of minority group members, self-contained special classes were to be indicted on several counts, including but not limiting beliefs (a) that minority group children were overrepresented in special classes, particularly for the mentally retarded; (b) that assessment prctices are biased; (c) that special education labels are stigmatizing; and (d) that teachers hold negative attitudes towards the potential of minority group children. These views, reinforced by professional special educators in some instances, have served to highlight for many minority parents and professionals the view that institutionalized racism is part and parcel of educational practice.

Samuda (1984) points out that in Canada "the most serious problems exist in the assessment, testing, placement and counselling of ethnic minorities..." and although "as the result of our research in Ontario schools have shown, the use of IQ tests have been abandoned in some schools...the teacher remains the arbiter in placement decisions" (Samuda and Crawford, 1980). Porter (1965), Bowles and Gintis (1972), Lauter and Howe (1970), Ryan (1971) and several other researchers (Karabel and Hasley, 1979) have shown how inequality in society, plus the practices of labelling and grouping in schools not only encourage but expect large numbers of students to perceive themselves as being "stupid", "slow-learners", and "non-verbal". Other research findings indicate how policies, practice and interaction patterns in some multicultural schools negatively effect minority students' self-concept, achievement and social mobility (Verma and Bagley, 1982).

The self-concept of ability approach and achievement research has also been concerned with many issues mentioned above. Particularly, Brookover and Erickson (1969), the prominent researchers in this area, challenged the beliefs of some psychologists who argued "that the differences in academic achievement are best explained by differences in capacity to learn, which are relatively fixed." Their work, along with others, provided a fresh look at the IQ controversy initiated by Jensen (1969), and contrary to Jensen, reinforced the optimistic view that human learning ability was not fixed; that it could be expanded under correct social conditions; and that success in the school was crucial to the on-going debate about equal educational opportunity and social mobility (Singh, 1977).

A few words about teacher characteristics and the schools are in order. Teachers as a group cannot be isolated as the sole cause of student under-achievement in the school. Teachers do not constitute a homogenous group. Not all teachers behave in a similar way toward students (Brophy and Good, 1974). Students have very uncanny perceptions of their teachers. They perceive some teachers as being helpful, cooperative and understanding, others just the opposite (Martin, 1984). Some teachers are relatively more "Pygmalion-prone" or "high-bias" than others, reflecting perhaps a dogmatic personality and need for greater control (Cooper and Good, 1983). Similarly, schools vary in their functions, structures and goals. For example, the city school may tend to teach students to renounce the past and acquire a new way of life; the suburban school may emphasize the fact that the child be oriented toward the future; and the village school or the school in a small community may want to see that the child is held close to tradition (Brembeck, 1971). Further, some schools may unintentionally encourage racial/ethnic segregation and discrimination, and they may implement policies and follow practices based on assumptions that contradict the equal opportunity goals. In contrast, other schools may genuinely foster integration, multiculturalism and equal educational opportunity (Brookover, *et al.*, 1974; Ogbu, 1978). Certainly, the larger system in which the school is embedded has much to do with the failure of the school. Not teachers alone, but many others – principals, school board officials, universities, business communities, governments at all levels, individual parents, the community as a whole – play an important role in effecting positive or negative outcomes in the school.

The last issue revolves around the meaning of multiculturalism, multicultural education and cultural differences. In another article (Singh, 1984) I have discussed the meaning of these concepts as they relate to the expectations of significant others, including teachers, the development of self-concept, achievement in schools, and life chances of individuals in detail. It suffices here to mention that significant others are people (or ideas, social movements, etc.) who are important in our lives and whose expectations of ourselves greatly affect our behaviours and self-concepts.

Most societies like Canada are characterized by the presence of social classes. Max Weber (1946) believed that social class is based on wealth, that a chance to acquire wealth is just as important as wealth itself, and that wealth is acquired by making profit in the marketplace. For most Canadians, the most important life chance is the opportunity to have a successful and dignified occupation or career that provides an adequate income. But, in order to increase one's life chances, one needs to have an advanced education, special skill, or a talent or service to sell in the marketplace. McLeod (1984) conceptualizes multiculturalism in Canada in terms of lifestyle, way of life and life chances. Wilson (1984) writes, and rightly so, that "the distinction between life chances and lifestyles is at the heart of the multicultural dilemma."

What, then, is the effect of identifying cross-cultural differences? Does this process enhance the life chances of people who are labelled different? It should be recognized that the habit of describing the smallest differences in the behaviors of others and the insistence on the self-evident truth that people are different will not solve the problems of the "vertical mosaic" image of Canadian society or soothe the injuries of class structure. What causes the problem is the significance of the difference. Are the differences being treated as deviant behavior, i.e., in negative, stigmatizing and stereotypic ways? Or are they being looked at and talked about in a positive, supportive and encouraging way? Brookover, *et al.* (1974) point out that

the maximizing of individual differences and the differentiation of educational programs for different children is commonly advocated without regard to the effect of such education on the social structure or the opportunities for social mobility. These programs and policies do not recognize that equality of opportunity is not facilitated by highly differentiated educational programs based upon the presumed differences between lower-class and middle-class children. One does not achieve equality by enchancing the differences in children and thus allocating them to different social status.

I now return to further elaboration of the self-concept of ability and expectation research approaches in education.

Some Insights and Implementation

Several insights derived from these two research approaches in education have implications for structuring the school, enhancing the potential of human resource currently available to Canadian society, and attaining the twin goals of excellence in education with equity. At the macro level, we may begin to use a change-oriented vocabulary that conceptualizes human educability in terms of an open-ended process, as opposed to the limited and the fixed entity conception of human abilities to learn (Singh, 1977). Both society and individuals, through interaction between them, can learn and grow to close the "human gap" or "cultural lag". According to Botkin, *et al.* (1979), "the human gap is the distance between the growing complexity of society (and culture) and our capacity (individuals) to cope with it." There are no limits to society's and an individual's abilities to learn. Peccei (see Botkin, *et al.*, 1979) points out that "the average person, even when living in deprivation and obscurity, is endowed with an innate brain capacity, and has on hand a *learning ability*, which can be stimulated and enhanced far beyond the current relatively modest levels." Botkin, *et al.* (1979) draw our attention to the fact that "human potential is being artifically constrained and vastly under-utilized, so much so that for all practical purposes there appear to be virtually no limits to learning." Artificial constraints are structured social inequalities that exist between nations and various groups within a nation (Karabel and Halsey, 1970; Porter, 1965). Further, by raising the expectation levels of its people, each society creates its own ability and achievement levels. Moreover, human learning takes place when all people are teachers, when there is universality of expectations and homogeneity of models, and when teaching is continuous, followed by consistent and repeated use of approval and disapproval or reward and punishment for appropriate and expected behavior (Brookover and Erickson, 1969).

Unfortunately, as Brookover and several other scholars point out, "in most discussions of the goals of education, educational leaders tend to emphasize the importance of educating the individual to 'the limits of his capacity'." Similarly, college and university administrators talk about educating anyone who has the potential or who can profit by such experience. Such discussion reflects the notion of dimension. However, we have no vocabulary which posits the concept of change or expansion or development of intelligence through the creation of appropriate environmental experiences. The concept of a varying and pliable learning ability is therefore very difficult to introduce, and it is not easy for us to comprehend such an idea without a vocabulary with which to discuss it (Brookover and Erickson, 1969).

If we want to achieve a high rate of success in our school, we must move away from the idea that human ability is fixed. Instead, we should develop attitudes based on the belief that almost all human beings can learn whatever any particular person can learn if they are encouraged, expected to learn and provided with the appropriate environment. Now we turn to the school or microlevel implications of expectation research.

Cooper and Good (1983) extensively review the research and state that "the relations between teacher expectations, teacher behavior, and student performance have been, and continue to be, active research areas." Brophy and Good (see Cooper and Good, 1983) did detailed analyses of the sequential relationship between teacher expectation and student performance. Their model involved four steps:

1) The teacher develops an expectation, predicting specific behaviour and achievement for each student.
2) Because of these expectations, the teacher behaves differently toward each student.
3) This treatment informs each student about the behaviour and achievement expected from him/her and affects the students' self-concept, achievements, motivation and level of aspiration.
4) If teacher treatment is consistent over time and students are behaviourally compliant, the students' achievement will come to correspond or remain correspondent with teachers' belief about the students. High teacher expectations will lead to or sustain student achievement at high levels, while low expectations will diminish or support low student achievement.

Good and Brophy (1980, cited in Cooper and Good, pp.10-11) report twelve of the more common ways teachers' action can vary with expectations:

1) Seating low-expectation students far from the teacher and/or seating them in a group.
2) Paying less attention to lows in classroom situations (smiling less often and maintaining eye contact).
3) Calling on lows less often to answer classroom questions or to make public demonstrations.
4) Waiting less time for lows to answer questions.
5) Not staying with lows in failure situations (i.e., providing fewer clues, asking fewer follow-up questions).
6) Criticizing lows more frequently than highs for incorrect public responses.
7) Praising lows less frequently than highs after successful public responses.
8) Praising lows more frequently than highs for marginal or inadequate responses.
9) Providing lows with less accurate and less detailed feedback than highs.
10) Failing to provide lows with feedback about their responses as highs.
11) Demanding less work and effort from lows than from highs.
12) Interrupting performance of lows more frequently than highs.

Rosenthal and Jacobson (1968) in their well-known study concluded that teachers' expectations had subtly influenced their students' performance. Their study highlighted a classic example of the self-fulfilling prophecy; it occurs when people behave in a way that makes their predictions likely to come true. Cooper and Good (1983) extensively review the works of Rosenthal (1968; 1974), Brophy and Good (1974) and many other researchers in this area.

Brookover and Erickson (1969) report that adult expectations held for students vary in norms from one school to another and, in fact, from one classroom to another. The relationship between expectations held by significant others (e.g., teachers, parents, peers, etc.), students' self-concept of ability and students' achievement has been well supported by research in many countries (Brookover and Erickson, 1975).

It is unlikely that the "vertical mosaic" nature of Canadian society will drastically change in the near future, though many significant changes in its social structure may be anticipated due to the presence of these factors: the new charter of rights; a heightened appreciation of democratic principles among citizens; the revolution of rising expectations; demand for self-respect, self-reliance, equity, justice; protection of human rights; increasing participation on the part of many minority groups in petitioning the government to remove structural and institutional racism to their social mobility; and increasing involvement of courts in making decisions regarding social policies and issues. The same can be said about the educational system. It is true, in general, that educational systems as social institutions, may continue to reproduce the Canadian social structure or structure of any other society in which they are embedded.

However, there is no reason to believe that they would not respond to the aspirations and expectations of people in society (Meyer, 1977). Also, it appears that the current international marketplace and economic interdependence make it imperative for societies like Canada to continue to develop their vast multicultural human resource within the framework of a pluralistic society. There is room for change at various levels of schooling in Canada, because schools, teachers, school boards, faculties of education, outside communities, and so on, vary in terms of their visions, creativities, interests, commitment and moral energies. Certainly, it appears that some schools, teachers, school boards, parents, and other groups in the community are relatively more interested than others in changing the social structure and the climate in schools to ensure successful outcomes for all children. Also, it seems that some of them are relatively more interested, committed and active than others in enhancing the life chances of pupils in multicultural school settings.

Let us continue to focus on the micro level, i.e., at the level of social structures in the school, the climate in the school, and the changing nature of the school in larger cities in North America. The population of these cities is largely composed of working-class white ethnics, blacks, Hispanic and other minorities. Teaching in the inner-city schools is a difficult task. There are numerous conflicts within the school which sometimes reflect all the tensions in the surrounding adult environment in the community. Yet, Edmonds and his associates (1979) point out that this picture of inner-city schools as a conflict-ridden institution may be overdrawn. They found out that many schools and students do reach their academic goals and many more could experience success. They report that in successful schools: 1) administrative leadership was strong; 2) all children were expected to achieve highly and no child was permitted to fall below minimum levels; and 3) an orderly and quiet atmosphere (though not rigid or possessive) prevailed. Coleman's (1981) study also indicated that private schools had similar characteristics. Edmonds (1972) states that "we can whenever, and wherever we choose, successfully teach all children whose schooling is of interest to us. We already know more than we need in order to do this. Whether we do it must finally depend on how we feel about the fact that we haven't so far." The school system is embedded in the larger social system. Rich (1983) observed that involvement of outsiders (i.e., parents, police and business people) in the school resolved serious behaviour problems of students and thus improved their test scores greatly.That outside involvement – in the form of a university-public-school partnership – could be beneficial under some circumstances was also supported by the Yale University's Child Study Center and two inner-city elementary schools in New Haven, Connecticut (Comer, 1980). The researchers in this study looked at the school as a total setting in which teacher and staff worked *with* the students, and found that three things accounted for solving the serious behaviour problems and increased test scores of the students.These were: changes in the expectations of teachers; creation of a calm atmosphere for learning; and letting the students know that they were able to do the school work.

Similarly, Brookover and his associates (1979) point out how the school climate can be changed to ensure success for all children. They note that "the conclusion of social researchers (Jenks, et al., 1972, and Hauser, Sewell, and Alwin, 1976) that schools do not and/or cannot make a difference in the achievement outcomes has been based on inadequate evidence." Based on their extensive research over the years, they identified school characteristics that encourage success for almost all students regardless of their family, ethnic, race and socioeconomic backgrounds. According to them, schools in which students enjoy a relatively high level of academic success tend to have certain characteristics. For example, the school staff has a positive view of students' ability to learn, communicating this view to one another, to students and to parents. Also, teachers accept responsibility for students' failure to learn, constantly seeking ways to "reach" students who have difficulties. Brookover, *et al.* (1979) write:

> Briefly, the characteristics of the school social system which we hypothesize will produce high achievement and other desired outcomes may be summarized as follows: First of all, assume that all children can and will learn whatever the school defines as desirable and appropriate. Expect all children to learn these patterns of behavior rather than differentiate among those who are expected and those who are not expected to learn. Have common norms that apply to all children so that all members of the school social system, the patterns of interaction between teacher and pupil should be characterized by consistently appropriate and clearly recognized reinforcement of learning behavior. Failure

should be followed by immediate feedback and reinstruction rather than positive reinforcement. Positive reinforcement should be given only when correct responses are made. This type of school environment is best characterized by what has come to be known as the Mastery Model (Bloom, 1976). Mastery of each unit of instruction by all should be the goal and the total school social system should be mobilized to achieve that goal. Thus students, teachers, and all associated in that school social system should assume that all students can and will learn, should provide appropriate norms and expectations, and practice the appropriate patterns of reinforcement and instruction for all students. This may be facilitated by having students work in teams and compete with other teams rather than as individuals competing with each other.

In summing up, it appears that no research dealing with the organization of learning and teaching, and its consequences for large numbers of students, is one hundred percent perfect. I contend only that the present state of the art in the sociology and social psychology of education does, to a reasonable degree, provide us with some useful insights into how to develop strategies for effecting change in the school's multicultural social structure, so as to attain equity and excellence in educational systems embedded in pluralistic societies. In all the studies reviewed above, the researchers believed that the personal characteristics of students were not the most important causes of their behaviours and learning problems. Instead, such problems stemmed from the structure, the climate and the general environment of the school. Finally, they believed that schools can, with the help of teachers and others in the community, make a difference in the achievement outcomes of the millions of students who attend them.

References

Beauchamp, T., Faden, R., *et al.* (Eds.). (1982). *Ethical issues in social science research*. Baltimore: Johns Hopkins University Press.

Berg, I. (1970). *Education and jobs: the great train robbery*. New York: Praeger Publishers.

Blau, P. and Duncan. O. (1967). *The American occupational structure*. New York: Wiley.

Bloom, B. (1976). *Human characteristics and school learning*. New York: McGraw-Hill Book Company.

Botlin, J. *et al.* (1979). *No limits to learning: bridging the human gap – a report to the Club of Rome*. New York: Pergamon Press.

Bowles, S. and Gintis, H. (1972). IQ in the United States class structure. In A. Gauter, et al. (Eds.), *The new assault on equality: IQ and social stratification*. New York: Harper and Row.

Bowles, S. and Gintis, H. (1976). *Schooling in capitalist America*. New York: Basic Books.

Brembeck, C. (1971). *Social foundations of education: environment influences in teaching and learning, 2nd edition*. New York: Wiley.

Brophy, J. and Good, T. (1974). *Teacher-student relationship: causes and consequences*. New York: Holt.

Brookover, W. and Erickson, E. (1969). *Society, schools and learning*. Boston: Allyn and Bacon.

Brookover, W., et al. (1974). Quality of education attainment, standardized testing, assessment, and accountability. In *Uses of sociology of education*. The Seventy-Third Yearbook of the National Society for the Study of Education, Part 11.

Brookover, W. and Erickson, E. (1975). *Sociology of education*. Homewood, Illinois: The Dorsey Press.

Brookover, W. and Beady, C., et al. (1979). *School social systems and student achievement: schools can make a difference*. Brooklyn, New York: J.F. Bergin Publishers.

Collins, R. (1979). *The credential society: an historical sociology of education and stratification*. New York: Academic Press.

Comer, J. (1980). *School power implications of an intervention project*. New York: Free Press.

Cooper, H. and Good, T. (1983). *Pygmalion grows up. Studies in the expectation communication process*. New York and London: Longman.

Edmonds, R. (1979). Some schools work and more can. In *Social policy*, March-April, 28-32.

Faris, R. (1961). The ability dimension in human society. In *American sociological review*. Friedricks, R. (1970). *A sociology of sociology*. New York: Free Press.

Good, T. and Brophy, J. (1980). *Educational psychology: a realistic approach, 2nd ed.* New York: Holt.

Hauser, R., Sewell, W. and Alwin, D. (1976). High school effects on achievement. In Sewell, Hauser, and Fettman, *School and academic achievement in American society*. New York: Academic Press.

Hamnett, M. and Singh, A., et al. (1984). *Ethics, politics, and international social science research: from critique to praxis*. Honolulu: The University of Hawaii Press.

Jenks, C., et al. (1972). *Inequality: a reassessment of the effect of family and schooling in America*. New York: Basic Books.

Jenks, C. (1979). *Who gets ahead? The determinant of economic success in America*. New York: Basic Books.

Jensen, A. (1969). How much can we boost IQ and scholastic achievement? In *Harvard Educational Review, XXXIX, 1* (Winter).

Karabel, J. and Halsey, A. (Eds.). (1979). *Power and ideology in education*. Oxford: Oxford University Press, Inc. (3rd printing.)

Lauter, P. and Howe, F. (1970). How the school system is rigged for failure. In *The New York Review of Books, XIV,* (June)

McLeod, K. (1984). Multiculturalism: lifestyle, way of life, life chances. In *Multiculturalism,, 12*(2), 19-21.

Mead, G.(1934). *Mind, self, and society*. Chicago: The University of Chicago Press.

Meyer, J. (1977). The effects of education as an institution. In *American Journal of Sociology, 83*, 55-77.

Ogbu, J.(1978). *Minority education and caste: the American system in cross-cultural perspective*. New York: Academic Press.

102

Porter, J. (1965). *The vertical mosaic*. Toronto: University of Toronto Press.

Reginald, L. (Ed.). (1976). *Mainstreaming and the minority child*. Minneapolis, Minnesota: The Council for Exceptional Children.

Rosenthal, R. and Jacobson. (1968). *Pygmalion in the classroom: teacher expectation and pupils' intellectual development*. New York: Holt.

Rosenthal, R. (1974). *On the social psychology of the self-fulfilling prophecy: further evidence for Pygmalion effects and their mediating mechanisms*. New York: MSS Modular.

Rich, E. (1983). Making it happen: turning a high school around. In *Social Policy*. Winter, 40-43.

Ryan, W. (1971). *Blaming the victim*. New York: Vantage Books.

Samuda, R. (1975). *Psychological testing of American minorities*. New York: Harper and Row.

Samuda, R. and Crawford, D. (1980). *Testing, assessment, counselling and placement of ethnic minority students: current methods in Ontario*. Toronto: Ministry of Education.

Samuda, R. (1984). The Canadian brand of multiculturalism: social and educational implications. In D. Modgil, G. Verma, and G. Modgil (Eds.), *Multicultural education: the interminable debate*. Barcombe Lewes, Sussex: Folwer Press Ltd.

Singh, A. (1977). Self-concept of ability and school achievement – an alternative to the fixed ability model of education. In R. Carlton et al. (Eds.), *Education change and society – a sociology of Canadian education*. Toronto: Gage Educational Publishing, 320-334.

Singh, A. (1984). The self and social change: multiculturalism and human educability. In *Multiculturalism*, *8*(1), 22-29.

Sjoberg, G. (Ed.). (1967). *Ethics, politics, and social research*. Cambridge, Mass.: Schenkman Publishing.

Verma, K. and Bagley, C. (Eds.). (1982). *Self-concept, achievement and multicultural education*. London: MacMillan.

Weber, M. (1946). *From Max Weber: essays in sociology*. H. Gerth and C. Mills (Eds. and Trans.). New York: Oxford University Press.

Wilson, J. (1984). Multicultural programmes in Canadian education. In R. Samuda, *et al*. (Eds.), *Multiculturalism in Canada: Social and educational perspectives*. Toronto: Allyn and Bacon.

PART III

Curriculum Development

Guidelines for Curriculum Writing in a Multicultural Milieu

Ahmed Ijaz

I n the past decade, considerable progress has been made in the re-moval of overtly racially offensive content from textbooks and instructional materials used in classrooms. While such materials are beginning to be increasingly free from derogatory references based on ethnic or racial stereotypes, ethnic and racial minority groups continue to be underrepresented, often to the degree of total exclusion. The federal policy of Multiculturalism within a Bilingual Framework which espouses the cultural freedom and equality of all Canadians and asserts that no ethnic group should take precedence over any other still remains an ideal as far as classroom instruction and the vehicle of that instruction are concerned. Visible minorities, in particular, remain invisible in curriculum materials. The lack of information on the contributions made by ethnic minorities to the development of Canadian and world social, political and economic history, science, technology, arts, etc., ex-plicitly or implicitly convey to students the message that (a) a certain race or cultural group is innately more Canadian than others, and (b) that minority cultures/races have made little or no contribution to Canadian or world development. Furthermore, the relative absence of ethnic minority members in curriculum materials reinforces the notion that since such Canadians belong to cultures that are neither English nor French, they are not Canadian. Visible minority Canadians, in particular, who are "raised in either a French or English milieu ... are still perceived to be from another culture by other Canadians. Regardless of how long (they) have been in this country, they are perceived to have been here for a short time" (*Equality Now*, p. 5).

In view of the slow progress made by Canadian publishers in developing curriculum materials which more effectively represent the multicultural/multiethnic composition of Canadian society, a number of school boards in major urban centres have taken the initiative in developing suitable materials. However, in most instances, the products of such initiatives have remained confined to the respective school jurisdictions. The distribution of such materials across other school boards tends to occur somewhat incidentally on the basis of word of mouth recommendations rather than systematically through a central clearing-house. There is an impelling need for Ministries of Education to publicize local initiatives in the development of multicultural learning materials in order to assist all school boards in obtaining access to such materials, to avoid unnecessary duplication, and to encourage the development of a wider range of such materials.

The following guidelines have been designed to assist curriculum writers at the local school and board levels in developing curriculum materials with an unbiased multicultural focus. For easy reference, these guidelines are presented in point form rather than in the form of detailed descriptive text.

Basic Principles for a Multicultural Curriculum

The content of books and other learning materials can influence the attitudes of students toward others and themselves. Evidence to this effect has been reviewed by Pratt and McDiarmid (1971) and Preiswerk (1980) who have shown that racial, cultural, and religious minorities were not only underrepresented in Canadian textbooks but also misrepresented. In a publication entitled *Race and Culture in Ontario School Materials*, the Ontario Ministry of Education has provided a framework of four basic principles for developing learning materials that represent racial, religious, and cultural minorities:

1) Learning materials should reflect fully and accurately the reality of Canada's racial and cultural diversity.
   - They should reflect the range of lifestyles, customs, and traditions of all races, cultures, and religions represented in Canadian society without romanticizing or patronizing minorities.
2) Learning materials should facilitate the development of mutual awareness, understanding and appreciation among all races, religions, and cultural groups in Canadian society.
   - They should explain the role, value, and meaning of behavioural patterns, customs and traditions in the life of each race and culture.

- They should show people of all races, cultures and religions as being "capable of contributing to the society and institutions within the context in which they function" (p.25).
- They should "raise issues and promote discussion in order to provide students with an understanding of situations that involve bias, prejudice and discrimination" (p.14).
- They should "help students analyse racial, cultural, and religious tensions and conflict fairly, frankly, objectively and sensitively at their level of maturity and understanding" (p.14).

3) Learning materials should recognize the universality of the human experience and interdependence of all human beings and communities.
   - While people of different races, cultures and religions may differ in their ways of meeting common needs because of differential value systems, they should be shown as sharing in a common human experience.

4) Learning materials should contribute to a feeling of self-worth in all students.
   - They should "contain a variety of cultural symbols to which all Canadian children can relate. Every student should be able to recognize something of his or her own life. The message that lifestyles, customs and religious beliefs that are different from one's own can have intrinsic worth should be clear" (p.13).
   - They should present the achievements and contributions of all races, cultures, and religions to the life and culture of Canada so that all students may develop pride in their heritages.

Guidelines for Presenting Information

It is often assumed that more information about other cultures produces better intergroup attitudes. Research shows that this is not necessarily the case. A number of studies investigating programs which focused on imparting information about other cultures found negative attitudinal effects whereas others found a positive effect or no effect. John Kehoe in his book A Handbook for Enhancing the Multicultural Climate of the School (p.74) provides the following guidelines for presenting information:

1) Emphasize positive achievements more than hardships and persecutions of ethnic minorities.

2) Place less emphasis on the exotic, bizarre, and different, and place more emphasis on similarities among cultures.
3) Present information from an insider's point of view, with an emphasis on a "we" rather than a "they" perspective.
4) Place less emphasis on poverty.
5) Emphasize family life and the nature of everyday life in other cultures.
6) Develop the concepts of prejudice, ethnocentrism, and stereotyping, and provide an opportunity to examine their harmful effects.

Prejudice is an attitude which implies a (generally unfavourable) judgement on a person, attributing to that person a variety of characteristics which are ascribed to a group of which the person is a member.
Ethnocentrism is an opinion that one's own race or culture is the most important and the other cultures are wrong or inferior because they do things differently.
Stereotype is a fixed, oversimplified image attributing certain, often false, characteristics to a person, thing or idea.
Bias is an inclination toward a specific opinion of or attitude toward certain things or people which is formed without adequate reason.

Background Information and Research

– Obtain the latest materials and statistics.
– Wherever possible, primary sources should be consulted.
– Consult sources with a wide range of viewpoints and perspectives.
– Try to identify and avoid sources which provide a biased treatment of minorities and an ethnocentric description or interpretation of events.
– Consult with local community organizations, professionals from minority groups, and relevant scholarly authorities to verify the accuracy of information.

Storyline and Description of Characters

Watch for subtle (covert) forms of bias toward racial and cultural groups.

Equal Participation in Society

– Reflect in title and content the equal participation of minorities in all areas of life and in a variety of situations.

- Racial and cultural minorities should be portrayed as authority figures as well as in supportive roles.

Heroes

- Heroes should belong equally to minority groups as to the establishment.
- When minority heroes appear, they should be admirable for the qualities that have made white heroes famous and not because they have done something that has benefitted white people.

Standard for Behaviour and Success

- Avoid making "white" Anglo-Canadian behaviour the standard for acceptability and success.
- To gain acceptance and approval, minorities should not have to exhibit extraordinary qualities, e.g., excel in sports, academics, etc.
- Ensure that minorities are portrayed as equally capable, intelligent, resourceful, self-confident, imaginative, and independent as the majority group.

Role of Women

- Sex roles should be incidental rather than crucial for characterization and plot.
- The achievements of girls and women should be based on their own initiative and intelligence and not shown to be the result of their good looks and their relationship with males.

Lifestyles

- Minority persons and their setting must be depicted in such a way that they do not contrast unfavourably with the norm of the white middle-class.
- If a minority is depicted as "different", ensure that no negative value judgment is implied.
- If the illustrations and text attempt to depict another culture, avoid over-simplifications and stereotypes.

– Be accurate in the description of clothing, customs, and behaviour.
– Avoid focussing exclusively on the exotic aspects of culture.

Decision-Making

– People of all races, cultures and religions should be shown as capable of making decisions concerning the issues that affect their lives.
– Do not present "Third World" peoples consistently as a burden to the rest of the world, without any effort at self-help and no initiative in finding solutions to problems.

Resolutions of Problems

– In the presentation and resolution of problems, avoid making minority people the problem.
– In the resolution of a particular problem faced by a minority person, avoid the benevolent intervention of a white person.

Language

– Language has great power to shape opinions and attitudes. Handle it carefully not to reinforce inaccurate images of minority groups and foreign countries but to stimulate understanding and respect.

Stereotypes

– Avoid expressions that imply that all attributes are shared by all members of an ethnic group (e.g., inscrutable Orientals, happy-go-lucky Blacks, frugal Scots, amorous Frenchmen, nature-loving Natives).

Insidious Bias

– Avoid loaded adjectives with derogatory connotations in relation with minority groups or indigenous people, e.g., "lazy", "primitive", "savage", "backward", "uncivilized", "conniving", "treacherous", "wily", "crafty", "inscrutable", "hostile", "superstitious", "war-like", "docile".

Group Identity

– Avoid descriptions of ethnic and racial groups through external characteristics (e.g., facial features, dress, skin, colour). Instead, describe groups according to their country of origin. For example, avoid referring to Japanese, Chinese, Koreans, Filipinos, etc. collectively as Orientals, but provide each with a separate group identity.

Colour Terms

– Only make reference to skin colour if the information is necessary for clarity. Do not use colour terms in a pejorative way. De-emphasize the negative connotations traditionally associated with the colour *black* by associating it with positive attributes.

Use of Personal Names

– Use accurate and current names rather than Anglicized names. Avoid obsolete names and names that would generate a negative reaction in the reader. For example, Sri Lanka is no longer known as "Ceylon"; Moslems practice the religion of Islam, not "Mohammedanism"; "Englishman" is an acceptable term, but "Chinaman" has derogatory connotations.
– Be aware of the self-identification preferences of racial and cultural groups (e.g., "Native Canadian" is preferable to "Canadian Indians", and "Inuit" to "Eskimo").
– Make sure that names are spelled correctly.

Sex Stereotyping

– Avoid sex-role stereotyping by excluding statements or expressions which imply inferior or limited roles for women.
– Avoid the use of the so-called generic pronoun (he) to refer to either

sex. Replace it by "she/he" or "they" or reword to eliminate the gender reference.

For example, instead of Every student must complete *his* project by Friday. USE Every student must complete *the* project by Friday.
– Avoid exclusionary terms and expressions involving the word "man" in its generic sense.

Instead of man-made; the common man; manpower; mankind; USE synthetic; manufactured; the average person; workforce; human resources; human race; people.
– Avoid demeaning words and expressions which trivialize or patronize women and their contribution to society, or identify them only through their relationship to man.

For example, instead of authoress; girl/gal Friday; old wives tales; USE author; writer assistant; superstitions; beliefs; ideas.
– Use parallel structures in reference which include both sexes.

For example, instead of ladies and men; man and wife; USE ladies and gentlemen; husband and wife; man and woman.

Illustrations

Drawings tend to be stylistic and simplified and particularly lend themselves to generating stereotypes.
– Particular care must be taken to avoid inadvertent caricatures or cliches, such as Orientals smiling inscrutably, happy-go-lucky Blacks with wide toothy grins, the naked savage Native Indian and his "squaw", etc.
– Avoid tokenism. Make sure that racial minority characters do not look just like whites except for being coloured in. Moreover, minority faces should not look stereotypically alike, but they should be depicted as genuine individuals with distinctive features. The use of photographs instead of drawings may eliminate some of these problems.
– Minorities should not be shown in subservient or passive roles but in a variety of situations and functions.

Developing Positive Intergroup Attitudes

Attitudes are a complex psychological phenomenon. To modify

intergroup attitudes, a variety of approaches has to be used which address not only the cognitions but also the affects.

1) Break down stereotypes
   a) by providing positive examples for other-group members;
   b) by providing examples that do not fit the stereotype (e.g., instead of showing Chinese as laundry or restaurant workers, provide examples of Mr. Chu, doctor; Mr. Chan, lawyer; etc.);
   c) by emphasizing individual variations within the other-group as well as in the own-group and similarities between both groups;
   d) by emphasizing diversity of attributes in individuals of the own-group and other-group.
2) Reduce unfamiliarity and ambiguity of people from other cultures and races
   a) by providing exposure to unfamiliar faces and by associating them with certain names and backgrounds;
   b) by highlighting the individuality of faces within the other-group;
   c) by using cross-cultural pictures depicting a variety of emotions in different situations.
3) Create greater understanding of the lifestyles, behavioural patterns and value systems of other-group members
   a) by providing the relevant information;
   b) by teaching students to see things from the perspective of another person, not just their own.
4) Develop empathy to better understand what a person from another culture is feeling
   a) by explaining different value systems;
   b) by identifying emotions felt from facial cues and from being familiar with the other's situation.

Multicultural components should be integrated into the different areas of the curriculum such as social studies, language and literature, science, mathematics and the arts. Such an integrated presentation of multicultural content not only provides pupils with stimulating new settings for study but can also improve retention in the skills areas, while simultaneously refining sensitivities and increasing knowledge.

References

Canada, House of Commons. (1984). *Equality now*. Ottawa: Report of the Special Committee on Visible Minorities in Canadian Society.

Council of Interracial Books for Children. *10 quick ways to analyze children's books for racism and sexism*. New York.

Ijaz, A.(1984). Ethnic attitude change: A multidimensional approach. In R. Samuda, J. Berry and M. Laferriere (Eds.), *Multiculturalism in Canada: Social and educational perspectives*. Toronto: Allyn and Bacon.

Kehoe, J. (1984). *A handbook for enhancing the multicultural climate of the school*. Vancouver: University of British Columbia, Faculty of Education.

Multiculturalism Canada. ( ). *Visible minorities in government communications: A matter of balance*. Ottawa. Ontario Ministry of Education. (1980). *Race, religion and culture in Ontario schools: Suggestions for authors and publishers*.

Ontario Secondary School Teachers' Federation, Status of Women Committee. ( ). *Count me in: Equality through language*. Guidelines for Non-Sexist Language Use.

Pratt, D. and McDiarmid, G. (1971). *Teaching prejudice: A content analysis of social studies textbooks authorized for use in Ontario*. Report to the Ontario Human Rights Commission. Toronto: Ontario Institute for Studies in Education.

Preiswerk, R. (1980). *Slant of the pen: Racism in childdren's books.*Geneva: World Council of Churches.

Methods of Integrating Ethnic Studies Into The Curriculum

Bridglal Pachai

I f the topic under discussion here is correctly interpreted, the starting point is the complete acceptance of the value of ethnic studies and an exploration of how they can be integrated into the curriculum. With this in mind, it would be convenient to recall a practical definition of ethnic studies as a feature in the curriculum.

> Ethnic studies is a study of ethnic groups, the ethnic experience, and the impact of ethnicity on Canadian society and culture. The field spans the traditional boundaries of disciplines such as art, history, literature, theology, psychology, sociology, linguistics, political science, cultural anthropology and music. Some of the topics within the focus of ethnic studies are immigration history and the immigrant experience; settlement patterns; the history, culture and social patterns of individual groups; intra- and inter- group relations; society; and questions of public policy related to bilingualism, multiculturalism, immigration and native land claims.
>
> (Wood, 1978)

A cursory analysis of this definition raises daunting questions such as: How many ethnic groups should be included? Will the disciplines chosen lend themselves to proper coverage? Would such a field of study, if manageable, not lead to counterproductive compartmentalization? And, given the immense task of eliminating ethnocentrism, stereotyping, prejudice and discrimination, would the inclusion of ethnic studies in the curriculum (and, by extension, in the school system) be able to do the job alone? If not, how should the curriculum introduce features of ethnic studies into the classroom – by requiring, say, one period per week for such topics as human relations, communications, vocational training, library training and study skills; or by means of a concerted yearly effort, culminating in a Human Rights Week or a Multicultural Week?

116

Indeed, any approach is equally good grist for the mill. However, given the limitations of the classroom timetable, and the urgency and necessity of integrating ethnic studies in the curriculum, certain practical decisions are necessary as prerequisites for the implementation process. If it is agreed that the knowledge and concerns derived from ethnic studies can be directed to the promotion of multiculturalism through education, then it can also be understood that the implementation process must take place in an atmosphere which recognizes that ethnic studies can promote multiculturalism on an ongoing basis, extending formally and informally from the first day in the classroom to the last day. It must be reflected in the attitudes, utterances and beliefs of educators, learners, administrators, politicians and parents.

> Multiculturalism, we might say, is like a radio station transmitting all day every day. If we are turned on and tuned in, our receivers will pick up the programs and the messages transmitted. But, of we're on a different wave length or if we are turned off, we'll never hear the programs or the messages.
>
> (Johnstone, 1981)

For the teacher and the school who are "turned on" and "tuned in," certain subject areas are readily available that can benefit from an inclusion of material derived from ethnic studies. These include social studies, literature, home economics, physical education, art, music, industrial arts and the sciences. Details of how these disciplines can incorporate ethnic studies and what methods and strategies can best serve the needs of multicultural education will depend on the resources available inside and outside a given school. When one considers that the area of interest covered by ethnic studies is such an extensive one and that there are scores of ethnic groups, each with a legitimate claim to a place in the Canadian mosaic, the situation calls for strategies that will stretch the resources and the ingenuity of educators and administrators. In the end, it may be a question of considering the environment in which the learning/ teaching/living process takes place as a crucial factor in selecting what ground is to be covered, what examples used, and what features stressed. Nor should the immediate environment be considered as the only factor, since schools are not islands unto themselves and will have to interact at some point with the larger Canadian reality and beyond. We can turn, once again, to Dr. Johnstone's telling remarks on this latter feature of our concern:

> The fact that nations have cultures as well as sub-cultures is often overlooked by us today, in our external government relations and in our dealings with

international trade and commerce.Despite its importance to us as an exporting nation, our ability to understand our trading partners or competitors remains largely underdeveloped.We cannot afford such neglect, since our survival and improvement depends on it. This has implications regarding whether or how well we train , for example managers of our multinational corporations or government staff who work in the international arena. But it also raises educational questions about how much our provincial education systems teach our students about the world they live in.

(Johnstone, 1981)

A thematic treatment could perhaps be devised to cover specific subject areas in a kind of concentric-circle approach, starting with the local unit and moving in stages to the provincial, regional, national, continental and international arenas.

To use the subject areas mentioned earlier to effectively bring about change "all day every day," textbook material would need to be drastically overhauled and not simply revised to effect minor adjustments. The inclusion of a greater proportion/depth of ethnic material in texts cannot be achieved easily, however, since commercial publishers have to be persuaded to cooperate. If and when this might be achieved is another area of uncertainty and points to the inadequacy on the part of educators to organize themselves sufficiently to use what valuable material exists. However, the question of providing suitable material in acceptable texts will continue to be an unsettling and disturbing issue for some time to come. In short, the process of integration could turn out to be a long and tedious one, calling for considerable patience, tolerance, ingenuity and perseverance.

The methods so far discussed of integrating ethnic studies into the curriculum are: the study of related disciplines, an implementation process that utilizes every opportunity, and the development of proper text materials that promote the dignity and worth of different cultures in an effort to eliminate ethnocentrism, stereotyping, prejudice and discrimination. These three methods or approaches need to be reinforced by complementary strategies that involve students, local communities and teachers in ways which, according to one informed source:

Relate the student's own life concerns and lifestyle to all class activities. As such, they convey to the student that the classroom is a place where he can learn to express, understand and evaluate the personal and social facts of his existence. A total system of organic learning, in which students continually project into the classroom and into the curriculum those events and selves, those problems and conflicts which they need to master, while the teacher continually guides them in the direction of a more general recognition of the historic roots and the wide implications of their personal concerns.

(Dickman, 1973)

Students, local communities and teachers are resources in the area of ethnic studies which need to be utilized in order to achieve the objectives of a school curriculum aimed at developing right thinking and right living.

Students are an excellent resource for integrating ethnic studies into the curriculum since they, as learners, need to improve their self-image and since the curriculum functions to prepare them for life. Their active contribution to the school curriculum could include material presented in class discussions and in various school functions and activities such as debates, speeches, drama, arts and crafts, sports, home economics, social studies and music. When all learners are encouraged to participate, the gap between the minority and majority groups is narrowed. As representatives of society, students provide a link between the school and the community at large. What takes place in the school spills over into the community:

> In school districts characterized by ethnic diversity, the use of student-generated concerns and the discussion of student experience within the classroom has an added power. It forces all students to focus on each other's ethnic identities and their consequences. By so doing, the classroom demonstrates that respect for diversity which it wishes to teach the students.
>
> (Dickeman, 1973).

Adult members of the community can be used to reinforce the students' classroom presentations with accounts of their own diverse experiences in the outside world, experiences as new or old immigrants, as members of advantaged or disadvantaged groups. In addition, as members of ethnic organizations, they have an obligation to operate as watchdogs over their concerns and aspirations. They can contribute meaningful material to that corpus of information known as ethnic studies for use in the classroom and beyond.

Two interesting case studies of community involvement have salutary lessons for us all. The first concerns the experiences of a young Canadian educator from a WASP background who worked between 1969 and 1974 to prepare a curriculum for schools in the Northwest Territories in close collaboration with the communities involved. The results were spectacular. Recalling the remarkable community involvement he writes: "In total, over a five-year period, one new item came off the printing press every other week, much of it in colour, some of it in two or more languages and virtually all of it created by individuals who wanted to see their stories, histories and perceptions in print." (Robinson, 1981). This educator's experience provided him with a moral which he has since shared widely and beneficially:

I have often thought of that proverb of giving people fish and you feed them for a day.Teach people how to fish and they will feed themselves for a lifetime. Multicultural approaches to education should provide similar lasting understanding and skill. The preparation of a book, the collaboration necessary in developing a curriculum provide those opportunities. Once people learn something of how an education system works, how their ideas can be brought to life on the screen or the printed page you have provided knowledge that no one can eradicate. You have opened the door to self-reliance.

(Robinson, 1981).

If the integration of ethnic studies into the curriculum can serve to promote self-reliance, it can also be used to encourage the sharing of experiences, even in a situation where minority ethnic groups are almost absent. This was the case in the second of our examples, occurring on an Indian reservation school in the United States where three members of the community formed a subcommittee to evaluate textbooks for cultural bias. Their findings are all too familiar to us, but their formula for effecting corrections was refreshingly direct: "If we are going to improve, we are going to have to do it ourselves. It has been done for us for so long that the people have no initiative. What do we need? We need allies, first of all, but we need allies to help on our terms" (Dunfee, 1969).

Community groups, then, either alone or in concert, can influence the shape and the content as well as the operation of the curriculum. Their involvement is an important link in the integrative chain.

The foremost link, however, is the teacher. He or she is the one who sits in the pilot's seat and is in charge of the controls. It is this educator who has to make the crucial decisions and see that they are carried out. Unhappily for many a teacher, the task of servicing multicultural education is often too formidable, sometimes undesirable, always very difficult. The reasons are well known. Ethnic studies is a relatively recent concern. For some people, multicultural education, cross-cultural communication, intercultural concerns and multicultural living belong to a category known as "airy-fairy" or "Mickey Mouse" concerns. Unless the teacher is well and truly committed, even if he or she is not well-informed, the attempt to integrate ethnic studies into the curriculum will not meet with the desired results. However, with the right commitment, the science teacher would be able to assist the social studies teacher; literature, arts, home economics, music are all amenable to an interdisciplinary approach managed by a team effort.

The case for integrating ethnic studies into the curriculum is a strong one. The alternatives of providing for separate ethnic studies as a separate course of of providing elective courses in certain ethnic areas have not received similar support since their effectiveness is doubted.

An integrated approach, handled thematically, arranged along interdisciplinary lines, equipped with appropriate text material, assisted by resource materials in the form of contributions by students and community members, guided by teachers committed to the promotion of multicultural education, can draw attention to the good uses to which ethnic studies can be put.

Some fifteen years ago certain questions were raised on the subject of ethnic studies in the curriculum. To recall them today is not a futile exercise since it is still easier to ask questions than to find the right answers to fit all situations. If they are recalled here, in summary and in conclusion, they may afford us all an opportunity for reaching our own that will most closely approximate our individual situations and expectations.

1) Should curriculum modification provided for ethnic emphases meet short-term or long-term goals?
2) With what school age children should these modifications be first introduced?
3) What comes first – modification of the curriculum or modification of teacher attitudes and perceptions?
4) Are modifications to curriculum adequate or is it necessary to completely overhaul the existing curriculum?
5) To whom is the modified curriculum aimed – a minority, a majority, everyone?
6) Is the preferred approach a separatist one, an integrative one, or both?
7) To whom should the responsibility of effecting the modifications be entrusted?
8) Should the function of the school curriculum be one of transmitting culture or of transforming culture?

Every school system, along with its concerned personnel, needs to find its own answer to these and other questions when attempting to define an approach and method of integrating ethnic studies into the curriculum. While the means to the end may greatly vary, the end result hoped for is the creation of a healthy society based on the concept of unity in diversity.

References

Dickeman, M. (1973). Teaching cultural pluralism. In J.A. Banks, *Teaching ethnic studies concepts and strategies.*

Dunfee, M. (1969). *Ethnic modification of the curriculum.*

Johnstone, P.A. (1981). Multiculturalism through education: A search for understanding. In Peter L. McCreath (Ed.), *Multiculturalism: A handbook for teachers.*

Robinson, P. (1981). Multiculturalism - The curriculum, the community and the school. In Peter L. McCreath (Ed.), *Multiculturalism: A handbook for teachers.*

Wood, D. (1978). *Multicultural Canada: A teacher's guide to ethnic studies.*

Integrating Multiculturalism in Early Childhood Education from Theory to Practice

Karen Mock

In writing a paper on integrating multiculturalism into Early Childhood Education, an important distinction must be made between the learning needs of young children and the learning needs of their teachers. The rationale for multicultural education for very young children is to be found in what we know about how children develop and how they learn. That is, it is now generally accepted by early childhood educators in Canada that quality programming for young children requires a recognition of individual differences in order to design a program based on sound cognitive-developmental learning principles combined with humanistic strategies for fostering socialization. As such, a case can be made for infusing multicultural content throughout the curriculum in order to build on every child's background experiences and cognitive skills to enhance learning and to foster a positive self-concept. In other words, for young children, multiculturalism must not be a separate topic or subject, but a natural part of all early learning as a reflection of the Canadian context and their own experience. Such an integration of multiculturalism in early childhood education is the logical implication of widely accepted theories of child development and learning, *if* those theories were to be put into effective practice in early childhood classrooms.

However, the learning needs of teachers and student teachers are very different from the learning needs of the young children they teach. Practitioners want more information about the culture and practices of specific ethnocultural groups and need to know how and where to get that information. In addition, they must learn to understand their own cultural values and assumptions and how those assumptions about child rearing, discipline, parenting, education, communication, and other important cultural variables affect their interaction with children and families. They must become intimately aware of the effects of immigration, stereotyping, prejudice, and racism on human behaviour and know something of the historical developments in these areas in Canada, and also how they impact on the education of young children.Early childhood educators must develop skills for detecting cultural biases in curriculum, media, and assessment tools, and they must also learn how to adapt them where appropriate and necessary. Unlike young children, teachers and student teachers must have specific instruction in multicultural education in order to address both theoretical and practical issues with enough depth to ensure effective implementation in their classrooms.

The theoretical rationale for multicultural early childhood education has been elaborated in more depth elsewhere (Mock, 1981, 1982), and a course for teachers described at some length (Mock, 1983). The present paper will bridge from the theoretical rationale to practical strategies for integrating multiculturalism in the education of young children, and then focus on the implications of multiculturalism for the preparation of early childhood educators at the college and university levels.

Multicultural Education for Young Children

A summary of the developmental literature on racism recently led the Urban Alliance on Race Relations (1983) to conclude that by the age of four, children have a well-developed conception of race and racial differences in terms of the consequences of those differences in our society (cf Goodman, 1964; Milner, 1975). For example, many children are aware, by the time they enter school, that different roles are usually ascribed to people of different colours.They learn from seeing how groups are depicted in the first books they read, or even from an unconscious awareness that certain groups are not depicted at all in the primers, comics, or pictures and posters in their environment. Visible minorities are virtually invisible in much of the material available to young children in early childhood settings. Visual aids that accurately depict our multiracial and multicultural society are not readily available. It is clear that at a very early age, children are exposed to a wide variety of media that teach them that certain groups are more important than others in our society.Not only does this dramatically affect the identity and self-concept of the child who is made to feel less significant by not seeing him or herself reflected in the environment, but it results in many children having already developed well defined racist attitudes by the time they get to school. Unless early childhood programs are modified to reflect the multicultural and multiracial population of Canada, they will continue to be a part of the problem, rather than be instrumental in the solution.

Ramsey (1982), in making a case for multicultural education in early childhood, cites compelling evidence that in order to influence children's basic racial and cultural attitudes, we must start with the very young. All early childhood educators are aware of the importance of the early years in shaping attitudes, values, and habits of social behaviour. Good preschool education has been shown to have a lasting influence on later social and emotional behaviour and even on future life chances of children who participate in them (Schweinhart and Weikart, 1984).

Most early childhood educators today consider a "good" program to be one that recognizes individual differences of the child and builds on the child's experiences as the foundation for learning, while providing opportunities for physical, social, emotional and intellectual growth in a safe and secure environment. However, those same early childhood teachers rarely reflect upon the cultural biases that are inherent in our current notions of good programming for even the very youngest children. The overall goals of the program itself may not be met for the child whose cultural background does not match the culturally shaped expectations of the teacher.

But when one does examine the program closely, several sources of bias are evident, including the curriculum, methods and materials used, and assessment instruments and procedures. For example, one goal of a cognitively-oriented curriculum might be to help the children to become independent learners. Another goal may be to encourage participation in discussion, planning, and "hands on" activities. How odd this must seem to parents who raise children to obey authority and wait to be told exactly what to do, to be seen and not heard, particularly in the presence of elders or teachers, and to learn from demonstration and didactic instruction rather than from active participation! Our current views on early childhood curriculum stem from modern western philosophy, psychology, and pedagogy. Ethnocentrism dictates that we believe our theories and practices to be the "right" ones and even the "best" ones, while others are deemed to be "wrong" or at least not as good, and therefore in need of change through education. However, such a conclusion runs contrary to a very important aspect of early childhood programming that is currently accepted, that is, adapting the program to the child, not the child to the program. Cultural background, ethnicity, and race are all aspects of individual difference that must be taken into consideration when designing an educational plan for any child.

A teacher who, with good intentions, believes that all children should be treated the same, regardless of their cultural background, is one who is paying mere lip-service to the concept of individual differences. Teachers should attempt to meet children's individual needs, whatever they are, so that they have an equal chance to learn and develop and succeed in the system. That is, an attempt to give children equal opportunity in education necessitates treating them differently. The recognition of cultural difference and building on that diversity is an essential component of quality early childhood education in Canada today.

Practical Classroom Strategies

Multicultural education does not mean a set of activities tacked on to the curriculum. It is an attitude, an underlying ethic, a commitment to broaden the cultural base of curriculum, methods, materials, and assessment strategies. Simple examples include commemorating a wide variety of holidays, festivals, and celebrations, not just those with which the teacher is most familiar. In this way, every child feels that he or she belongs in the group; and, in keeping with cognitive developmental theory, the teacher builds concepts from the child's existing experience. Similarly, if every child is to have an opportunity for dramatic play, role-playing, and working through familiar or emotional social situations, then the doll or house centre that is intended for such activity must include props and costumes that reflect all the children's home experiences, not just some. Snacks should include a diversity of foods so that all children have an opportunity to try new things and all children have an equal chance of recognizing very familiar foods or treats. Different assessment tools must be used for different children and administered in the appropriate language, or at least by someone who is sensitive to the cultural biases inherent in most of our presently used instruments. One must be absolutely sure that the relevant developmental characteristic has been isolated and is being evaluated effectively, rather than the child's cultural background or language experience. Remembering the importance of context in learning new material, the early childhood teacher should select books, posters, music, and all other curriculum aids with a view to ensuring that all the children can identify with at least some of the material being used, and that all children will be exposed to the unfamiliar, rather than the minority group children always being the ones to have to adapt to the novel or strange and sometimes bewildering environment.

Multiculturalism also requires a commitment to develop and to use a wide variety of communication techniques, verbal and non-verbal, with parents and children so they feel genuinely accepted and have an equal chance of developing a self-concept as healthy as those of the so-called dominant or majority culture. The early childhood teacher has the advantage of close contact with parents, grandparents and other caregivers who can participate in the program and share many cultural events and experiences with the children.

To design an effective multicultural program, the early childhood educator must learn about the racial, cultural, and socioeconomic background of the children in his or her care, including what experiences they have had with people from other groups and their attitudes towards their own and other groups. Then the teacher can respond to these variations, both by enhancing the multicultural climate in the classroom through appropriate multicultural materials, displays and teaching strategies, and also by striving to enhance cooperation and acceptance among the children. The teacher must take an active role, as these behaviours are too important to be left to chance or for the children to work out on their own. An example will illustrate this point. The author recently had occasion to test a 7-year-old girl of Chinese origin who explained that she had to go out for recess to help her friends fight back against some children who were calling them names.

> They call us 'chinky' and say nonsense sounds that they think sound like Chinese, and they say they don't like us because we're good in class. So I don't like them and we're trying to figure out how to fight back. It hurts our feelings. I wish we could be friends.

Discussion with the child revealed that nothing was being done to prevent this kind of behaviour in the schoolyard or in the classroom, and that "if we told the teacher, she'd get mad, and then they would hate us more." Rather than ignoring the situation or blaming the children for it, the teacher should have been in tune with the attitudes of the children in the class and addressed them in a preventative manner with effective multicultural curriculum resources and intercultural communication techniques both to increase awareness and sensitivity among the children and to foster more effective race relations within and outside the classroom.

In keeping with what we know about how young children learn, multicultural early childhood education must not consist of lessons or information about exotic places or "other cultures" remote from the child's experience. This approach emphasizes differences, and the children have no context into which to place the information. All currently trained early childhood teachers understand that this is not how children learn best. A far more effective approach is to emphasize the shared experience of all people through an examination of similarities and differences in everyday, common experiences of the children themselves. This is the approach taken in the resource book entitled *Multicultural Early Childhood Education* edited by Keith McLeod (1984) and such an integrated approach is consistent with the cognitive-developmental philosophy of early childhood programming.

Multiculturalism must be an integral and continuous part of the curriculum, just as it is a fundamental part of Canadian society today. However, there are some educators who labour under the misconception that multicultural education is only important in classes and neighbour-hoods in which a variety of cultural and/or racial groups are represented or where race or ethnicity is a source of concern to the teacher. Multicultural education is relevant to all Canadian classrooms regard-less of the ethnic or racial composition of the pupils, because it builds on cultural diversity as a strength in Canadian society. We know that early experience influences later development. If young children are exposed to diverse ethnic groups and multicultural material as an integral part of their programs right from the beginning, they will learn, at an early age, that cultural diversity is an integral part of Canadian life. Regardless of their own race or ethnicity, this will facilitate their increased later participation as accepting, well-adjusted adults in Canada's multicultur-al society.

Multicultural Education for Early Childhood Teachers

What are the implications of multiculturalism for the programs in colleges and universities that are designed to prepare early childhood educators to teach and care for young children, and how can multicultur-alism be integrated into these programs? While in the United States multicultural education has become part of the compulsory require-ments for teacher certification in every state, and while several Canadian educators have emphasized the necessity of effective multi-cultural teacher education in this volume and elsewhere (Ray, 1980; Mallea and Young, 1980; Mock, 1981, 1982, 1983; Chud, 1983 among others), a recent survey of multiculturalism in early childhood education programs (Mock, 1984) reveals that most provinces have a long way to go in ensuring that early childhood educators are effectively prepared to meet the demands of teaching in our multicultural Canadian society. There is, however, consensus among those currently involved in multicultural teacher education that there are certain key components that must be included in teacher preparation in Canada today. They may be summarized as follows:

1) *Intercultural awareness* – this includes an examination of one's own ethno-cultural heritage and identity as well as the study of other communities, in order to increase awareness of the teacher's own values and assumptions and to develop an understanding of how these affect one's interactions and relationships with other people.

2) *Cross-cultural child rearing practices* – an examination of how culture shapes and influences the development of the child, increasing awareness that universal values may be played out in very different parenting practices and an understanding by the teacher that there is no one "right" way to raise or teach children.

3) *Family and community resources* – an understanding of various family structures and dynamics from a cross-cultural perspective, and how immigration and resettlement affects the family; increasing awareness of what resources are available in the ethnic and minority communities to assist families and also teachers.

4) *Language development* - familiarity with developmental stages of language acquisition, including psycholinguistic and sociolinguistic perspectives; and understanding of the effects of second language learning, dialect differences, and an understanding of current issues and programs (e.g. ESL/D, Heritage Languages, Bilingualism, etc.).

5) *Multicultural curriculum development* - programming suggestions to enhance the multicultural nature of the classroom environment and activities; introduction to diverse curriculum resources.

6) *Historical aspects of immigration and multiculturalism* – Canada's immigration patterns and policies and their impact on schooling, various approaches to resettlement and integration (e.g. assimilation, absorption, acculturation, multiculturalism, etc.).

7) *Stereotyping, prejudice, racism* - definitions, theories and research; increased awareness of prejudice, racism and discrimination as it occurs in education and society; development of skills in dealing with problems and issues as they arise in the teacher's personal and professional life; incresed understanding of the real effects of racism.

8) *Interpersonal experience* - a practicum or other opportunity for direct contact and interaction with members of a variety of cultural, racial, or ethnic groups; ample opportunity for discussion and personal involvement without feeling threatened or inhibited; coming to terms with one's own feelings, values, attitudes, and personal growth and awareness.

The above list suggests that effective multicultural teacher education is interdisciplinary and multidimensional. Multicultural education must involve experiential learning and skill development or training, as well as material presented in a more traditional academic style. Teacher education faculties and colleges are particularly well suited for integrating the theoretical foundation with very practical strategies that have been found to be most successful in multicultural education. Having had the unique opportunity of developing and teaching a compulsory pre-service course in multicultural education for early childhood students, I can recall many incidents that illustrate the importance of a flexible and eclectic approach to such material. For example, it was not unusual for some students to demonstrate a lack of understanding and lack of empathy (sometimes bordering on overt bigotry and hostility) at the beginning of the course, but many of those same students develop considerably more insight and apparent under-standing as well as reduced stereotyping after completing a required practicum.

Student teachers should be required to work in a multicultural setting, such as an inner city school, parent/child drop-in centre, ethnic community centre, and ESL or ESD program, or an alternative or parochial school, in order to have first-hand experience with young children from a cultural background different from their own. Such a practicum must be carefully planned, monitored and assessed so that the students become familiar with the needs and the values of the community served, with the political structure of the setting (e.g. funding, role in the community, supervisory differences, participation of the parents, etc.), and so that the students will have ample opportunity for feedback, as well as reflection of personal attitudes and personal growth over time. It is important to provide material on education as a social and cultural system, so that the students can develop an awareness of the context in which they find themselves in educational and social service agencies, and at least a beginning understanding of the mechanisms of change within such institutions in Canadian society.

Personal contact and interaction indeed appear to have had the most impact on student teachers in the author's preservice course on multiculturalism (Mock, 1983). Student evaluations consistently revealed that although all were valued, none of the strategies used in the course (readings, lectures, workshops, films, role-playing, simulations) was quite as effective as personal interaction with members of minority and/or ethnic groups both through guest speakers and through the practicum experience. Chud (1983) also emphasizes the importance of involving many resource people in such a course for early childhood teachers, to ensure that the content is developed and presented by people with expertise and relevant personal experience related to the various topics. Willing volunteers, guest speakers, or resource personnel can often be found from the various communities. Support by the administration is important when attempting to integrate multiculturalism into the program, and support by policies of multicultural education and race relations even better. By becoming personally acquainted with individuals committed to this field, students recognize the value of the multidisciplinary and the multicultural approach. However, unless support goes beyond the committed individuals involved directly in the program, when they leave or move on, the program may disappear.

In order to achieve the goals of multicultural education for teachers, traditional methods of university and college teaching should be modified. For example, material on multiculturalism or race and ethnic relations is very value-laden and evokes many emotional reactions in students. As such, it should not be presented in the traditional linear fashion in which most university courses are presented. Successful teaching strategies include personal interaction with members of ethnic groups, self-awareness exercises, group problem-solving, modifying curriculum to suit individual needs and backgrounds, simulations and other forms of experiential learning, as well as some traditional presentation of content through lectures, readings, and formal presentations. It is important for the teacher educator to model effective teaching strategies, that is, to put into practice the very content about which he or she is teaching. This would mean a more personal style of teaching would be most effective, taking individual difference in cultural background and learning style into consideration to a much greater extent than is customary in large post-secondary institutions. The instructor must display an active commitment to multiculturalism and be prepared to defend the content and the strategies constructively, demonstrating their efficacy; because it is not unusual for these and other successful multicultural teaching strategies to be considered suspect by superiors and colleagues who may be resistant to the material. Just as the student teachers must become aware of the context of education and the mechanisms of change, so must the multicultural teacher educator develop an understanding of the system and be flexible in designing and implementing a program to meet the needs of the individuals, the group, and the institution. This flexibility in teaching style and communication style is extremely important for the success of integrating multiculturalism into any education program with teachers or with children.

It is possible, even at the college level, to teach in a way that meets individual needs and acknowledges the diverse backgrounds of students without compromising the standards of the program. With multicultural education, not only is it possible, it is essential to "practice what you preach". When a student teacher has the emotional experience of being taught in a way that meets individual students where they are in their thinking and development in an accepting way, it becomes far easier to teach that way upon graduation. If there are students in the class who have had previous cultural or educational experiences that are interfering with their completing the requirements successfully, then they need a different approach that will give them as much chance as the majority of their classmates to meet the requirements. Or if there is a student who displays hostility or bigotry, the instructor must utilize his or her skills in race relations to communicate effectively, diffuse the hostility, meet the student where he or she is on the issue, and work from there, providing the appropriate experiences for that student to move a little closer to where you would like that student to be. In other words, just as the design and implementation of multicultural education for young children rests primarily on the attitudes, skills and knowledge of the teacher (Ramsey, 1983), so does the design and implementation of multicultural education for teachers rest on the attitudes, skills and knowledge of the teacher educator. The success of effective multicultural education for teachers depends upon the support and sensitivity of the college or university administration, indicating the necessity of multicultural awareness at every level of the system and the importance of the entrenchment of the ideals of multiculturalism as policy in all of our educational institutions.

The recent report of the Special Committee on Visible Minorities in Canadian Society (*Equality Now*, 1984) highlights Early Childhood Education as an area worthy of attention by the proposed Ministry of Multiculturalism. Specifically, the recommendations of the parliamentary committee regarding Early Childhood Education call for:

1) Minimum standards for working in early childhood education.
2) Multicultural teaching materials for use in training programs.
3) Curriculum materials that would positively influence attitudes and values during the period of early childhood education.

This kind of emphasis may provide the additional support that is necessary for integrating multiculturalism into our early childhood and teacher education programs across the country. It appears, then, that the time is now to make some important strides in integrating multiculturalism in early childhood education, that is, putting sound theory into effective practice.

> *Multiculturalism* means understanding and functioning comfortably within more than one cultural context. It begins in the preschool with everyday experiences in play, language, art, music, etc. - not 'lessons' about people and places remote from the child's experience. - *Young Children in Action*

References

Chud, G. (1983). Working with ESL preschoolers: Meeting the needs of the whole child. *Teal Occasional Papers, 7*, 61-68.

Goodman, M. (1964). *Race awareness in young children*. New York: Collier.

Mallea, J. and Young. (1980). Teacher education for a multicultural society. In K. McLeod (Ed.), *Intercultural education and community development*. Toronto: Faculty of Education, University of Toronto, 87-93.

McLeod, K. (Ed.) (1984). *Multicultural early childhood education*. Toronto: Guidance Centre, Faculty of Education, University of Toronto.

Milner, D. (1975). *Children and race*. London: Penguin.

Mock, R. (1981). Multicultural education at the early childhood level: A developmental rationale. Paper presented at the National Conference on Multicultural Education, Winnipeg. Published in *Multicultural early childhood education*. Toronto: Guidance Centre, Faculty of Education, University of Toronto, 1984.

Mock, K. (1982). Early childhood education in a multicultural society. *Multiculturalism, 5*(4), 3-6.

Mock, K. (1983). The successful multicultural teacher. *The History and Social Science Teacher, 19*(2), 87-97.

Mock, K. (1984). *Status report on multicultural education in early childhood education*. Ottawa: Secretary of State, Multiculturalism Directorate.

Ramsey, P. (1982). Multicultural education in early childhood. *Young Children*. January, 13-23.

Ray, D. (1980). Multiculturalism in teacher education. In K. McLeod (Ed.), *Intercultural education and community development*. Toronto: Faculty of Education, University of Toronto.

Schweinhart, L. and Weikart, D. (1984). Changed lives: The effects of the Perry

134

Preschool Program on youths through age 19. Ypsilanti, Mich.: High/Scope Research Foundation.

Special Commission on Visible Minorities in Canadian Society. (1984). Bob Daudlin (Chairman). *Equality now!* Hull, Quebec: Queen's Printer.

Urban Alliance on Race Relations. (1984). Brief to the Special Committee on Visible Minorities in Canadian Society, as cited in *Equality Now!*

Methods for Integrating Multiculturalism in Elementary Schools

Jean Augustine and Helen Bochar

E ducational practice plays a major role in developing multiculturalism as an ideological reality in Canadian society. In elementary schools, educational practice includes consideration of how
curriculum and curriculum materials are organized and of how teachers'
and students' perceptions of themselves, as principal actors in today's
society, affect the world about them.

The principal is the key and critical person in making the school truly
multicultural. The principal sets the tone, atmosphere and pace of events
in the school. The principal controls and influences the factors that
affect both the classroom and school experiences of the child as well as
the student's experiences outside the school. The principal as curriculum leader, school manager/administrator, and public relations person
(deflecting pressures from outside) has the responsibility of ensuring
that the curricula in the school are efficiently implemented in a manner
appropriate to the age and level of the individual child. R.T. Macaulay
in a position paper to the Ontario Association of Education Administrative Officials on *The Role of the Principal* discuss eight areas in which
the principal impacts:

1) Scheduling and Working Conditions
2) Curriculum Development
3) Teacher-Student Involvement
4) Community Relations
5) Professional Development
6) Budget and Ceilings
7) Professional and Fraternal Associations
8) Public Relations

It is the duty of the principal to ensure that the school board's guidelines and goals of the system are implemented. In creating a school atmosphere with multicultural values the following are concrete evidence: work displayed; pictures in view; discipline used; encouragement given or self-esteem stressed; decorum and code behaviour with emphasis on respect for each other; visible sign of community persons in the school; deliberate attempts to provide role models; use of ethnic visual and creative art forms on an equal footing with the conventional forms.

Key areas to consider in an elementary school are: (1) Parent Reporting and (2) Assessment and Counselling. Care must be taken that written language in a report is not too technical for parents' understanding. Teachers must be aware of non-verbal communication. Interpreters might be essential for some interviews. Overtures to involve parents in parent-teacher committees and to familiarize them with the majority culture and an understanding of the school system are necessary.

In addition to pedagogical considerations and teacher/student perceptions, other key factors to be examined are the physical arrangement of the classroom and co-curricular activities which contribute to the overall atmosphere. And lastly, the teacher's ability to interact effectively with students and "translate" curriculum in a manner which not only mediates cultural differences but enhances cross-cultural understanding, establishing him/her as a role model for multiculturalism in action. In developing curriculum, methods for integrating multiculturalism in elementary schools must interrelate to all aspects of the teaching/ learning environment.

Organization of Curriculum and Curriculum Materials

It is important that the teacher as curriculum developer has a global perspective and is able to appreciate the interdependence of all cultural groups in society. Each segment of society – no matter how large or how small – is only part of a whole. It is the total picture which portrays the Canadian reality. To portray social activity in Canada from a singular perspective only is not being true to the Canadian identity. One of the major concerns of educators in developing curriculum from a multicultural perspective is safeguarding against hidden and implied messages which are counter-productive to the goals, aims, and objectives of a multicultural society. In order to safeguard against this, educators must review curriculum and view curriculum analytically and critically. Curriculum materials, besides being attractive and geared to the cultural tastes of students at the primary, junior and intermediate levels, need to be examined in terms of their capacity to develop multicultural principles in students. As a guide, teachers should ask, "Do the schools' curriculum and curriculum materials fulfill the following?"

1) Do the illustrations in the texts, kits and other visual aids represent a multicultural society?
2) Do minority groups have equal billing in terms of their visibility?
3) Do characters provide positive role-modelling for all students?
4) Do the families and their activities and other social structures reflect a multicultural society?
5) Are minority groups illustrated as principal actors in contributing positively to a Canadian society?
6) In fairytales and other fictional stories, are antagonists characterized in a manner that is offensive and prejudicial to any cultural group?
7) In historical accounts and other documentary realities, are minority groups illustrated as exotic – as outside the norm?

If the materials are found to be lacking in any particular area, then measures need to be taken to remedy the situation. This can be done by adding additional resources (pictures, books, filmstrips, posters, etc.) to the program. Or in some cases, specific stories and their illustrations can be deleted from the curriculum and replaced with others.

When specific units of study are being developed, the role of language and the manner in which knowledge is woven are key areas of concern. These areas are critical since the content of lessons provides a ground for developing pedagogical techniques and thinking processes. All subject areas are avenues for developing students' minds and perspective. In addition to the questions asked earlier, the educator as curriculum developer needs to address the following when dealing with written materials.

Language Arts

1) Do names of characters reflect a multicultural society?
2) Are characters from minority groups represented positively in influencing the environment, community or society?
3) Is there evidence of intercultural activity where acceptance of each group is a focus?
4) Are conflicts resolved in a manner which enhances cross-cultural understanding?

5) Are folklore stories presented as an adjunct to the "regular" curriculum or are there structures in the program to facilitate integration?
6) Does the program provide exposure to a variety of family units, activities as well as other social structures which enhance cross-cultural understanding?

Social Sciences and Other Documentary Realities

1) Are historical accounts and other descriptions of people free of prejudice and bias?
2) Do accounts suffer from ethnocentrism?
3) Do sociological accounts of people at a particular moment in history contribute to the stereotyping of those groups in contemporary society?
4) Do accounts include the contributions of all cultural groups to the development of Canadian society?

Mathematics

1) In problem-solving, do names of persons, activities and events represent a multicultural society?

Teacher and Student Perceptions of the World About Them

In order to integrate multiculturalism into school curricula, the teacher must develop a global view of reality. In order to facilitate this, curriculum packages may need to include comprehensive self-teaching units – either as a supplementary written section or as an audio-visual kit. In some instances, publishers and curriculum writers may need to work with other professionals in the field of multicultural education before their specific projects are initiated. In-service has become a vehicle for professional development which stresses the interdependence of cultural communities. Teachers are made aware that each culture has the same institutional structures – only the complexities of each may differ. The institutional structures focus upon the family, socialization and education, laws and economics. Each culture has ritual ceremonies and traditions. Every culture is based on a logic where contradictions are mediated through an ideology and a power structure. Individual cultures may prioritize issues differently, but basically each culture is organized in a similar fashion. A method for integrating multiculturalism, then, is to focus on the similarities among cultures while acknowledging the individual differences in carrying out specific routines.

In addition to developing teachers' perspective, curriculum must accommodate the various levels of abstraction of students in elementary schools. Multicultural themes and perspectives must be housed within the conceptual framework of students. Content-wise the curriculum starts with issues dealing with the student and members of the family. As the student matures, he/she is gradually moved out of the family setting and is introduced to the community and its helpers as well as other environmental factors. The movement extends to rural and urban settings, then to environments in other provincial jurisdictions and outside Canada. It must be remembered that a concept of a global reality starts to develop in the intermediate division. Each environment, its social organization and its interactive capabilities should not only be viewed from a common ground (not from an ethnocentric perspective) but within the realm of the conceptual capabilities of the students.

Classroom Organization and Co-Curricular Activities

Fruits of students' labour should be displayed! Visual clues contribute to the overall atmosphere of the classroom. By organizing units of work around multicultural themes, the teacher can guide students' efforts and mindsets in a manner that develops the concept of multiculturalism as a Canadian reality. Many of the foci presented earlier in the chapter lend themselves to creative activities, e.g., art, charts, display tables, written work, etc. Thus, students will be in an environment which is conducive to cross-cultural and intercultural understanding. Co-curricular activities can further enhance growth in this area by having students actively participate in co-curricular programs which integrate multicultural themes.

Teacher as a Role Model

The teacher plays a major role in integrating multiculturalism into the curriculum. The teacher's ability to interact with students in an effective and meaningful manner which promotes multicultural understanding contributes to students' further growth and development. The teacher's ability to visualize commonalities among cultures; to take advantage of opportunities to use the students' distinct backgrounds and experiences as a resource; to promote understanding and encourage friendships between students establishes himself/herself as a role model for multiculturalism in action. Continued professional development can be provided when teachers seek out to update background information. A focus on open-ended questions will allow students not only to express themselves but will allow teachers to interact more effectively. Teacher/ student and student/student interaction which lends itself to comparing and contrasting activities, explaining a process or event, demonstrating cause and effect relationships provides the ground for the conceptual tools needed to integrate multiculturalism into the elementary school.

Appropriate Multicultural Pedagogy and Its Implementation in the High School

Richard Butt

Introduction

This paper will attempt to answer two practical questions that are of fundamental importance to multicultural education. First, how should one teach multicultural education: that is, what pedagogy exists to help high school pupils learn desirable outcomes, particularly those related to the minimization of racism and prejudice? Second, how might teachers go about successfully implementing desirable multicultural pedagogy?

Possible answers to the first question were derived from an examination and interpretation of selected research literature. The various teaching strategies that emerged from this exercise were then organized into clusters of similar approaches. This facilitated two tasks. First, the clusters of teaching/learning strategies could be organized roughly into a sequence ranging from those strategies most easy to use to those most difficult to use. Second, the clustering and sequencing process facilitated a deeper analysis of the generic pedagogy underlying each cluster of teaching/learning approaches and, subsequently, the whole sequence of teaching techniques.

Using a Transitional Curriculum in the Classroom

Most of the teaching/learning approaches that appear to be useful for multicultural education are experiential in nature. Since most conventional classrooms still use direct teaching as the predominant pedagogy, some significant classroom change will be required to implement desirable multicultural pedagogy. It is therefore necessary to discuss the approach to classroom implementation and change before considering desirable pedagogy in order that the reader might understand why and how the clusters of teaching techniques are arranged the way they are.

The approach to classroom change is based on the notion of the *transitional curriculum* (Butt, 1981). This approach is based on several assumptions:

1) The implementation of new practices in the classroom require both teachers and pupils to become learners in order to acquire new roles and interactions.
2) New pedagogical approaches need to be broken down into small enough steps to allow both pupils and teachers to learn successfully, unencumbered by other issues.
3) These pedagogical learning steps need to be arranged in some sort of logical sequence, whereby those strategies closest to a teacher's existing pedagogy and easiest to implement are attempted first. More difficult and complex approaches that might subsume earlier approaches are attempted later.
4) These changes need to be approached gradually using a mastery approach, whereby the teaching strategy in each step is repeatedly used when appropriate, until both teacher and students have learned the necessary roles and interactions. They would then move on to the next step in the transitional curriculum.
5) An important concept in learning that has been applied particularly in British primary schools is the notion of readiness, or the students' preparedness for the learning of a particular skill, concept or attitude. This readiness may depend on such factors as the developmental level in pertinent areas (moral, cognitive, attitudinal and psychomotor) maturation (a combination of learning and development), previous experiences, specific skill levels, and the like.

The concept of readiness equally applies to learning in multicultural education. The evolutionary nature of the development of desirable attitudes, values and interpersonal communication skills, and the need for a gradual opening towards self-examination, require a teacher to be sensitive about whether students have enough background experience, skills and openness to handle a particular pedagogy. For example, to ask neophytes to multiculturalism to begin by participating in in-depth roleplaying would be inappropriate. The transitional curriculum, then, carries with it the notion that despite student and teacher familiarity with the roles and interactions of a particular pedagogy, they should not move on to more demanding classroom activities until they are personally prepared for the content and processes involved.

The teaching strategies in this paper have been organized into an example of a transitional curriculum for classroom change. It should not, however, be considered a recipe. All teachers should decide the nature of their current classroom transactions, where they would like to be, and design their own transitional plan for change accordingly.

Prior to examining specific teaching techniques that have been organized into an illustrative transitional curriculum, it is important to emphasize several characteristics of multicultural education which are necessary for providing a healthy atmosphere in which the benefits of multicultural pedagogy can take root.

Regardless of whether prejudice and racism are learned, natural to human beings, or both, the following guidelines are recommended (Kalin, 1984, pp. 119-424):

1) Multicultural education must commence with very young children and continue through high school to maximize the development of healthy attitudes through learning, maturation and experience, and to maximize the benefits of logical thought applied to and derived from healthy attitudes and values (Buchignani, 1984).
2) Multicultural education must emphasize critical thinking, especially applied to learners' attitudes, values and behaviours with respect to other groups.
3) Multicultural education must enable the individual to identify prejudices as soon as personal readiness allows and to confront them directly.
4) Education needs to continue to emphasize the development of self-concept and self-esteem in children (particularly for low achievers and working-class children) (Kehoe, 1984; Tiedt, 1979; Verma et al., 1983; Bagley, Verma and Evan-Wong, 1977).
5) The derivation of self-importance from to superordination of oneself or one's cultural group or, conversely, from the subordination of other groups should be discouraged (Berry, 1984).

Limitations

This paper is based on an interpretation of research literature that is necessarily speculative in nature since some findings are still contentious. Other findings have not, as yet, been shown to generalize across age groups. Some strategies are extrapolations from the research. As well, any strategy, if not used in an appropriate way for a particular group of learners, may not work well. If pupils are not at a minimal level of readiness or if their social context makes it inappropriate, a strategy will not be useful. In a sense, then, particular strategies are in themselves still mere hypotheses until the teacher tries them out in the classroom. This applies to the notion of combinations, hypothesized synergies and sequences of methods represented by the traditional curriculum.

Multicultural Pedagogy in a Transitional Curriculum

Cluster One: Enhanced Direct Teaching

A. *Direct teaching with a change in content emphasis*
If we assume that the teacher who has chosen to implement multicultural education in her high school class usually uses a conventional teacher-centred or direct teaching approach, then one of the easiest changes to make would be to alter content emphasis rather than pupil/teacher interactions.

Much multicultural education has focussed on providing information about the differences among ethnic groups with regards to food, dress, dance, ritual and the like. These differences may or may not be trivial in themselves, but they certainly could be trivialized by superficial examination either in the instructional material or classroom treatment or both. Ironically, the approach of giving information in order to reduce ignorance seldom leads to a reduction in racist or prejudiced attitudes (Stenhouse, 1975; Verma and MacDonald, 1971; Ijaz and Ijaz, 1982; Hayes and Conklin, 1953; Kehoe, 1978; Katz, 1976; Parkinson and MacDonald, 1972; Bagley and Verma, 1972). In fact, in certain cases, it can cause prejudice to increase rather than to decrease (Miller, 1969). Conversely, moving from a content emphasis on differences to an emphasis on similarities *does* lead to improved attitudes (Kehoe and Hood, 1978; Litcher and Johnson, 1969; Verma and Bagley, 1979; Salyachivin, 1972, 1973). Moving completely to an emphasis of similarities, however, might negate the valuing of ethnic uniqueness and steer individuals more towards a melting pot than towards a valued cultural mosaic. One might suggest, then, that content would need to be manipulated by the teacher (Werner, 1985) to include:

1) a balanced emphasis of differences *and* similarities, not only in the superficial facets of ethnicity but in deeper features;

2) the political, economic, religious, historical, geographical and social contexts in which these similarities and differences evolved;

3) a treatment that emphasizes critical understanding and not simply the glib notion that "everyone is just like me" or that "our common humanity" will overcome all differences.

Undoubtedly, there are human experiences that are similar, especially within the context of one country, but at the same time there are also fundamental differences in values and means that cause us to interpret similar experiences quite differently.

B. *Direct teaching plus critical discussion*
One of the first ways a teacher might wish to supplement direct teaching in a conventional classroom and begin gradually changing classroom processes is through the use of critical discussion. This might serve to animate personal thinking as well as to prepare students and teacher for a more interactive classroom.

Carefully crafted discussion that focusses on pertinent questions relating to multicultural issues, racism and prejudice has been shown to encourage attitudinal change with respect to tolerance and understanding of other groups (Katz, 1965; Kagan, 1952; Verma and Bagley, 1979).

If students and teacher are not used to open discussions, a facilitating framework to focus critical thinking and structure and encourage participation would be needed. One way to proceed might be to provide an unfinished list of issues and questions that might be identified from the direct teaching of content outlined in the previous step. During and after the direct teaching, students would be asked to identify additional issues and questions, as well as to formulate their own dispositions on an individual basis. After this, to encourage participation, they would be asked to share and discuss their individual thoughts in small groups. As this is repeated, the guiding issues and questions would tap more personal experiences and practices, and group size could be increased to include the whole class. This type of discussion, with the teacher encouraging critical thinking, could deepen the understanding of significant differences and similarities among various ethnic groups (see Werner, 1985, for further examples).

C. *Direct teaching of acceptable behaviour*
Direct teaching, through the emphasis of "partisan" logical arguments

for healthy multicultural attitudes and behaviour, can encourage healthy attitudes (Verma and Bagley, 1979). Behaviour modification techniques have also been shown to influence multicultural attitudes (Bagley and Verma, 1975; Worchal and Cooper, 1976). Undoubtedly, many of us as teachers have elements of this approach within much of our personal "pedagogical styles." One suspects, however, that deliberate accentuation of these human tendencies into an indoctrinating system of behaviour modification, though it may be successful in the short term, may in the long term be thwarted with the demonstrably negative effects of *authoritarianism* instilling unexamined beliefs (Bagley et al., 1977). It has also been shown that a partisan or exhortative approach is, in the end, less effective than chairing pupils' critical discussion in a neutral manner (Bagley and Verma, 1981). However, the partisan approach might be acceptable, if it were practised in *moderation* and *in necessary combination* with other approaches that lead to personal growth and education. In this way the behaviour modification acts as a useful support system for the practical implementation of self-enlightenment and personally chosen beliefs (McDougall, 1985).

On the other hand, it has been argued that, since some individuals evolve entrenched racist attitudes and behaviours that are difficult or impossible to change, classroom and school rules should be very clear as to what is "right" and "wrong" – that is, discriminatory and racist acts should be prohibited outright (Buchignani, 1984).

Cluster Two: Reality and Minds

A. *Films, video and other media*
In implementing multicultural education in the classroom, one of the easier steps for a teacher to take to move away from conventional direct teaching is to use film or video. These media have proved useful in changing pupils attitudes (Kehoe and Hood, 1978; Hood, 1980; Kehoe, 1979; Echols, 1981; Silvern, Waterman, Sobesky and Ryan, 1979), especially if they take an inside and real perspective.They can be excellent and evocative representations of reality. They can also invite the viewer, through vicarious experience, into the worlds of other groups and the heart of interracial problems. A reverse approach, whereby students view film and other media to discern racial stereotypes, provide students with critical capabilities (see Simon *et al.*, 1985 and Werner, 1985).

One could extrapolate that carefully selected or posed still photographs or colourful graphics depicting real-life situations pertinent to multicultural issues would also prove effective. These materials are of the type that Paulo Freire or Jaime Diaz might use as evocative stimulants to discussion in their adult education endeavours in Third World countries.

B. *Case Studies*

Another approach that reflects reality and provides a focus for pupil thinking and discussion is the case study. Real situations concerning members of a particular group, whether the day-by-day events that a community member undertakes or instances depicting daily prejudices, can provide a concrete focus for discussion and lead to attitudinal improvement (Triandis *et al.*, 1972 and Werner, 1985). One of the ways in which the case study and various media can be used with neophytes in multicultural education is to provide a view from a distance of people like themselves in prejudicial situations. This is perhaps a gentle and effective way to begin helping pupils to confront themselves – a way to help them get over the habit of uncritical self-examination and self-insight. None of the teaching approaches outlined here should be considered as "stand alone" panaceas. We can always achieve better results when a variety of techniques are woven into a synergistic pedagogical fabric. The usefulness of the above techniques will be greatly enhanced if combined with carefully structured role-taking exercises and discussion.

C. *Role-taking or role exchange*

In order to fully actualize the natural role taking (McDougall, 1985) that might take place during the examination of case study material or the viewing of films, pupils could be given some very simple exercises. These exercises are not meant to lead to public role-playing: instead they require the pupil to place himself or herself in the place of individuals in a case study or film situation and to "live through" the experience personally. A series of questions would guide the pupil in the experience of role taking and would make conscious and explicit the results of that experience. The outcomes of exercises such as these would provide rich substance for pupil discussion. Support for this approach is found in Hohn (1973), Weiner and Wright (1973), Gray and Ashmore (1975), Kehoe and Rogers (1978), and Ridley, Vaughn and Wittman (1982).

D. *Class discussion and inquiry: a non-directive approach*

In order to maximize potential attitudinal development in multicultural education, the above strategies – case studies, films and role taking –

can be combined with critical discussion. One method for class discussion and inquiry that has proven effective is one where the teacher acts as a neutral, non-directive, non-sanctioning chairman (Verma and MacDonald, 1972; Verma and Bagley, 1973). He or she asks questions in a non-sanctioning tone to cause pupils to reflect on and inquire into their own dispositions.

This cluster of teaching strategies is aimed at bringing excerpts from concrete and real experiences into the minds of pupils in evocative ways. At the neophyte stage the aim is to begin the process of self-examination in a positive manner, rather than a confronting one that might lead to defensive postures and self-justification. Case studies and film serve to initiate that process through a representation of self through others at a distance. In the process of role-taking the pupil may begin to apprehend and empathize with others' realities. Through such activities, combined with critical discussion in a neutral, non-sanctioning climate, pupils may themselves begin to gain insights as to their own dispositions and learn to become self critical.

Cluster Three: Ethnic Interaction – Community and Classroom

A teacher may begin to think of introducing a more structured and deliberate approach to encouraging ethnic interaction in both the classroom and the community. Various strategies have proved effective in this regard (Sherif et al., 1961). Buchignani (1984) again has emphasized, however, that no pedagogical approach is a panacea. Each has to be carefully fashioned to suit the context, situation and state of readiness of students. Inappropriately applied or forced interracial interaction *can* give rise to increased prejudice (Valien, 1954; Cambell, 1958; Webster, 1961).

A. *Visits to the classroom by high status ethnic members*
Of benefit to all pupils would be visits to the classroom by high-status individuals from minority groups. This approach has been used successfully to improve multicultural attitudes and behaviours. Visitors would relate their personal histories – how they managed to overcome some of the usual hurdles in life, how they handled special problems of prejudice and racism – which would be of great pertinence and interest to students. The students could then utilize the experience gained through other multicultural educational strategies to pose questions to the guest speakers and to engage in discussion of identified issues.

B. *Interethnic work groups*
One relatively easy change to make in the classroom would be to place children of different ethnic backgrounds on teams and groups for various activities (plays, games, projects, discussion groups, debates, teams etc.) that require significant interaction and cooperation. This approach has proven effective (Rogers *et al.*, 1981 and Hansell and Slavin, (1981).

C. *Inter-home visits*
Inter-home visits of pupils from different ethnic groups under the auspices of some form of project might improve understanding and valuing of other lifestyles in an enjoyable experiential activity. This type of active interchange serves to individualize and personalize a person's experience of another group; and it tends to help break down amorphous categories and stereotyping (Kalin, 1984).

D. *Pupil creation of case studies, oral histories and biographies*
As part of studies of ethnicity in the community, pupils could conduct, record and create case studies of the current lived realities of certain members of ethnic groups. The student could take oral histories and create mini-biographies of interesting or typical individuals. The teacher would need, of course, to train pupils in the techniques for these activities and instruct them in how the techniques might be used. Pupils could train themselves using each other as subjects, if they are ready; or, having conducted community studies, go on to in-depth studies of one another or of themselves. These case studies could also be used for class discussion.

Cluster Four: Cooperative Learning

Various types of carefully designed group activities have been shown to promote the learning of attitudes, values and skills conducive to healthy, multicultural interaction (Amir, 1976; Bridgeman, 1981; Johnson and Johnson, 1983; DeVries *et al.*, 1978 and Weigal *et al.*, 1975). These activities require somewhat more complex pre-organization and pre-paration than some of the earlier activities mentioned. Activities that involve cooperative learning are jigsaw groups and group projects.

A. *Jigsaw groups*
Jigsaw group work developed by Aronson *et al.*, (1978) has led to

improved ethnic attitudes (Kalin, 1984). The essence of this technique is not just that pupils work in groups but that each member of a group of 4-6 pupils has a piece of information or material that is different than the information of the other members and, most importantly, that is essential to the group's task. In this way each member of the group is an "expert" in a particular facet of the activity. In order to fulfill their task, it is necessary, then, for the individuals to cooperate and share with each other. Each person's contribution is essential and is valued more or less equally in an interdependent climate (McDougall, 1985). One way of organizing this technique is as follows:

1) Form heterogenous groups by ethnicity and other factors.
2) Distribute topic segments, roles, materials and information to individuals.
3) The pupils then study their materials independently.
4) They join with other classmates who have the same information to share, elaborate, discuss and critique their comprehension and presentation.
5) Pupils then return to their original groups and tutor one another on their particular pieces in order to accomplish the group task. It should be noted that four and five require a structured approach to self education and peer education through tutoring.

B. *The group investigation model or thematic approach*
This approach requires that students have developed skills in independent learning. The teacher (or students) describe a theme, general problem or a cluster of issues, and provide sufficient information to students so that they can select individual subtopics of interest. Two possibilities for forming groups exist: the teacher might form groups either of like interest or of dissimilar but complementary interests that form an integrated whole (somewhat like the jigsaw technique). Teacher and pupils jointly plan how they can complete their group tasks. The development of individual group contracts might provide a useful structure for pupils' tasks and for the teacher to monitor activity. Eventually, teams will present or display their findings to the class. Their efforts are then criticized and jointly assessed (McDougall, 1985).

Cooperative learning is related to the development of interpersonal empathy among individuals, but multicultural empathy, in particular, can greatly enhanced by three techniques. First, by forming "inter-ethnic" groups, second, by creating group tasks that treat multicultural context, issues and concerns; third, by creating tasks that require the use of multicultural attitudes, skills and processes. One should also look to the possibilities of combining other teaching techniques (such as role playing, psychodrama and case studies) with the cooperative approaches. Johnson *et al.* (1984) describes in more detail how cooperative learning might be implemented in the classroom.

Cluster Five: Personal Expressive Activities

A. *Creation of role playing and psychodrama vignettes*
When pupils (and the teacher) are ready, role-playing and psychodrama provide a means for pupils to explore, in greater depth, feelings and expressions of prejudice and the experience of being a victim in such situations. The activity can also be used to express positive aspects of a culture. Such activities, in carefully selected contexts, have proven to have positive effects (Culbertson, 1957; Breckheimer and Nelson, 1976; Ijaz, 1980, 1982; Verma and Bagley, 1979; Silvern *et al.*, 1979; and McDougall, 1985), although in other instances they had no appreciable effects. An initial approach might be to have individuals or pairs of students from the same group to act out a personal experience or prejudice. The role of their peers in this would also be active in that they would be asked to role-take as well as to critically assess the role playing and issues that arise. A second approach might be to organize multi-ethnic groups in role-playing, whereby group members act out a prejudicial situation that one of the group members has experienced. This individual would act as a resource person and coach his or her peers to try to get authentic expression of the experience through empathy. Suggestions and benefits of peer tutoring are provided by McDougall (1984). This technique is not an easy one to engage in and one that must be undertaken very carefully. Teachers interested in this technique would be advised to participate in workshops and engage in careful personal preparation before implementing such an approach (Buchignani, 1984).

B. *Creative projects: Literature, drama and the arts*
The intent of this teaching strategy is to provide pupils personal experience with each others' cultures through active participation in the creation and/or performance of various forms of literature, drama and other expressive arts (Ijaz, 1980, 1982). Instead of utilizing such activities to highlight differences, it is suggested that the teacher choose a set of themes or values common to a number of cultures, and use the

expressive arts and critical examination to enable pupils to understand the unique ways in which various groups pursue the same or similar ideals. This might lead to apprehension of the aspects of human culture that is relatively common to most groups.

Cluster Six: Interpersonal Communication and Personal Development

This cluster of strategies is still somewhat speculative but there has been some research into the question of whether techniques typically advocated for interpersonal communication development can also be used to enhance multicultural attitudes, particularly empathy and the like. Ridley *et al.* (1982) was able to help children develop a greater capacity to feel the way others do through the use of some direct teaching combined with a hierarchy of examples of emotional states, personally relevant and evocative situations, other people's emotional states (starting with persons close to the pupils and gradually moving away) and, finally, more complex social situations. Children were able to attain successfully higher level skills in empathy through this approach.

Conclusion

In order to understand how the foregoing techniques might work and how to make them part of our pedagogical thinking and problem solving in the classroom when we adapt materials or create further techniques for multicultural activity, it is important to discuss the common characteristics of the techniques and consider why they hold promise.

It is fairly easy to understand why techniques such as those examined in the first cluster lead to acceptable changes in behaviour. Basically, these approaches work due to the reinforcement theory and the principles of behaviour modification. The position taken is that these approaches are useful only if supported by other techniques that emphasize education rather than training. Only then will there be lasting, longterm and authentic benefits. Here, then, we will focus on pedagogy that will educate rather than just train the individual pupil.

In working through the teaching activities from the first cluster to the fourth cluster, it generally appears that subsequent clusters subsume characteristics of previous clusters, although this does not prevent the reverse being true.

One suspects that the first activity in the first cluster is useful because it emphasizes similarities across cultures rather than curious differences, or the metaculture of humans; that is, that essentially we are alike in a significant number of human values. If prejudice results, in part, because we cannot take another group's perspective because of differences, then an emphasis of similarities might overcome that barrier.

When critical discussion is added to direct teaching that emphasizes similarities as well as differences, it seems natural that self-reflection focussed on appropriate values coupled with the use of logic would produce insight and growth.

Techniques such as case studies and film can begin to represent and simulate the real-life world of the pupil in a concrete way. Through evocative, vicarious experience it is possible to enable the pupil to begin taking other group members' perspectives, to role-take and experience empathy in a somewhat distanced, non-threatening way. Role-taking enhances empathy and positive, multicultural attitudes. Learning from appropriate film pieces and case studies can probably be maximized if we add structured role-taking exercises, which enhance empathy and self-reflection, and critical analysis and discussion. Hopefully, this process would lead to insight and personal growth through the choice of better, more positive values.

The third cluster begins to utilize the potential of what is known in the literature as the contact hypothesis, whereby the greater appropriate inter-ethnic contact there is, the lower the degree of prejudice and racism. I prefer to rename this concept, the *interaction* phenomenon. Interaction more clearly describes the personal experiences involved. This type of pedagogy capitalizes on real concrete experiences of ethnic groups, initially in the school and classroom, but also in the real world of the home and the community. As well as providing the above advantages, case studies, oral histories and biographies also provide the pupils with a chance to elaborate their experience into a more organized and explicit type of knowledge that might be of use to their peers.

Cooperative learning may have all of the advantages of cluster three techniques, but it is carefully structured to maximize appropriate interethnic interaction in *groups*. This technique is also fashioned to encourage interpersonal valuing, cooperation and interdependence. Groups practise living together through tasks, resolving conflicts, developing consensus and the like. It is hoped that, by this stage, the pupils have moved beyond simple role-taking to the development of shared perspectives which might contribute to cross-cultural inter-subjective meaning.

154

The expressive activities in cluster five take real and concrete experiences into further depth. Role playing, psychodrama and creative projects enable pupils to probe deeply into personally experienced culture or experiences of racism of individual members of ethnic groups.

The final group of techniques, which focusses on personal growth and interpersonal communication skills, can be used in conjunction with any other cluster as necessary and as the pupils are ready for it.

The overall nature of the pedagogy portrayed here is that it emphasizes experience, critical self-reflection and personal growth through self-education. The experiences are real, experiential, interactive, affective and cognitive, and are personally and socially relevant. They emphasize peer learning and cooperation using media that stimulate all the senses, feelings and emotions. These pedagogical characteristics add up to a very Deweyan notion of education.

As was noted earlier, this transitional curriculum is but a hypothesis based on some positive findings in research. Furthermore, the situation-specific nature of teaching makes it highly improbable that what might work in one classroom will work as well in another: adaptations are always needed. What this paper attempts to present is a way teachers might think about pedagogical questions in multiculturalism and of how they might implement their own ideas in the classroom. Obviously, there may be other general sequences and combinations of teaching strategies that optimize multicultural learning in clearly recognizable circumstances. We need both formal research and the day-to-day action research of classroom teachers to contribute this knowledge.

References

Amir, Y.(1976). The role of intergroup contact in change of prejudice and ethnic relations. In P.A. Katz (Ed.), *Towards the elimination of racism*. New York: Pergammon.

Aronson, E., Blaney, N., Stephean, C., Sikes, J. and Snapp, M. (1978). *The jigsaw classroom*. Beverley Hills, CA: Sage.

Bagley, C. and Verma, G. (1972). Some effects of teaching designed to promote understanding of racial issues in adolescence. *Journal of Moral Education, 1*(3), 231-238.

Bagley, C., Verma, G. and Evan-Wong, L. (1979). Prejudice in culture, social system and personality. In Verma and Bagley (Eds.), *Race, education, and identity*. London: MacMillan.

Bagley, C. and Verma, G. (1981). Self concept and the longterm effects of teaching race relations. In Verma and Bagley (Eds.), *Self concept, achievement and multicultural education*. London: MacMillan.

Bem, D. (1970). *Beliefs, attitudes and human affairs*. Belmont, CA: Brookes/Cole.

Berry, J.W. (1984). Multicultural attitudes and education. In R. Samuda, J. Berry and M. Laferriere (Eds.), *Multiculturalism in Canada*. Toronto: Allyn and Bacon.

Breckheimer, S.E. and Nelson, R. (1976). Group methods for reducing racial prejudice and discrimination. *Psychological Report, 39*, 1259-1268.

Bridgeman, D.L. (1981). Enhanced role taking through cooperative interdependence: A field study. *Child Development, 52*, 1231-1238.

Buchignani, N. (1984). Educational strategies to increase racial tolerance. Unpublished manuscript. University of Lethbridge.

Butt, R.L. (1981). The transitional curriculum. *Educational Leadership*. November, 117-119.

Cambell, E. (1958). Some social psychological correlates of direction in attitude change. *Social Forces, 36*, 335-340.

Culbertson, F. (1957). Modification of an emotionally held attitude through role playing. *Journal of Abnormal and Social Psychology, 54*, 230-234.

DeVries, D.L., Edwards, K.J. and Slavin, R. Biracial learning teams and race relations in the classroom. *Journal of Educational Psychology, 70*, 356-362.

Echols, F. (1981). An evaluation of exploring likenesses and differences. Unpublished manuscript. Vancouver: University of British Columbia.

Gray, D. and Ashmore, R. (1975). Comparing the effects of informational, role-playing and vale discrepancy treatment of racial attitudes. *Journal of Applied Social Psychology, 5*(3), 262-281.

Hansell, S. and Slowin, R. (1981). Cooperative learning and the structure of interracial friendship.*Social Education, 54*(2), 98-105.

Hayes, M. and Conklin, M. (1953). Intergroup attitudes and experimental change. *Journal of Experimental Education, 22*, 19-36.

Hohn, R.(1973). Perceptual training and its effects on racial preferences of kindergarten children. *Psychological Reports, 32*, 435-441.

Hood, B.(1980). *Exploring likenesses and differences in film*. Vancouver: National Film Board of Canada.

Ijaz, M.(1980). Ethnic attitudes of elementary school children towards Blacks and East Indians and the effect of a cultural program on these attitudes. Ed.D. Dissertation, University of Toronto.

Ijaz, M. and Ijaz, H. We can change our children's racial attitudes. *Multiculturalism, 5*(2), 11-17.

Johnson, R. and Johnson, D. (1983). Effects of cooperative, competitive, and individualistic learning experiences on social development. *Exceptional Children, 49*, 323-329.

Johnson, D., Johnson, R., Johnson-Holubec, E. and Roy, P. (1984). *Circles of learning: Cooperation in the classroom*. Alexandria, Virginia: Association for Supervision and Curriculum Development.

Kagan, H. (1952). *Changing the attitudes of Christians towards Jews: A psychological approach through religion*. New York: Columbia University Press.

Kalin, R. (1984). The development of ethnic attitudes. In R. Samuda, J. Berry and M. Laferriere (Eds.), *Multiculturalism in Canada*. Toronto: Allyn and Bacon.

Katz, I. (1965). *Conflict and harmony in an adolescent interracial group*. New York: New York University Press. Kehoe, J. and Hood, B. (1978). An evaluation of an antiprejudice film program. Unpublished paper. Vancouver: University of British Columbia.

156

Kehoe, J. and Rogers, T. (1978). The effect of principle testing discussion. *Canadian Journal of Education*, *3*, p.4.

Kehoe, J. (1979). An evaluation of explaining likenesses and differences. Unpublished manuscript. Vancouver: University of British Columbia.

Kehoe, J. (1984). Achieving the goals of multicultural education in the classroom. In R. Samuda, J. Berry and M. Laferriere (Eds.), *Multiculturalism in Canada*. Toronto: Allyn and Bacon.

Litcher, J. and Johnson, D. (1969). Changes in attitude toward negroes of white elementary school students after use of a multiethnic reader. *Journal of Educational Psychology*, *60*, 148-152.

McDougall, D. (1985). Teaching empathy and the reduction of prejudice. *Multiculturalism Education Journal*, *3*(1), 5-13.

Miller, H. (1969). The effectiveness of teaching techniques for reducing colour prejudice.*Liberal Education*, *16*, 25-31.

Parkinson, J. and MacDonald, B. (1972). Teaching race relations neutrally. *Race*, *13*(3), 299-313.

Ridley, C., Vaughn, S. and Whittman, S. (1982). Developing empathic skills: A model for preschool children. *Child Study*, *12*, 89-97.

Rogers, M. et al. (1981). Cooperative games as an intervention to promote cross racial acceptance. *American Educational Research Journal*, *18*, 513-516.

Salyachivim, S. (1979). Change in international understanding as a function of perceived similarity, conceptual level, and primary effect. Ph.D. Dissertation. Toronto: University of Toronto.

Salyachivim, S. (1973). Strategies for international understanding. *Edge*, *1*(1), 9-10.

Sherif, F. et al. (1961). *Intergroup conflict and cooperation*. Norman: University of Oklahoma.

Silvern, L., Waterman, J., Sobesky, W. and Ryan, V. (1979). Effects of a developmental model of perspective teaching training. *Child Development*, *50*, 243-246.

Simon, R., Brown, J., Lee, E. and Young, J. (1985). Decoding discrimination: A study through film. Ottawa: Multicultural Education Materials Animation Project and the Secretary of State.

Stenhouse, L. (1975). Problems of researching teaching about race relations. In Verma and Bagley (Eds.), *Race relations across cultures*. London: Heinemann.

Tiedt, P. and Tiedt, I. (1979). *Multicultural teaching: A handbook of activities, information and resources*. Boston: Allyn and Bacon.

Triandis, H., Vassilion, V., Tanaka, Y. and Sharmugan, A. (1972). *The analysis of subjective culture*. New York: Wiley.

Valien B. (1954). Community in chaos: Cairo, Illinois. In R. Williams and M. Ryan (Eds.), *Schools in transition*. Chapel Hill: University Press of America.

Verma, G. and MacDonald, B. (1972). *Teaching race in schools*. *Race*, *13*(2), 187-202.

Verma, G. and Bagley, C. (1973). Changing racial attitudes in adolescents: An experimental English study. *International Journal of Psychology*, *8*, 55-58.

Verma, G. and Bagley, C. (1979). Measured change in racial attitudes following the use of ultra different teaching methods. In Verma and Bagley (Eds.), *Race, education and identity*. London: MacMillan.

Webster, S. (1961). Some social psychological correlates of direction in attitude change. *Social Forces*, *36*, 335-340.

Weigal, R.H., Wiser, P.C. and Cook, S.W. (1975). Impact of cooperative learning experiences on cross ethnic relations and attitudes. *Journal of Social Issues, 31*, 219-245.

Weiner, M.J. and Wright, F.E. (1973).Effects of undergoing arbitrary discrimination upon subsequent attitudes toward a minority group. *Journal of Applied Social Psychology, 3*, 94-102.

Werner, W. (In press). *The media and multiculturalism: Teaching critical mindedness.* Ottawa: Multicultural Education Materials Animation Project and Secretary of State.

Worchel, S. and Cooper, J. (1976). *Understanding social psychology.* Homewood, IL: Dorsey Press. Verma, G. et al. (1983)

Integrating Multiculturalism in Correctional Schools

John Lewis

The incarceration of minorities has been a reality in Canada for many years. Racial and ethnic minorities made up of largely poor, uneducated members have a high rate of incarceration in the correctional institutions. Hilton (1982) revealed that in the province of Saskatchewan, adult male treaty Indians were 37 times more likely to be in prison than non-natives. The figure for female natives was eight times that of non-native females. Métis populations suffer the same fate in a diminished form. They are eight times more likely to be incarcerated than non-native people. In recent years there has been a high percentage of native people in particular, in the Canadian penitentiaries. There has also been a noticeable rise of ethnic minority prisoners. Recent census statistics (1981) reveal that 13 percent of incarcerated felons are non-Caucasian. Over half of this number are native Indians or Métis. An observable rise in prisoners from the Caribbean has taken place in recent years. Canada has a multicultural policy and, as such, has had an influx of ethnic minorities from Europe, Latin America and South East Asia in the last ten years. This influence has permeated the social structure of the country, and it is only just recently that the influence of this ethnic and racial mix has been felt in the educational system and, more recently, in the prisons. The influx of foreign inmates has created incredible complexity in a system that already has a diversified population.

A teacher can expect to encounter Canadian and American blacks, Native Indians, French Canadians, Europeans, South East Asians, Caribbeans and the majority white, English-speaking Canadians in the classroom. The latest census figures reveal that 87 percent of Canadian prisoners are Caucasian. This figure, however, can lead to false assumptions for it is indeed a fact that within this large group of

Caucasian inmates there exists a quite marked within-group difference. That is to say, the Caucasian group is made up of ethnic minorities from Europe as well as Canadian-born Caucasians. Various nationalities are represented that range from English, Irish, Scottish, French and other northern European countries to some of the southern European countries like Portugal, Italy and Greece. The multicultural mix described above is also affected by many interacting variables. These variables, such as differences in ancestry, family life and geographic region are very evident in a large group of "Caucasians." The interaction of these various factors can affect the educational process.

The following discussion examines a sample of the issues to which correctional educators are exposed. For the most part this discussion will be centred around the correctional school setting in the Ontario region, even more specifically, the Kingston region which, in fact, houses most of the inmates in eastern and central Canada. The developments there will be used as a model to discuss the issues of multiculturalism in correctional schools.

Kingston is a major area for many prisons in Ontario; there are in the neighbourhood of ten institutions within fifteen miles of the city. Since 1980, the Frontenac County Board of Education has been contracted to supply services to five of the correctional institutions in the region. These services fall under the rubric of Community and Continuing Education. At the present time, a separate division called Correctional Services has been formed to deal specifically with educational needs of each institution. The Board of Education employs teachers contracted to supply services to the institutions. The full range of services include elementary and secondary courses. Students can fulfill all the requirements necessary to obtain their secondary school diplomas; and at the elementary level there are specialized services offered in basic literacy. Credit in this system is, of course, awarded by the Frontenac County Board of Education and follows the same curriculum guidelines as mainstream schools.

The curriculum for high school students is based upon the Ontario Schools' Intermediate and Senior Division (OSIS) 1984 document which outlines the program and diploma requirements for secondary students. In this document, thirteen goals of education, which run the gamut from skill acquisition to learning are given. In fact the OSIS document specifically says that a student must be helped to "develop esteem for the customs, cultures and beliefs of a wide variety of societal groups." The document states that cultural diversity and national identity and unity are issues demanding attention in the school curriculum and even further outlines very specific policies under the heading of "Multiculturalism." Schools must demonstrate their commitment to the ideals and principles of multiculturalism.

These ideals and principles must be infused into curriculum materials and teaching methods. By extension, the policy must also apply to the correctional setting since the basic structure of awarding credits to prisoners is the the same as that of awarding credits to mainstream students. The question arises of how one can write about correctional education and, more specifically, multicultural methods in the prison, if prison students and high school students are to be treated alike. Surely, one might argue, the issues and methods remain the same. Obviously, however, although many of the methods and issues are similar between "inside" and "outside" schools, clear differences do exist.

First, the prison school population consists primarily of adults. The students range from 17 years of age to the late 50s. Most students in the prison schools,in fact, are beyond normal school-leaving age.

This situation compels correctional educators to be fully aware of the significance of age differences. The teacher has to be aware of adult developmental issues and of normal aging sequences when dealing with these students. Levinson (1978) has illustrated most clearly the sequential cycles of adult development. Failure to realize the student as an adult and to adjust curriculum and teaching methods accordingly will lead to diminished educating power. The effect this age diversity has in prison schools can be quite startling: a typical classroom, for instance, could have an 18-year-old, a 35-year-old and a 50-year-old. Each of these students represents a different generation. As such, multicultural issues have differing impacts on each.The 18-year-old may have been exposed to multiculturalism from an early age within the context of growing up.He may have lived in a multicultural milieu. The change in Canadian immigration policy over the last twenty years is partly accountable for this. By contrast, an older prisoner may have had less exposure to this type of mixed population, and stereotyped images of some minority groups could still be firmly ingrained, especially in the case of the oldest group.

The second difference between mainstream and correctional methods centres around the personality characteristics of prisoners and the debate over whether inmates have cognitive styles different from mainstream students. A great deal has been written about the nature of the criminal personality. Wishnie (1977) has demonstrated that inmates tend to be illogical and irrational. He states that criminals are more prone to stereotypic thinking and, in fact, tend to see other people as two-dimensional and predictable. I recently showed a film about three families from different geographical locations in the world to a group of inmates. Most of them displayed stereotypic conceptions of the different cultures. They tended to view the cultures from a detached perspective and to make clichéd comments like "all blacks behave like that." The perspective and stance taken by the inmates were ethnocentric and categorical in nature; the limited range of responses revealed that the cultures under study were misunderstood. Campbell (1980) in a study of Canadian inmates found that many prisoners displayed an impulsive approach to decision-making and were basically field dependent. Impulsiveness is prevalent among inmate students and manifests itself in an impulsive learning style. This style can result in tendency to jumping to conclusions to make hasty generalizations based upon limited information. These faulty logical processes directly affect attitudes towards minority issues: conclusions about cultures and minority individuals are arrived at with limited foreknowledge; and very often these conclusions are negative and are based on isolated encounters with a particular culture or individual.

Yochelson and Samenow (1979) studied the criminal personality extensively and discovered cognitive deficiencies in most inmates. A study by Narrol et al. (1982), carried out in a Kingston-area penitentiary, also showed marked cognitive deficiencies among the inmate student population. In many cases, these deficiencies are the basis for faulty comparative thinking, simplified generalizations, and a lack of deductive and inductive reasoning. In turn, these undeveloped cognitive functions translate into intolerance for differences in people and things and resistance to new ideas and concepts.

How then, does one teach multiculturalism in accordance with the policies and philosophical positions of the OSIS; and yet still be aware of the age differences, multicultural mix and special characteristics of inmate students? The issue becomes a two-faceted question: How does one teach ethnic minority prisoners, and how does one change prejudice and stereotypic thinking among prisoners? These two issues will be dealt with separately.

The multicultural constitution of the inmate population places demands upon correctional schools. Assessment for placement in the schools becomes an important aspect of correctional education. Samuda (1975) and Sundberg (1980) both both have pointed out the necessity for sensitivity in assessing minority students. The validity of conventional placement tests has been questioned when used with minority students. The correctional teacher must first and foremost determine the extent to which standardized tests have had an impact on the placement of particular inmates. Some inmates may have been inappropriately slotted into programs and grades on the basis of low scores obtained on tests that are culturally unfair. Dynamic testing paradigms might prove to be the most useful approach when assessing students for school placement. Several guidelines appear to be appropriate in the assessment of inmate students. First, the assessment should provide an accurate appraisal of a student's current level of functioning within his cultural context and taking into account his prior experiences; second, the student's specific educational needs must be identified; third, his strengths and assets must be identified and emphasized through the assessment process; fourth, the assessment must be dynamic and ongoing.

The placement of students into grade levels must take all the aforementioned assessment concerns into consideration. Once the minority student is placed into a particular class or grade level, the onus is on the teacher to fine-tune the placement process – he or she is the best person to judge the effectiveness of the. Once a student has been placed into the program, many issues may surface. A key concern is the language facility of minority students.

The degree of language facility will, for the most part, determine whether a student will be classified as basic, general or advanced level. This categorization in the prison schools is based on facility in the English language. Teachers should be sensitive to cross-cultural language variables as outlined by Sue and Sue (1977). The confusion between ability and achievement needs to be clarified, and teachers should not automatically consider basic level courses to be the only courses suitable for inmate students with a language-ability problem. The dynamic assessment technique could, perhaps, provide more insight into the progress that a minority student makes. Once in a program, the cultural experiences of a minority student could provide valuable material for discussion and comparison.

The placement of minority students into programs along with predominant Anglo-Celtic inmates creates a cultural mix that can provide an interesting classroom experience. This interaction of culturally different inmates demands more focussed curriculum planning. Several practical methodologies are suggested below.
1) The use of interdisciplinary courses is an area that has not been explored fully in the correctional setting. An ethnic group could be examined in the context of a course that cuts across curriculum lines. For instance a study of native Canadians could be offered dealing with such physical manifestations of the culture as food, dance and

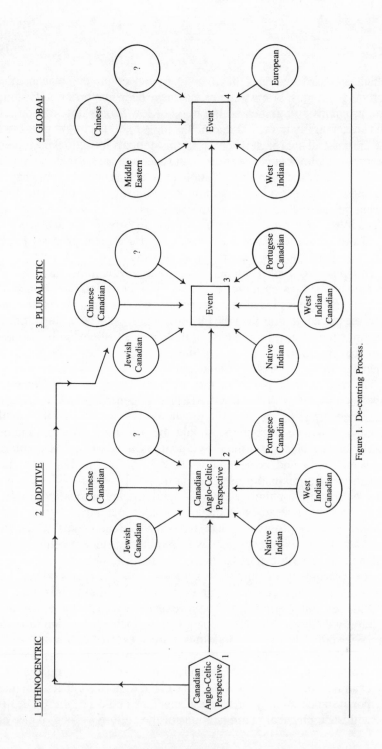

Figure 1. De-centring Process.

art. The study could also include an examination of the power, communication patterns and social connections within various native groups. Within-group similarities and differences rather than a categorical comparison with the dominant culture, could be stressed. Through such an the interdisciplinary approach, a comprehensive study of native Canadian or other groups would be accomplished.

2) The implementation of team teaching would allow several perspectives to be presented on identical or similar issues. It is the sharing of divergent and convergent views on selected multicultural topics that allow for open dialogue and increased cross-cultural awareness among students. Team teaching could be used in the context of a single course or in a general approach where teachers constantly present their views on selected topics across the curriculum.

3) The development of a fluid, progressive model of the curriculum should be undertaken. Banks (1983) formulated a model for curriculum change in ethnic studies that could be modified and utilized in correctional schools for multicultural content. This model, which has been adapted for Canadian correctional school programs, is illustrated in Figure 1.

The first facet of the model demonstrates the ethnocentric curriculum approach. This is the format that maintains the status quo of curriculum. It advocates that the majority Anglo-Celtic perspective be used in course material and that all cross-cultural issues be viewed from this narrow perspective. This approach is, of course, the traditional metholodology used in both non-prison and prison educational settings. Much of the curriculum still uses this model since it requires no additional planning for incorporating multicultural aims and goals.

The development of an additive model is an attempt to add multicultural content to the existing curriculum. More often than not, this is the method used in the initial stages of curriculum reform since it fulfills some of the aims of the OSIS document. In this paradigm, the dominant Anglo-Celtic perspective forms the core of the curriculum. Units on native Canadians, Chinese Canadians and so on, are developed in order to be attached to the core content. In correctional schools these units can incorporate any or all of the aspects cocerning interdisciplinary approaches discussed above. Very often, the technique most useful here is simply a discussion of similarities and differences between groups. More emphasis is placed on between-group rather than within-group differences.

The third model is the pluralistic approach. In this model events are studied from several ethnic or plural viewpoints. This approach allows for the study of significant events or topics from the traditional Anglo-Celtic perspective, along with other ethnically varied viewpoints: each viewpoint is given equal status so that differences and similarities between viewpoints can be examined. This model allows for both a between-group and within-group perspective. For instance, the implementation of a controversial government law could be examined from a pluralistic viewpoint. This approach allows students to discuss topics from their own ethnic viewpoints or to research issues from culturally different orientations.

The last stage in the fluid development of a multicultural model is the global perspective. This is the ideal form for curriculum studies and views social or historical occurrences from a multinational perspective.

At this stage, some of the correctional schools in Ontario have implemented the additive model for multicultural education but have progressed no further; the author feels that movement towards pluralistic and global approaches is necessary. The curriculum could move in progressive stages from intermediate to senior levels; certainly by the senior level, the global perspective would be a useful curriculum approach. As one progresses through the curriculum stages of ethnocentric, additive, pluralistic and global views, a complex de-centreing process is bound to occur in students.They, therefore, move from an ethnocentric position towards more flexible viewpoints. The resultant effect could be more tolerant thinking and action among prison inmates and less stereotyped conceptions of culture. It is also hoped that prejudicial thinking would be reduced.

The teaching of critical thinking skills, values education, personal life management and guidance courses should be increased. Many of the concepts in these areas form a substratum for dealing with issues connected to stereotypic thinking and racism, and many could be offered for credit. This issue is more fully disscussed in Lewis and McKechnie (1980, 1981). The implications for implementing multiculturalism in the prison school setting are extensive.

Curriculum materials must be chosen with care. Overt and covert forms of bias and racism in textbooks and materials must be eliminated; at the very least, the curriculum materials with bias must not be used. Pratt (1983) has pointed out many examples of bias in books and their effect on student attitudes and values. Language, which can shape values and attitudes, must be used in a culturally sensitive and appropriate fashion to eliminate stereotyping and prejudice. Ijaz (1985) delineates these issues more fully and outlines the guidelines for curriculum writing in multicultural settings.

Summary

The prison system is faced with an increase in the numbers of minority inmates; many of these inmates will pursue educational endeavors while incarcerated. The school systems in Ontario, especially, have Ministry guidelines applicable to mainstream and inmate students. These guidelines reflect a thrust toward multicultural education. While inmate students should receive basically the same methodological treatment as mainstream pupils, certain differences between the two groups do exist. Correctional education must be able to view the differences and similarities as a fact of life.

Within correctional settings, sensitivity in the assessment and placement of culturally diverse students is necessary. The process of teaching must be modified to incorporate multicultural ideals. A more comprehensive fluid model of curriculum change must be implemented, and courses dealing with cognitive and moral issues should be incorporated into the existing syllabus. Care must to be exercised in choosing materials used in the classroom.

The prison school setting offers an opportunity to formulate and implement multicultural programs in a way that will have real benefit for the people involved. It is hoped that practical work in this area will increase in the future.

References

Banks, J. (1983). Ethnicity and curriculum reform. In R. Samuda, and S. Woods (Eds.), *Perspectives in immigrant and minority education*. Lanham, MD.: University Press of America.

Campbell, D. and Davis, R. (1981). Understanding impulsivity and related cognitive styles in inmate studies. Report submitted to the Ministry of the Solicitor General of Canada.

Government of Canada. (1981). Justice Statistics 1980-81, Ottawa.

Government of Ontario. (1984). Ministry of Education. Ontario Schools Intermediate and Senior Divisions (O.S.I.S.), Toronto.

Hylton, J. (1982). The Native offender in Saskatchewan: Some implications for crime prevention programming. *Canadian Journal of Criminology*, 24(2).

Ijaz, A. (1985). Guidelines for curriculum writing in a multicultural milieu. Unpub-

168

lished manuscript presented at the Invitational Symposium on Teaching Methods in a Multicultural Society. Kingston.

Levinson, D. (1978). *Seasons of a man's life*. New York: Knopf.

Lewis, J. and McKechnie, M. (1981). The need for a cognitively based education in prison settings. Unpublished manuscript presented at the Ontario Institute for Studies in Education.

Lewis, J. and McKechnie. (1980). Moral education in prison: A cognitive approach. Proceedings of the National Conference on Prison Education. Victoria: University of Victoria Press.

Naroll, H., Silverman, H. and Waksman.M. (1982). Developing cognitive potential in vocational high school students. *Journal of Educational Research*, 76(2), 107-112.

Pratt, D. (1982). Bias in textbooks: Progress and problems. In R. Samuda, J. Berry, and M. Laferriere (Eds.), *Multiculturalism in Canada: Social and educational perspectives*. Toronto: Allyn and Bacon.

Sue, D.W. and Sue, D. (1977). Barriers to effective cross-cultural counselling. *Journal of Counselling Psychology*, 24(5), 426-429.

Sundberg, N. and Gonzales, L. (1981). Cross-cultural assessment: Overview and issues. In McReynolds (Ed.) *Advances in psychological assessment, Volume 5*. San Francisco: Jossey Bass.

Wishnie, H. (1977). *The impulsive personality*. New York: Plenum.

Yochelson, S. and Samenow, S. (1976). *The criminal personality, Volume 1*. New York: Aronson.

PART IV

Teaching Methods

Preparing Teachers of French for Multicultural Schools

André Obadia

The teaching profession is no sinecure. Anyone who has spent six or seven hours a day teaching a class of thirty school children, not to mention looking after their social and emotional needs, is left with no illusions that the task is simple. However, some teachers appear to meet the challenge better than others and never lose their drive and enthusiasm. They are known as "immersion teachers", a term that is becoming increasingly well known across Canada.

French immersion, a relatively new method for teaching French to Anglophone children, has been the subject of a great deal of discussion over the past twenty years. In light of the many studies of the remarkable results obtained through this method, it is time we examined in more detail the role played by the teachers themselves. These teachers usually remained on the sidelines of the socio-political and administrative upheavals that accompanied (and still accompany) the early years of the programme, and of the contagious euphoria of parents enthused with the positive results of this type of education.

Conscious of the responsibilities with which they were entrusted, teachers bent to the winds of change and stood quietly by while some of the most eminent Canadian researchers conducted their studies from coast to coast. Even today, little research is being done on the needs, concerns, problems, responsibilities and success of the teachers themselves.

However, since the early days of immersion, the success of the programme has rested mainly on the teacher. Even if the first generation of children who began kindergarten in French without knowing a single word of the language were perhaps confused, they were certainly not alone. Well aware of the challenges and risks posed by this completely new and perhaps unique approach to education, the teachers themselves felt even more "immersed".

Those same teachers soon became the focal point of emotional and worried Anglophone parents and of condescending but somewhat incredulous administrators. They were put in front of classes without receiving any precise pedagogical directives or specialized training.

Since they were themselves usually bilingual, the teachers knew deep down that the objective being sought was achievable. Their main concern was the groups of children they had to teach. They knew the experiment could succeed because they felt it in their bones.

But how should they proceed? What tools would they use? Should they rely on the programmes and manuals of the French schools in Quebec, or on those of core French classes in which Anglophone children spent only between 15 and 30 minutes a day learning French? The first approach appeared too difficult, especially for the early part of the year; the second was too rigid and too monotonous to be used throughout the school year. There was only one solution, discovered by the veterans of this period and perhaps to a lesser degree, by those teaching immersion today. They had to sit down at their desks with a pot of coffee and spend many hours establishing goals and objectives, a programme for the year and the classes for the day. These unknown pioneers burned a great deal of midnight oil.

School boards equipped with a coordinator or counsellor moved heaven and earth to try to make the teachers' work a little easier. School boards in Montreal and Ottawa-Carleton in particular carried out a phenomenal amount of work, feverishly researching and writing to produce a complete curriculum outline. Thanks to additional funding from the Department of the Secretary of State, hastily assembled courses of study began to see the light of day. A great deal of progress has been made since those first years; instead of a few sheets of paper, the boards today proudly display volumes of 500 and 1500 pages supplemented with original teaching material.

After prudently waiting to see which way the wind was blowing, publishing houses began to show an interest in the growth of bilingualism, a typically Canadian phenomenon at least in primary and secondary schools. The professional journals began to advertise publications (books and textbooks) that could be used in immersion classes. Increasingly, the publications that focused on immersion classes had to draw inspiration directly from the experience of this type of schooling instead of borrowing ideas from materials designed for Francophone students. It became increasingly apparent that the language needs and difficulties for Francophones and immersion classes were quite different.

Today, French immersion teachers are supported in their efforts by better informed and more organized parents, many of whom are members of an association known as Canadian Parents for French (CPF). Such parents are deeply involved in their children's education and give one another invaluable support. Similarly, the immersion teachers themselves founded the Canadian Association of Immersion Teachers (CAIT), which today has 1200 members. Provincial associations of the CAIT have been established and this will undoubtedly help improve communications between members. One need only attend the annual meetings of the CPF or the CAIT to be aware of the commitment, drive and optimism of participants. The first tentative years are now in the past and teachers are no longer on their own. The progress has been enormous over a mere twenty year period. This success story is largely due to the efforts of teachers who, in the early days, had no specialized training, no teaching materials, nothing. Imagine what could be done if everything were available!

Will teachers and parents lose some of their enthusiasm over the years and, if so, will this have an impact on students? An answer to this question is difficult to predict. What is certain, however, is that strong support is still being given to this method, for which there is an increasing number of active practitioners in small towns.

From a sociological standpoint, it is interesting to see the impact of immersion on families. Some parents begin to take French courses, visit areas in which French is spoken and grow closer to Francophones. These points were revealed by a study we conducted in Canada.

Profile of the Immersion Teacher

Who are these key players, where do they come from and what training have they received? The majority of French immersion teachers are French-Canadians; some are Francophones from Europe, Africa or other countries; and, increasingly, we find more Anglo-phones from Canada and other countries using this teaching method. Overall, these teachers are a reflection of Canada's mosaic.

Our recent study (Obadia, Roy, Saunders, Tafler and Wilton, 1983) revealed the following breakdown of immersion teachers in Canada; 73 percent Francophone, 20 percent Anglophone, 5 percent Allophone and 2 percent claiming equal proficiency in both official languages. The greatest concentration of Anglophones is found in British Columbia (40 percent) and Ontario (33 percent); the smallest concentration is in Quebec (3 percent) and Saskatchewan (5 percent).

Drawing on data from 400 questionnaires, the study also revealed that 44 percent of all immersion teachers have taken their education training in French, 28 percent in English and 27 percent in both languages.

Teaching positions, which are today few and far between, continue to attract bilingual candidates who, thanks to immersion programmes, will have better chances of finding a job.

The teachers surveyed in this study had an average of 1.9 university degrees or teaching certificates and 9.4 years of experience. This is surprising when compared to the national average which is 12.5 years (Statistics Canada 1981-82). Given the fact that immersion is a recent phenomenon in Canada, we might have expected less experience; however, the programme appears to attract experienced teachers who have taught in other fields.

Compared with the average age of teachers in elementary and secondary schools, immersion teachers are younger. Fourteen percent are 25 years of age or under, as compared to 4 percent nationally for the same age group (Statistics Canada, 1981-1982). Sixty-four percent are 35 years of age or under, as compared to 42 percent for the teaching profession as a whole.

The majority (69 percent) teach all day in French to pupils who began immersion either between kindergarten and grade 3 (81 percent), or between grades 4 and 6 (10 percent) or in grades 7 or 8 (8 percent).

The methods used to train immersion teachers are still tentative. Clearly it is not enough simply to have mastered the French language. If we accept the definition that "immersion is a means of educating a child mainly in a language other than his mother tongue" (Coulombe, 1983), we see that these are not the usual "foreign-language" classes, but an approach to education that also gives attention to the child's physical, cognitive and emotional development. We therefore need a fully rounded educator, a teacher who has received both general and specialized training and who is not simply a language teacher.

Core French and French Immersion Teachers

It is important to make a distinction between the role of the teachers of core French and the very different responsibilities of the immersion teachers.

In 15- to 30-minute daily periods, the former try to teach the rudiments of the language to seven or eight classes, in other words to approximately 300 pupils a day. Their purpose is to teach them to communicate orally, and to a lesser degree, to read and write the language. They try to create situations in which the pupil is asked to use a relatively limited number of structures and as functional a vocabulary as possible. The rhythm of the lesson and the motivation and attention of pupils have to be maintained at all times. Variety is the key element and teachers are constantly the focal point of such classes. They must be careful how they use language, and their vocabulary must remain within the scope of the pupils. They need imagination, a sense of humour and a great deal of patience; and, of course, they must be realistic about the language objectives they can attain.

The situation of elementary immersion teachers is quite different. First, they work with only about 30 pupils for the emtire day. Their objective goes beyond teaching the French language and includes such subjects as science, mathematics, history, geography and so on. The second language becomes the natural vehicle of communication for the entire day and for all activities. Pupils very quickly realize they can manipulate another language without too much difficulty and that they are expanding and improving their knowledge from day to day in a real context.

The language enables them to learn algebraic equations, the history of Confederation, the principle of communicating vessels and the geography of Canada. It becomes a working tool based on subject content rather than on language. Both the student and the teacher make progress. The linguistic results obtained in an immersion class are more tangible and therefore more satisfying and encouraging for the teacher and pupil than those obtained in a traditional core French class.

Training

Most immersion teachers are graduates of French or English faculties of education which train their students to teach in the child's mother tongue. Additional courses on second language teaching (French or English) are usually given during this traditional period of training. A study (Coulombe, 1983) on the training of immersion teachers has revealed that 36 percent of faculties of education already offer one or more specialized courses for immersion teachers and that, particularly west of Ontario, 16 percent intend to follow suit over the next five years. However, the time devoted to immersion as compared to traditional training courses varies from 9 percent to 67 percent, positive proof that much still needs to be done and that overall organization is lacking.

The time spent on practice teaching also varies, student teachers spending from one week to six months in immersion classes. These practice teaching periods may be part of the traditional classic training year or may be taken as additional periods. The number of student teachers planning to teach immersion in Canada rose from 428 in 1979 to 790 in 1982, an increase of 84.6 percent. Fifty-six percent of faculties of education forecast a rise in enrolment and 50 percent are planning to increase the number of professors responsible for such training.

The length of the training periods, the number and content of courses and the proliferation of student teachers all reflect a gap that is, paradoxically, the result of delays and perhaps surprise on the part of faculties and ministries of education responsible for teacher training and the granting of teaching certificates.

According to the study cited above (Obadia, Roy, Saunders, Tafler and Wilton, 1983), immersion teachers found that courses dealing with methodology, techniques and practice teaching were "the most valuable and must useful." Immersion teaching and methodology were also the most popular choices for in-service programmes. More specifically, they would like to learn more about activity methods, remedial teaching, and the teaching of oral expression and reading skills. From a list of 33 subjects, computers rank 14th and linguistics only 29th!

Training French Teachers: A Unique Approach at Simon Fraser

The training programme for teachers of French as a second language (immersion or core) at the Faculty of Education at Simon Fraser University is based on a model that is unique in Canada. The originality of the approach is as much in the structure of the staff, which goes back to the creation of the university in 1965, as in the way the twelve months of professional training are organized.

The staff is made up of:
- *university professors* whose role is similar to that of professors at any other university;
- *faculty associates*, seconded from their school board for one or two years. These teachers take on teaching tasks of a primarily practical and support nature related to the student teacher at the primary and

secondary level. Each associate is responsible for about a dozen students;
– *school associates*, each of whom takes one or two trainees in his or her class.

The training of the student teacher, which is at the heart of this trio, takes place in a climate of continuous exchange between theory and practice, a dynamic cycle from which all four participants benefit.

The Twelve Months of Training

The year is divided overall into six months of course work and six months of practice teaching.

Course 401: In September, after a week of orientation at the Faculty of Education, student teachers are placed in a classroom situation for a period of about two months. This is a true "immersion" experience, a term which is in fact frequently used during this period.

These first two months spent in the classroom allow student teachers to determine if teaching is really their vocation, and, once they return to the university, enables them to relate their courses to a real situation they recently experienced.

French immersion trainees also have the opportunity to spend about 25 percent of their time in English classes.

Course 402: The students then take a series of five courses, two of which are in French and deal with the basic elements of general education, special education and psychology.

Course 405: Four months of practice teaching. Students, under the supervision of the faculty associate, teach for four months in a French immersion class, or, if they prefer, in a French class for Francophones.

Course 404: Returning to the university, students do a further four-month period of academic study.

By the end of their year of training, student teachers have spent approximately 80 percent of their time in French-language education courses dealing with immersion and in practice teaching in French immersion. The rest of the time is spent on English-language education courses.

Language criteria: Any student wishing to enrol in immersion must take an oral test. Only those who demonstrate a very solid mastery of the French language, equivalent to that of a native speaker, and who pass a written test, are accepted into the programme. Candidates wishing to teach core French must also take an entrance test.

The Need for Coordination

Very soon, we shall have to coordinate all these efforts and adapt to this new concept of "immersion teacher" which some trainers of language teachers still have difficulty in understanding.

In light of existing research and experience, specialists are increasingly convinced that pedagogical preparation for immersion should be part of a formal training programme and not be conducted on a piecemeal, ad hoc basis. It should have its own structure, philosophy and pedagogy like any traditional training for English or French schools. French immersion, as we know it in Canada, is a very effective technique which has proven its worth and, in terms of teacher training, should now be given its letters of credential.

Although immersion is not, of course, the only method for making pupils bilingual, it does appear to correspond to the wishes of parents and the objectives of educators. It also satisfies the pupils themselves. Whether they begin in kindergarten or grade 7, they are clearly proud of their accomplishments and grateful to their parents for having provided them with an oportunity to master their mother tongue like any other Anglophone of their age and to handle with ease the other official language of Canada.

Immersion is like a rough-hewn sculpture on which refinements are now required. Although we have not yet seen the full impact of this programme, its early results suggest that it can help contribute to a more harmonious society in Canada.

References

Coulombe, D. (1983). *A survey of teacher training in French immersion in Canada.* Vancouver: Faculty of Education, Simon Fraser University.

Obadia, A., Roy, R., Saunders, B., Tafler, R. and Wilton, F. (1983). *Etude nationale sur la formation et le perfectionment du professeur d'immersion francais.* Canadian Association of Immersion Teachers.

Implementing Multiculturalism in French-As-A-Second-Language Education

Yvonne Hebert and Michael O'Sullivan

The implementation of multicultural education in the Canadian classroom is a complex challenge for all educators, regardless of their particular discipline. We consider this implementation to pervade every area of the educational school system (McLeod, 1981; Laferriere, 1981). To meet this challenge, teachers and teacher educators need consistent, effective practices in multicultural education that derive from an appropriate theory. For the teaching of French, a number of methodological approaches are currently available from which one can develop initiatives towards a suitable theory and practice of multicultural education.

As a modest step in this direction, this paper proposes methodological initiatives for implementing multiculturalism in the teaching of French as a second language in school programs known as Core French. Core French programs contain approximately 90 percent of Canadian students who enroll in French (LeBlanc, as quoted in Stern, 1984). It is proposed that teachers of this program can and should make a contribution to their students' cross-cultural awareness and encourage their openness to persons who have racial, religious, linguistic or cultural characteristics different from their own.

Cross-cultural objectives have long been an integral part of French language education in this country. The Saskatchewan Core French Curriculum (1984) is typical of Canadian provincial curricula in its policy:

> The Core French Program should enable students to develop an understanding and an appreciation of the French language culture, particularly as experienced in Canada.

Although sensitizing students who are largely non-Francophones to French cultures and subcultures is usual in French language instruction, this has not systematically been part of the curriculum. Stern (1983) comments that while the study of culture "has been recognized for a long time as an important component of foreign language curricula...the cultural component has...not been treated as a 'syllabus' with its own defined content, progression and mastery levels equivalent to the language syllabus." As a result, this for multicultural education, and our task as second-language and multicultural educators is to promote this idea with teachers, teacher educators and curriculum developers.

Our proposal is timely.The shortcomings of second language teaching methodologies not specifically designed to achieve communicative competence are now well recognized. Efforts are currently underway to develop national guidelines (notably, the Canadian Association of Second Language Teachers' National Study of Core French, 1985-1988) for necessary changes in Core French curricula. Every effort should be made to design and test curriculum materials that are consistent with the integration of Core French and multiculturalism, with a view of refining our thinking on the best means of achieving this.

In presenting our proposal, we will first examine the methodological bases for implementing multiculturalism in Core French instruction drawing on four sources:

1) key elements of the communicative approach in second language curriculum;
2) recent proposals for a multi-dimensional second language curriculum;
3) current trends towards the integration of subject matters;
4) current theoretical and practical developments in multicultural education.

In the second part of this paper, we briefly describe the emerging methodological initiatives, illustrating them with two sample activities which focus on the cultural diversity of Canada and on developing multicultural awareness in students.

The Methodological Bases

Current approaches to teaching French as a second language, classified under the broad rubric of communicative approaches, emerged during the sixties and seventies to try and attain the elusive goal of functional proficiency. These approaches have many common characteristics and follow a valuable new philosophy in language pedagogy; based on the recognition that there is no *one* definitive method for teaching second languages (Stern, 1983). The characteristics of communicative approaches, closely linked to theoretical bases, are as follows:

1) Language is viewed as social behaviour (Hymes, 1971).
2) The pedagogies concern themselves with the function of language to express ideas, to establish and maintain social relations, and to provide links between the self and situations (which include authentic texts) (Halliday, 1973; Firth, 1951, 1964; Candlin, 1977; Widdowson, 1978; Wilkins, 1976. Another approach is taken by Brown, 1984 and Jakobson, 1960).
3) The complexities of language are considered in context, taking into account such concerns as the appropriateness of the addressee's response with regard to the rules of interpretation prevailing in a given speech community (Searle, 1970; Austin, 1962).
4) Language is studied as a form of interaction in terms of its function in people's lives; for example, verbal strategies of interaction are examined, as revealed in turn-taking and other practices of conversational management (Gumperz and Cook-Gumperz, 1982).

From these characteristics and their foundations arise criteria for the curriculum and classroom. In selecting and developing curriculum materials, it is important to keep in mind that there is no such thing as an ideal textbook and that a range of options is possible between pre-packaged programs and the no-textbook situation. To determine the adequacy of curriculum materials representative of communicative approaches, Berns (1985) proposes the following criteria, adapted here for the teaching of French.

1) Utterances should be presented with sufficient context for the interpretation of meaning.
2) The relevant contextual features – that is, persons, objects, verbal and non-verbal behaviour, and effect – should be identifiable.
3) The insights gained into an instance of language use should be generalizable: that is, the learner should be able to make predictions or interpretations of meaning in similar situation types.
4) All three major functions of language – that is, the expression of ideas (the contextual function), the establishment and maintenance of social relations (the behavioural function), and the provision of links between self and situation (the textual function) – should be taken into account.

5) Texts and other materials should be authentic: that is, if they are not taken from original sources, they should be believable as representations of actual uses of French.
6) Options should be provided for the expression and interpretation of meaning.
7) More than the formulaic functions of language should be illustrated.
8) The interdependency of formal and functional meaning in a context, as opposed to simple equivalency of form and function, should be explicit.

In the second language classroom, a number of teaching techniques have been extremely valuable, such as problem-solving activities and information gaps (where participants in an exchange need to find out information that only other participants have). However, Gerngrob and Puchta (1984) suggest that if we really want our students "to do things with words" in a second language, the key curricular concept must be a pedagogical one, linking the students' selves with topics that are relevant to them. Materials and participant structures that enable students to act out language functions, such as complaining or apologizing, buying a ticket or making suggestions, satisfy the requirements of a communicative approach and help to develop cognitive processes. Language learning is vitally influenced by the effects of motivational and affective processes and of personality (cf., Hamers and Blanc, 1983; Dulay, Burt and Krashsen, 1982). Hence, we should strive to teach students using materials that foster classroom interaction dealing with students' immediate needs and, at the same time, fulfill objectives for a distant future.

According to Gerngrob and Puchta (1984), the focus of language teaching must be on the learner's self, integrating a "learn-by-doing" process that allows both second-language learning and acquisition. Participant structures and materials should provide learning experiences that engage students creatively, stimulating them to grow by exposure to a diversity of perceptions, ideas and emotions; and teaching them to share and express these ideas and emotions in the second language.

Recent proposals for a multidimensional second language curriculum, particularly for Core French, provide additional methodological bases from which to create initiatives for implementing multiculturalism (Stern, 1984, 1983b; Canadian Association of Second Language Teacher's three-year National Study of Core French in progress). In devising a curriculum for Core French or for other languages, Stern (1984, 1983b) proposes a shift from a relatively narrow focus or unidimensional curriculum to a broader, multidimensional and flexible focus. There are three reasons for supporting such a shift in focus:

1) French is widely recognized in Canada as an important part of basic literacy in schooling.
2) A second language cannot be acquired by formal study and practice alone.
3) Language learning includes the experience of communication, a meeting of minds, getting in touch with other people, and getting to know them.

Four components or syllabuses are proposed as the main building blocks for any second language curriculum at any level of schooling. These four components, which are complementary and integrative, are:

1) A language component, consisting of traditional study of the language and of forms, speech acts, notions, functions and discourse, which represent the language study principle.
2) A cultural component, referring to the life of a target community, the language's cultural communities and a local community.
3) A communicative component: that is, language use in real life as an integral part of the curriculum.
4) A general language education component, representing a reflective, more general perspective based on thinking about language, culture, community issues and oneself as a language learner.

Adoption of this multidimensional focus has considerable potential to broaden the Core French curriculum and to facilitate the integration of multiculturalism into the teaching of French as a second language. Current trends towards integrating subject matter right across the curriculum provide an additional impetus for implementing multiculturalism in the teaching of French. One model, proposed by Boyer (1983), identifies five characteristics of a functional integration of subject matter:

1) The integration is interdisciplinary: that is, it takes into account the entire content and orientation of a school program rather than being an aggregate of discrete subjects juxtaposed under a general thematic rubric.
2) It is functional within a framework of learning situations that are as authentic as possible with respect to students' experiences.
3) It adheres to the objectives in such a way that generalizations about

the integrated program objectives as a whole may also apply to the objectives of each component program.

4) It accounts for the nature and level of the objectives of each of the component programs, integrating the curricular aspects most feasible to structured integration.

5) It is practical in that it can proceed in stages and does not necessarily embrace all subject matters or school programs at once.

The integration of subject matters is more readily applicable to elementary schooling; however, secondary programs and even post-secondary teacher education programs can benefit from such integration. Implementing multiculturalism in the teaching of French at any level can be facilitated by this curricular and pedagogical approach.

Finally, and quite importantly, current theoretical and practical developments in multicultural education are available from which to develop methodological bases to facilitate the implementation of multiculturalism in the teaching of French as a second language. Grounded in a realistic knowledge of the nature of Canadian society, our recommendation is to take a cultural/intercultural approach that aims at developing skills, knowledge, attitudes and emotions in students so that they acquire a sense of confidence in their self and group identity a knowledge of cultures and subcultures, including their own and the facility to speak and function capably in more than one language and culture. Without having to rely upon the heterogeneity of a particular local community, the cultural/intercultural approach recognizes schools, libraries, families and programs as basic aspects of multi-culturalism. It provides students with necessary cognitive and affective bases for developing positive self-concepts, for valuing alternative lifestyles, for examining languages and cultures, for developing sound concepts of human and civil rights, for appreciating the cultural diversity of Canada, and for giving a greater meaning to the notion of Canadian citizenship.

Practical developments in multicultural education have arisen out of the greatest classroom successes that occurred when school staffs, sometimes in conjunction with parental and community representatives, came together to examine their educational goals, objectives and programs in light of the social diversity around them, included in their local community (McLeod, 1981; Ramsay et al., 1983; Kehoe, 1984). The needs of administration, programs, teachers, students, and the community have been considered as part of an overall picture.

Two findings are of particular relevance. One is the discovery that teachers are crucial to the implementation of multicultural education. It is teachers' attitudes and behaviours, preparation and emphases, techniques and capabilities that largely determine the success of implementation. Being educators and not curriculum developers, teachers also tend to teach or work from ready-made curricula.

The second finding is that certain types of curricular materials and pedagogical approaches are effective in developing multicultural awareness. Reading and discussing multicultural materials, with or without field experiences, is effective in creating attitudinal change among students, both at the elementary and secondary levels (studies reported in Kehoe, 1983, 1984; Black, 1973). Balanced materials not based on typical holiday and seasonal approaches, presented with reading and discussion, and with the teacher adopting the role of a neutral authority, have been effective in bringing about significant favourable changes in attitudes. Role-taking is another effective strategy for developing a child's ability to describe accurately what others see, feel, think, intend and like, and which is essential to the development of a non-prejudiced individual. The development of this ability is much more difficult than the development of social knowledge (Flavell, Botkin, et al., 1958, and other studies reported in Kehoe, 1984).

Methodological Initiatives

In our methodological initiatives, we propose pedagogies and curriculum materials that are:

1) *interactive*: i.e., students come together socially to exchange ideas, feelings, behaviours and skills in discussions and activities with common goals;
2) *authentic*: i.e., students' needs are respected and met as much as possible; materials and activities provide a link with students while being representative of the target language or culture;
3) *realizable*: i.e., integrated program objectives should be met within a framework of school-and community-based learning situations;
4) *functional*: i.e., sufficient context should be provided, including identifiable contextual features for communication while providing options for the expression and interpretation of meaning;
5) *generalizable*: i.e., balanced materials and pedagogies should develop generalizations relating to understanding, insight and

perspective in the social cognition of behaviours, languages and cultures.

These five qualitative principles form the basis of our ongoing work in this area, including two field-tested examples of curricular initiatives that will be presented and discussed next.

The two projects, *Je fais mes propres jouets* and *Le Centenaire de la rebellion de 1885*, represent modest efforts towards furthering the proposed cultural/intercultural approach and which provide teachers and teacher educators experience with this approach. Such projects can be easily integrated into present curricula without adding an unnecessary burden to teachers already labouring under the tight time constraints imposed by the material for which they are presently responsible.

The activity *Je fais mes propres jouets* is a communicative activity that fosters a relatively natural setting in which students are encouraged to speak and write French while having fun. In order to discuss the photographs and to explain their creations to classmates, students need to consult the French-English dictionary, and in doing so, learn new vocabulary and use new structures in a situation in which they are enjoying themselves.

From the point of view of the language teacher, the lesson has validity because it gets the students to talk about homemade toys and the pleasures of giving and receiving. From the point of view of multiculturalism, the lesson in an indirect way makes a powerful statement in that a child from a minority background becomes like any child with a homemade toy.

As a caution, it should be noted that such a lesson would be ineffective if it were taught to a class only once. With regards to multiculturalism, a one-time activity would be a token effort, quickly forgotten by the students; with regards to second-language learning, the activity would not greatly contribute to the students' ability to communicate competently in French. Exercises that encourage constant communication and that develop cross-cultural awareness must become a regular part of the class content.

The second project, *Le centenaire de la rebellion de 1885*, represents a different type of curriculum activity. From a language-learning point of view, it requires students to recognize the distinction between two past tense forms, *l'imparfait* et *le passe compose*, a distinction which English-speaking students often find difficult. Discussing an historical event requires students to make this distinction. This activity in fact underlies our opinion that such a mini-unit, far from creating an additional burden for the teacher, could be profitably substituted for the hours, even days spent on textbook exercises on this same lesson. From a multicultural point of view, the activity has the advantage of focussing the students' attention on the aspirations of the Metis in the early days of settlement, and the conflicts between them and Ottawa over the future of the West. Since the circumstances facing the Metis in Saskatchewan today can be traced directly to their defeat in 1885, engaging students in activities that expose them to Riel's perspective will contribute to their understanding of this aspect of Canadian history and of the distinction between Metis and Indian land claims.

The 1885 Metis Rebellion is a distinctly Canadian event and is therefore eminently suited to our purposes. Moreover, it was fought in French, lost in English, and involves an interculture and an interpeople. At present, it is considered specific to Saskatchewan and is usually taught only in or near Regina because of the Royal Canadian Mounted Police museum located there. However, the material could be readily modified for other regions of the country; and other local events, anniversaries and community issues could be used in the same way.

Although further development is needed with this particular unit, our preliminary results are positive, indicating that it contributes to the desired results from both a language-learning and a multicultural point of view.

A third type of initiative for integrating multiculturalism with Core French programs involves modules or mini-units focussing on the life of selected minority groups. Models for this, though they may be inadequate as presently constituted from a communicative point of view, exist in the form of curriculum material on life in Quebec. Further extensions could take the form of lessons in a module format on a diversity of cultural groups. These lessons would also include the desired communicative, language, cultural and general language syllabuses that constitute the multidimensional, communicative approach to the Core French curriculum.

Multiculturalism and French-as-a-second-language education can be readily integrated into the present curriculum if there is a commitment on the part of the classroom teacher to the development of communicative competence and cross-cultural sensitization. Overall results are likely to be more satisfactory, once initiatives started locally become provincial and national.

Conclusion

The cultural and racial heterogeneity of Canada places tremendous

188

responsibilities on educators to create a climate of tolerance in the classroom and beyond.As educators, we should take advantage of any opportunity to contribute to the creation of this climate. Core French, taught using the communicative approach and with a multidimensional perspective, lends itself remarkably well to contributing to this positive climate. The contribution made by Core French programs would increase even more dramatically if their strategies for multicultural education were formally adopted by the provinces and if the appropriate materials were made available. For the moment, however, teachers and educators involved in the preparation of curriculum materials for Core French are encouraged to continue developing materials which foster a multicultural perspective.

References

Austin, J. (1962). *How to do things with words*. Oxford: Clarendon Press.

Berns, M. (1984). Functional approaches to language and language teaching: Another look. In S.J. Savignon and M.S. Berns (Eds.), *Initiatives in communicative language teaching: A book of readings*. Don Mills: Addison-Wesley.

Black, J. The effects of instruction in general semantics on ethnic prejudice. *Research in the Teaching of English, 7*(1), 98-108.

Boyer, J-Y. (1983). Pour une approche fonctionelle de l'integration des matieres au primaire. *Revue des sciences de l'education, 9*(3), 433-452.

Brown, J. (1984). Communicative competence versus communicative cognisance: Jakobson's model revisited. *Canadian Modern Language Review, 40*(4), 599-615.

Candlin, C. (1977). Preface. In M. Coulthard, *An introduction to discourse analysis*. London: Longmans.

Dulay, H., Burt, M. and Krashen, S. (1982). *Language two*. New York: Oxford University Press.

Firth, J. (1951). Modes of meaning. *Essays and studies of the English Association, Nova Scotia, 4*, 118-149. Reprinted in *Papers in linguistics 1934-1951*. London: Oxford University Press.

Firth, J. (1964). *Tongues of men/speech*. London: Oxford University Press.

Flavell, J. and Botkin, P. et al. (1968). *The development of role taking and communication skills in children*. New York: Wiley.

Gerngrob, G. and Puchta, H. (1984). Beyond notions and functions: Language teaching or the art of letting go. In S. Savignon and M. Berns (Eds.), *Initiatives in communicative language teaching: A book of readings*. Don Mills: Addison-Wesley.

Gumperz, J. and Cook-Gumperz, J. (1982). Introduction: Language and the communication of social identity. In J. Gumperz (Ed.), *Language and social identity*. New York: Cambridge University Press.

Halliday, M. (1973). *Explorations in the functions of language*. London: Edward Arnold.

Halliday, M. (1978). *Language as a social semiotic: The social interpretation of language and meaning*. Baltimore: University Park Press.

Hamers, J. and Blanc, M. (1983). *Bilingualite et bilinguisme*. Bruxelles: Pierre Mardaga.

Hymes, D. (1971). Competence and performance in linguistic theory. In R. Huxley and E. Ingrams (Eds.), *Language acquisition: Models and methods*. London: Academic Press.

Jakobson, R. (1960). Linguistics and poetics. In T. Sebeok (Ed.), *Style in language*. Cambridge, Mass.: M.I.T. Press.

Kehoe, J. (1983). Strategies for human rights education. In D. Ray and V. D'Oyley (Eds.), *Human rights in Canadian education*. Dubuque, Iowa: Kendall/Hunt.

Kehoe, J. (1984). *A handbook for enhancing the multicultural climate of the school*. Vancouver: Alternatives to Racism, WEDGE Publications.

Laferriere, M: (1981). Education interculturelle et multi-culturalisme: Ambiguites et occultations. In *Education and Canadian multiculturalism: Some problems and some solutions*. Canadian Society for the Study of Education, Eighth Yearbook.

McLeod, K. (1981). Multiculturalism and multicultural education: Policy and practice. In *Education and Canadian multiculturalism: Some problems and some solutions*. Canadian Society for the Study of Education, Eighth Yearbook.

Ramsay, P., Sneddon, D., Grenfell, J. and Ford, I. (1983). "Successful versus "unsuccessful" schools: A grounded theory study of predominantly working class Polynesian schools in Southern Auckland, New Zealand. *Australia and New Zealand Journal of Sociology, 19*(1).

Saskatchewan Education. (1984). *A curriculum guide for divisions 111-1V: Core French*. Savignon, S. (1983). *Communicative competence: Theory and class-room practice*. Don Mills: Addison-Wesley.

Searle, J. (1970). *Speech acts*. Cambridge, England: Cambridge University Press.

Stern, H. (1983a). *Fundamental concepts of language teaching*. Toronto: Oxford University Press.

Stern, H. (1983b). Toward a multidimensional foreign language curriculum. In R. Mead (Ed.), *Foreign languages: Key links in the chain of learning*. Middlebury, VT: Northeast Conference.

Stern H. (1984). A quiet language revolution: Second-language teaching in Canadian contexts – achievements and new directions. *Canadian Modern Language Review, 40*(5), 506-524.

Widdowson, H. (1978). *Teaching language as communication*. Oxford: Oxford University Press.

Wilkins, D (1976). *Notional syllabuses*. Oxford: Oxford University Press.

Multiculturalism and Social Studies Instruction: Some Models and Guidelines

Dean Wood

Earlier chapters in this book have set the stage for this look at the teaching of multiculturalism in social studies courses at any grade level. The purposes of multicultural education have been overviewed and the curriculum issues have been addressed. Because of this already prepared background, this chapter will move quickly to instructional processes, with only a brief mention of a single curriculum issue.

Educators agree that the best way to reflect multiculturalism in the social studies curriculum is by specified content and objectives. In Alberta, for example, multiculturalism makes up about one-third of the program at each of five grade levels: grade 1 – Canadian families; grade 3 – lifestyles in culturally distinctive communities; grade 5 – Canada: exploration and settlement; grade 7 – Canada: a multicultural society; and grade 10 – human rights in Canada (Alberta Education, Curriculum Branch, 1981). While this formalized approach certainly has its advantages, multiculturalism can still be a part of the curriculum, even when there are no concrete prescriptions. Often, knowledge, skill and concept objectives are stated in general terms, with limited or no references to a particular body of content. As one way of meeting curriculum objectives, teachers can integrate multicultural material as they prepare instructional units based on these general statements.

As teachers, we tend to avoid general statements; we prefer to use concrete situations, illustrations or case studies whenever we can, and this chapter follows this approach as well. Accordingly, three sample lesson plans are presented to introduce the reader to the instructional processes being recommended. The very important question of perspective is also given considerable attention.

Sample Lesson 1

As teachers prepare lessons on multiculturalism, there is a temptation to select several immigrant groups and study each separately, beginning with its arrival in Canada and tracing its history to the present. This approach has limited motivational value, leads to an emphasis on differences, and does not provide the knowledge base for concept and generalization development. In addition, it is impossible for students to study all the ethnic groups that exist in Canada, so choices must be made. A thematic, comparative approach, on the other hand, based on concepts from the social sciences, ensures that the most significant aspects of the ethnic experience are studied and provides insights into the diversity of experiences of various groups in Canada. Teachers must carefully consider their selection criteria and ensure that they are providing a balanced representation of the groups, cultures, histories and experiences found in Canada.

The first sample lesson takes such an approach to the topic of the immigrant experience. Many other concepts, such as culture, change, ethnic community and discrimination, could be developed in the same way. The lesson uses a data retrieval chart, a basic two-way form that structures students' inquiry and organizes the data for higher level activities.

Topic The immigrant experience

Objectives To enable students:

1) to describe the experiences of three immigrant groups;
2) to assume the role of a character in each of the case studies and to write a letter to a relative in the homeland;
3) to compare and contrast the experiences of these groups;
4) to develop a generalization about the immigrant experience.

Student References
Burke, M.V. (1978). *The Ukrainian Canadians*. pp. 6-11, 14-26, 30-32.
Gutkin, H. (1983). *The Jewish Canadians*. pp. 8-10, 14-23.
Harris, H. and Sun, M. (1982). *The Chinese Canadians*. pp. 10-13, 16-24.

Teaching Strategies

1) The objectives can be approached in a number of ways, depending on the curriculum content and the level of the students. Students can

Figure 1
DATA RETRIEVAL CHART ON THE IMMIGRANT EXPEREINCE

Key Questions	Chinese Canadians	Jewish Canadians	Ukranian Canadians
Describe the home community			
What were the reasons for immigrating			
Describe the journey to Canada			
Describe the first month or so in Canada			
What problems were encountered during the first few years in Canada?			
Describe accomplishments during first years in Canada.			

be asked to generate guiding questions for the "Key Questions" section of the data retrieval chart; or they can be given the questions suggested below. The students can be divided into teams to study each immigrant group, and later, reorganized into new teams, each containing students from each of the original teams. An information-sharing session among members of the teams should then follow.

2) To reinforce their understanding of the content, students can participate in one of the creative activities suggested in the objectives above. The teacher should point out that there were very few photographs in the early periods of immigration in Canada and suggest that they might make their letters to their relatives more interesting by including some drawings reflecting their experiences in Canada.

3) Lead a discussion using the completed chart as the reference point. What similarities and differences do the students see in the experiences of the three groups? How would they explain them?

4) Through class discussion develop, test and revise generalizations in response to this question: "What was the nature of the immigrant experience in Canada around the turn of the century?"

Sample Lesson 2

Whenever possible, films and videotapes should be used in the study of multiculturalism. In contrast to written historical narratives, they create a sense of immediacy and portray the ethnic experience in a more personal manner, providing more meaningful insights to students. In addition, the use of such a medium provides opportunities for media literacy activities in a multicultural context. Because of the all-pervasive influence of the electronic media and their common failure to present Canada's ethnic diversity in a positive way, it is particularly important to promote media literacy in a multicultural context.

This lesson uses the film *Teach Me To Dance* (1978) to promote the development of media literacy, using a model developed by Carlos Cortes (1980), and to convey social studies content about intergroup relations. Set in rural Alberta in 1919, the film dramatizes anti-Ukrainian sentiment through the friendship between Lesia, a Ukrainian-Canadian girl, and Sarah, an English-Canadian girl. Sarah wishes to perform a Ukrainian dance with Lesia at the school Christmas concert. However, Sarah's father and teacher, reflecting the sentiments of the English-Canadian community, forbid the dance. At the end, despite the tensions in their community, the two girls are able to sustain their friendship.

Topic Intergroup relations and media literacy

Objectives Students should be able to:

1) define the concept of intergroup relations;
2) describe relations between Anglo-Canadians and Ukrainian-Canadians as portrayed in the film;
3) make inferences about the social factors contributing to intergroup tensions;
4) analyze the film according to a media literacy model.

Teaching Strategies

1) Briefly introduce the topic by explaining that relations develop between groups in a community, just as they do between individuals. These can be positive, based on mutual respect, or they can be negative, with one or more groups discriminating against others. Most immigrant groups have experienced some form of discrimination. At any one time in a community, there can be positive relations

between some groups and negative relations between others. In class periods, students can be introduced to the concepts of discrimination, assimilation, integration and segregation (Wood, 1978, pp. 19-21, 23-25).

2) Show the film and lead the class into a discussion, focussing on specific issues in order to clarify students' comprehension of the characters, their attitudes and reactions. Itemize the evidence relevant to the theme of intergroup relations.

3) Ask the students to make inferences about the reasons for the tensions between the Anglo-Canadians and Ukrainian-Canadians. List the responses on the board without any discussion, and then have students evaluate their inferences in light of the evidence that has been collected. A short teacher lecture from Howard Palmer's (1982) book *Patterns of Prejudice: A History of Nativism in Alberta* would be helpful for senior students. Follow up the discussion by having students write a short paragraph in their notebooks on this topic.

4) Tell students that they are now going to consider the film from another perspective. Point out that they spend a lot of time in literature classes studying style, theme, technique, and so on, but that they spend very little time studying electronic media as a means of communication. Show the film a second time and use the following questions based on Cortes' model to analyze the film.

   a) *Analysis of media content* What images of Ukrainian-Canadians are presented? What images of English Canadians? How are the images created?

   b) *Analysis of media communication structures* What are the characteristics of a historical drama? How does it differ from a documentary? Can a historical drama create false impressions? Could a viewer be led to making overgeneralizations from watching one?

   c) *Analysis of causation* Causation refers to the social forces which shape the media at any given time. Contrast the perspective of the film with the perspective of the letter to the editor cited in the film. Is the perspective of the film a common one in Canada today? What does it say about present intergroup relations and attitudes?

   d) *Analysis of self as viewer* What did students find most meaningful in the film? Which character had the most impact on them? Did the film confirm or contradict any of their ideas?

As an extension of this lesson, students can investigate television with the object of media literacy. First, the class can be divided into small groups, with each group assigned to the monitoring of a particular news program for a week. The students should report on what multicultural topics or issues were featured and which ethnic groups received coverage. Similar reports can be prepared, using advertisements, children's programs and various kinds of entertainment programs. Canadian and American networks and program types can be compared.

As in any classroom activity, it is the follow-up to the data gathering phase that is at the heart of the learning process.Students can analyze their data considering such questions as: When are ethnic groups and multiculturalism newsworthy? Are stereotypes of any groups perpetuated by television? Is Canadian society presented as diverse or homogenous? What implicit messages about ethnic groups can be identified? What attitudes will pre-schoolers acquire on the basis of their experiences with television?

Sample Lesson 3

Since the publication of McDiarmid and Pratt's (1971) landmark study, *Teaching Prejudice: A Content Analysis of Social Studies Textbooks Authorized for Use in Ontario*, researchers across Canada have been evaluating the portrayal of ethnic groups in school texts, particularly social studies texts. An investigation sponsored by the Manitoba Department of Education (1980) reached a conclusion in agreement with other studies:

> Canada's cultural and ethnic mosaic is not readily apparent. Although only 45 percent of Canadians are of Anglo-Saxon origin, stories of their culture and lifestyles predominate.Characters with French backgrounds and immigrants are almost non-existent in texts. Canada's native peoples receive slightly more recognition, but they are usually presented in traditional settings or in legends and myths.
>
> (p.4).

While significant efforts are underway to eliminate ethnic bias by omission and commission in texts, teachers should also prepare students to detect bias in texts and other information sources. A lesson such as this can be part of a basic skills unit, or it can be used at the start of a multicultural lesson using the media.

Topic Ethnic bias in texts

Objectives Students should be able to:

1) define bias;
2) identify ethnic bias in samples drawn from social studies texts;
3) compare and contrast objective and biased writing;
4) explain the impact of ethnic bias in texts on students and victimized groups.

Teaching Strategies

1) Give students a handout containing these statements:
   a) When Europeans discovered North America, they laid claim to the wilderness in the name of a European monarch.
   b) The primitive qualities of native cultures are best illustrated by their pagan beliefs.
   c) Big Bear, Wandering Spirit and their band of blood-thirsty Cree massacred nine innocent people at Frog Lake in April, 1885.
   Lead a general discussion on these three statements. What are their themes? Which words and phrases are the most powerful? Whose point of view is expressed? Have the students seen statements like these before? Do they find this style of writing acceptable? Define bias for students. Have them apply the definition to the statements.
2) While the statements above were specially prepared to dramatically demonstrate bias, the samples below are drawn from actual books in use across Canada. Discuss them with the class, using the questions from the above activity.
   a) "The missionaries travelled deep into the woods and lived among the Indians. They learned the Indian languages. They baptized the Indians and tried to teach them to be Christians. Many of the missionaries died in Indian raids and wars. They were proud to die while trying to bring their religion to the Indians. The missionaries who died were known as martyrs." (Neering and Garrod, *Life in New France*, 1975.)
   b) "Many of the newcomers from Europe were subjected to the abuse of Canadians, who resented their *foreign* dress, language and customs" (emphasis added). (Stewart and McLean, *Forming a Nation: The Story of Canada and Canadians*, 1978, Book 2.
   c) "The result was that tens of thousands of hopeful settlers came from central Europe, mostly from Russia and the Austro-Hungarian Empire, a *hodge-podge* of ethnic groups, languages, religions and social customs" (emphasis added). (Stewart and McLean, *Forming a Nation: The Story of Canada and Canadians*, 1978, Book 2.

If possible, either provide students with samples of bias from their texts and reference books, or have them collect samples.

3) Pass out the following list of three statements that are matched contrasts to statements in activity 1.

a) Without the help of the native peoples, the first Europeans could neither have survived nor explored North America.

b) The Crees worshipped their Creator "Manito"; everything in the universe was created by Him and was under His control.

c) Riel led a Metis and Indian struggle against the colonization of their lands and the accompanying destruction of their cultures.

Compare and contrast the statements in this activity with those in activity 1. Is the perspective in the second set different from that in the first? Is the language different? Compare and contrast the impact of each set. Which set appears more truthful?

4) Lead a discussion of the impact of ethnic bias in texts on readers. Are people's attitudes shaped without an awareness on their part? What impact does bias have on the victimized groups? How do the explicit and implicit messages of biased statements affect a child's sense of self-worth and his or her attitude towards his or her own ethnocultural group? This lesson can easily be extended to an exploration of bias in newspapers, magazines, television advertisements, news programs, documentaries and situation comedies.

The three preceding sample lessons illustrate some elements of a preferred instructional approach to multiculturalism in social studies. First, they utilize a thematic, comparative approach based upon key concepts and generalizations derived from the social sciences. Second, they emphasize the importance of a process orientation rather than exclusively a cognitive outcomes approach. Third, they focus on skill development in compliance with the objectives of all social studies curricula. Fourth, instruction in multiculturalism should, as indicated in the sample plans, emphasize the human experience rather than an impersonal, professedly objective historical account or general description of ethnic groups.

Perspective or point of view is the unifying concept for the guidelines that follow. Teachers and program developers often overlook the effects of their instructional choices upon students' perceptions of themselves and of social groups at the local, national and world levels. We can see this choice process reflected in Carter's (1981) definition of curriculum as "the school's version of the culture children are hopefully to learn and reproduce ... Curriculum is culture as distilled, arranged and presented to the young by the school" (pp. 162-163). In the same vein, instructional planning involves a deliberate selection and presentation of information to students in a simplified manner. As soon as certain topics and facts are selected and others rejected, there is a very real danger of distortion. Werner, Connors, Aoki and Dahlie (1977) point out that "program developers become the gate-keepers of reality definitions. They select, classify, and evaluate viewpoints and knowledge for inclusion within programs. Certain perspectives are legitimized to the exclusion of other points of view" (p. 48). Similarly, teachers, in their day-to-day planning, become a second level of gate-keepers.

Within this context there are a number of issues of perspective that should be considered in the planning and instructional activities of teachers.

1) *Similarities and differences.* For a number of reasons which are beyond the focus of this chapter, Canadians have a history of seeing ethnic groups in terms of what makes them different from the rest of society. However, the similarities are just as real as differences, and by learning to recognize such similarities students will begin to perceive the bonds that unite all peoples and to develop positive intergroup attitudes. Discuss the impact of these two sets of questions for young children.

   a) Compare an igloo with your house. Would you like to live in an igloo? Compare a settler's sod hut with your house. Would you like to live in a sod hut?

   b) Why did the settlers build sod huts and the Inuit build igloos? Can you see any similarities between sod huts and igloos in your list of reasons?

2) *Hyphenated Canadianism.* In most cases, people who identify with ethnic groups refer to themselves as "hyphenated" Canadians: Portuguese-Canadians, Japanese-Canadians or Indo-Canadians. Most texts and, quite likely, most teachers approach multicultural topics with primary emphasis on the *first* part of the hyphenated identity. Such an orientation is misleading and distorts the historical and sociological realities of the ethnic experience in Canada. Instead, we should re-define our focus or ensure that ethnic groups are portrayed as an integral part of Canadian society. What cultural patterns do *most* Canadians share? How do Jewish-Canadians, for example, maintain a Jewish identity and some Jewish culture within the larger context of Canadian society? Does a hyphenated identity mean a person is bicultural?

3) *Insider versus outsider.* Robert K. Merton's (1972) exploration of

the tension between the "insider" and "outsider" doctrines in the sociology of knowledge crystallize another issue of perspective. According to the insider doctrine, "authentic understanding of group life can be achieved only by those who are directly engaged as members in the life of the group" (p. 32). By contrast, the outsider doctrine holds that "knowledge about groups, unprejudiced by membership in them, is accessible only to outsiders" (p. 31). Teaching about ethnic groups is quite different from conducting research in social science, but much of what we do as teachers reflects the dispassionate, objective distance of the outsider doctrine. While the insider doctrine could negate much of what we do in multicultural studies, its exclusiveness should not lead teachers to reject it outright. In teaching, we draw upon the work of textbook authors and social science researchers, but mould their perspectives to our individual instructional planning. We should be conscious of the insider-outsider dichotomy and select our sources and activities so that students are exposed to both perspectives. What does this mean in practical terms? A study of arranged marriages in a Sikh community, for example, could be based upon anthropological research conducted from an outsider perspective; but it should also draw upon an insider perspective by including the views of Sikh men and women as expressed in various literary forms. The relocation of Japanese-Canadians can be studied from the perspective of outsider historians and textbook authors, but balance is only achieved when students encounter Japanese-Canadian reactions drawn from primary sources. Introducing students to multiple perspectives ensures a more comprehensive and personal outlook on multiculturalism.

4) Two concepts from the social sciences, ethnic community and intra-group diversity, also help to resolve issues of perspective. Often, we speak of *the* Ukrainian-Canadian or *the* Mennonite-Canadian, as if all the people of a particular origin can be relegated to a single group. In doing this, we cast such a wide net and gloss over so much diversity that, in reality, we can make very few meaningful statements about the group in its present form. In fact, internal differentiation increases according to the length of a group's history in Canada (Vallee, Schwartz, and Darkness, 1968, pp. 593-594). Correspondingly, the concept of "ethnic groups" becomes less and less useful in schools where the qualifications and subtleties of such classifications may well be lost on students.

In place of "ethnic group" as an organizing concept we should perhaps use "ethnic community" which refers to the people of one ethnic origin in a recognized population unit such as a town, city, or district of a city, like Toronto's west end. This concept provides a more accurate perspective because of its smaller scale and its emphasis upon observable elements in a single community. The attention to such aspects as interpersonal relations and organized social, cultural, welfare, recreational, religious, educational, commercial and political activities (Breton, 1964, p. 194), can replace the over-reliance on the large and rather vague concept of "culture" which, in the classroom, often becomes a study of folk arts, foods, crafts and other rather superficial, material aspects of a culture.

The previous mention of internal differentiation leads to the concept of intra-group diversity. Many ethnic groups were already internally diverse according to religion, dialect, class, occupation, and so forth, upon their arrival in Canada. Diversity grows with the influence of assimilation over time, and new waves of immigrants add to the complex dynamics of a group. A concern for a balanced and accurate perspective on ethnic groups necessitates the recognition of the concept of intra-group diversity and the changes it encompasses.

Additional suggestions that could be made on instruction in multiculturalism are many, varied and beyond the scope of this chapter. Resourceful teachers can always derive other learning activities from various sources and develop creative ones of their own; but a teacher's overall instructional orientation in multiculturalism is as significant as the specifics of his or her teaching strategy. Any individual lesson will be successful, if it reflects the social science-based teaching and learning principles, and the multicultural perspective expressed here.

References

Alberta Education, Curriculum Branch. *1981 Alberta social studies curriculum.*

Andrews, J. (1984). *Once the seed is sown: Potentials for the use of Canadian children's books in the strengthening of multiculturalism.* Ottawa: Multiculturalism Canada.

Banks, J. (1973). Teaching for ethnic literacy: A comparative approach. *Social Education, 37*(8), 738-750.

Banks, J. (1976). Ethnic studies as a process of curriculum reform. *Social Education, 40*(2), 76-80.

Banks, J., Cortes, C., Gay, G., Garcia, R. and Ochoa, A. (1976). *Curriculum guidelines for multiethnic education: Position statement.* Arlington, Virginia: National Council for the Social Studies.

202

Breton, R. (1964). Institutional completeness of ethnic communities and the personal relations of immigrants. *American Journal of Sociology, 70*, 193-205.

Britt, M. (Ed.) (1982). *Multiculturalism film and video catalogue*. Ottawa: Canadian Film Institute.

Burke, M. (1978). *The Ukrainian-Canadians*. Toronto: Van Nostrand Reinhold.

Carter, T. (1971). Cultural content for linguistically different learners. *Elementary English, 48*(2), 162-175.

Cortes, C. (1980). The role of media in multicultural education. *Viewpoints in Teaching and Learning, 56*(1), 38-49.

Dynneson, T. (1977). A cross-cultural approach to learning about the family. *Social Education, 41*(6), 482-483.

Gay, G. and Banks, J. (1975). Teaching the American Revolution: A multiethnic approach. *Social Education, 39*(7), 461-465.

Gutkin, H. (1983). *The Jewish Canadians*. Toronto: Nelson Canada.

Harris, H. and Sun, M. (1982). *The Chinese Canadians*. Toronto: Nelson Canada.

Hood, B. (1982). *Exploring likenesses and differences with film*. Montreal: National Film Board of Canada.

Kiely, M. (Ed.) (1984). *Multiculturalism multimedia catalogue – 1984*. Ottawa: Canadian Film Institute.

Manitoba Department of Education, Curriculum Branch. (1980). *Confronting the stereotypes for grades 4-6: A handbook on bias, Volume 2.*

McDiarmid, G. and Pratt, D. (1971). *Teaching prejudice: A content anaysis of social studies textbooks authorized for use in Ontario*. Toronto: Ontario Institute for Studies in Education.

McLeod, K. (Ed.) (1984). *Multicultural early childhood education*. Toronto: Guidance Centre, Faculty of Education, University of Toronto.

Merton, R. (1972). Insiders and outsiders: A chapter in the sociology of knowledge. *American Journal of Sociology, 78*, 9-47.

Neering, R. and Garrod, S. (1975). *Life in New France*. Markham: Fitzhenry and Whiteside.

O'Neill, P. (1984). Prejudice towards Indians in history textbooks: A 1984 profile.*The History and Social Science Teacher, 20*(1), 33-39.

Palmer,H. (1982). *Patterns of prejudice: A history of nativism in Alberta*. Toronto: McClelland and Stewart.

Stewart, R. and McLean, N. (1978). *Forming a nation: The story of Canada and Canadians* (Book 2). Toronto: Gage.

Vallee, F., Schwarz, M., and Darknell, F. (1968). Ethnic assimilation and differentiation in Canada. In R. Blisher et al., *Canadian society: Sociological perspectives* (3rd ed.). Toronto: Macmillan.

Werner, W., Connors, B., Aoki, T., and Dahlie, J. (1977). *Whose culture? Whose heritage?:Ethnicity within Canadian social studies curricula*. Vancouver: Centre for the Study of Curriculum and Instruction, Faculty of Education, University of British Columbia.

Wheeler, A. (Producer) (1978). *Teach me to dance*. (Film) Montreal: National Film Board.

Wood, D. (1978). *Multicultural Canada: A teacher's guide to ethnic studies*. Toronto: Ontario Institute for Studies in Education.

Wood, D. (1981). Social studies textbooks in a multicultural society. *The History and Social Science Teacher, 17*(1), 21-29.

Wood, D. (1983). Schools in a multi-ethnic society: Responding to prejudice and discrimination. *Canadian Ethnic Studies*, *15*(2), 125-129.

Wood, D. (1984). *Cross-cultural communication in a multicultural society: A resource book for awareness and training programs*. Edmonton: ACCESS.

Wood, D. and Remnant, R. (1980). *The people we are: Canada's multicultural society*. Agincourt: Gage.

Teaching Mathematics in Multicultural Schools

Ronald Ripley

A background in mathematics is essential for any high school student hoping to find employment in today's high-tech world. Yet many students have little or no interest in mathematics, are not enrolling in mathematics classes, or are making poor progress in the courses they take. This is a problem particularly affecting many students from minority groups.

Mathematics educators have been aware of this situation for some time. In 1976, the National Council of Teachers of Mathematics published this position statement:

> Every student should receive a meaningful and timely mathematics education and none should be excluded because of language or cultural differences. Schools should actively seek to identify the educational factors which diminish a student's opportunity to learn mathematics and to remove such barriers without disruption of the integrity of the student's cultural world. Special instruction in mathematics, using material in the primary language of the student, should be provided until the student can function adequately in a mathematics class conducted mainly in English or in the predominant language of the area. (Position statement on mathematics and bilingual/bicultural education, adopted by the N.C.T.M. in January 1976.)

Some Obstacles to Learning

What are the factors that might contribute to a student's difficulty with mathematics? Reasons that are often cited in the literature include mathematics anxiety, low motivation, a negative attitude towards the subject, no perceived use for mathematics in daily life, and inappropriate instruction. Students from minority groups face further problems, such as lack of role models and language or cultural barriers which distance them from the teacher and the majority of their class-mates.

Much of the research into why many minority students do not participate as much or do as well as their white counterparts has produced some questionable assumptions (Matthews, 1983). One is the assumption that all members of a racial group behave in the same way. This does not make allowances for such contributing factors as geographic location, socioeconomic status and family influences.

Another assumption is that all students from one racial background will behave alike, even when they are born in different countries and regions. Thus, racial groups are often lumped together for research purposes, even though Asian Americans include individuals from many different countries; Hispanic Americans come from Cuba, Puerto Rico and Mexico; and native Americans include students from many different tribes.

A third assumption is that there is consistency in mathematics learning at each level, and that this can be measured objectively and compared across the country. Matthews states that there are marked differences among schools and classrooms, and that these differences should be considered before comparisons can be made. He concludes by recommending changes in research methods, advocating small case studies which incorporate more background information and recommending that minorities be included on the research teams.

Two publications which can be of considerable help for the teaching of mathematics to minority groups are the special issue of the *Journal for Research in Mathematics Education*, 15(2) and *The Handbook for Conducting Equity Activities in Mathematics Education* (Cheek, 1984). The first publication presents useful information concerning mathematics education for different ethnic groups and discusses the factors which affect each group. One of these factors which has great significance is the effect of language differences on mathematics learning. One problem may be that the first language of the student may not possess words for the mathematics terms used in the classroom. For example, there are no words in the Navajo language for "if", "multiply" and "divide" (Bradley, 1984). The structure of some languages might inhibit problem-solving and concept formation (Bradley, 1984; Valverde, 1984). Since concept formation is the essence of mathematics and the ability to solve problems its goal, the language barrier could place a very serious handicap on some students. Valverde (1984) suggests that students should form these concepts in the language they are most proficient in. An additional language-related problem faces minority students when they must interpret the special mathematics terminology of of textbooks and take tests in their second language.

Curriculum content is another problem area for some minority students. The perceived usefulness of a subject often influences a student's course selection. Teachers must make certain that the mathematics presented in the classroom has applications in the real world (Valverde, 1984; Cheek, 1984). Further difficulties arise for immigrant children when the teacher is not familiar with the curriculum that they have been studying in their native countries and makes no provisions for their particular needs (Tsang, 1984).

Differences in learning styles can also add to the problem of learning mathematics. Children from some ethnic groups may be more field-dependent in their learning and see things holistically. This requires a different approach to teaching mathematics (Valverde, 1984).

Some Intervention Strategies

The *Handbook for Conducting Equity Activities in Mathematics Education* is particularly useful for teacher groups trying to improve their mathematics programs. Five successful intervention programs are described. These were designed to encourage students to continue their studies by showing how important mathematics can be in and for their future. One program, the Math Bridge Program (Birmingham, 1984) in Minneapolis, was created for Black, American Indian and Chicano students in grade eight. It includes a Saturday program at the University of Minnesota which, among other things, demonstrates the importance of college preparatory courses. At the university, the students learn about computer mathematics and attend special career seminars. There is a follow-up program throughout high school which is designed to sustain the interest in mathematics created by the program.

The AAA Math Program, implemented in two Tampa, Florida high schools, was designed to reduce math anxiety. The teams in each school, led by a guidance counsellor and a mathematics teacher, were directed at those students whose anxiety or lack of confidence affected their performance in mathematics. Each after-school session consisted of two hours of group counselling, career information and special tutoring in mathematics. Turner (1984) reports that there was positive evaluation of the project by both students and teachers. Witthuhn (1984) reports on a program, developed in Minneapolis public schools, to examine the achievement, participation and attitudes towards mathematics of American Indian girls, and to create interest in spcial programs and research for them. The handbook is particularly helpful to those about to initiate programs, because it gives examples of workshops which have already been developed to promote equity in mathematics education.

Some Suggestions for the Classroom Teacher

What do these recommendations suggest for the classroom teacher? First, the classroom should be a secure environment where students can learn, free from fear and anxiety. Second, careful consideration should be given to maintaining, or in some cases, developing, positive attitudes towards the subject of mathematics. Third, the course content should be modified to suit the needs and interests of the class, and should be presented in a variety of ways to accommodate the learning styles of each student. All three factors are closely related and affect one another.

The following section of the paper will present specific teaching suggestions for improving the performance in mathematics of minority students in particular, and all students in general. The first suggestion is to make the subject more relevant to those students who perceive mathematics as being unimportant to their lives. The second recommendation is to teach more multicultural and historical topics in the math class so that students learn of the many contributions made by various cultures and nations to the discipline. The third suggestion concerns classroom organization. And the last recommendation that will be discussed is to devote to the study of problem-solving and to teach it in a more collaborative and meaningful way.

Content Beyond the Textbook

One of the main reasons for student apathy towards mathematics is that they perceive it to lack relevance to their everyday lives (Ripley, 1981). To counteract this impression, the teacher needs to look beyond the textbook and to use common, everyday situations where mathematics is a necessary and useful tool. Consumer studies make a good starting point – we all have to eat and buy goods. Restaurant menus, store catalogues, advertisements and sports books all offer good examples of mathematics in everyday use.For instance, students who are interested in carpentry or construction can use lumber ads from the newspaper to find out the cost of building a recreation room. Batting averages and hockey statistics are useful ways for introducing decimals. Students can, using pizza bills, calculate the total cost of a meal and how much change they will receive in return, thus learning the need for addition, subtraction, decimals and place value. Catalogues, newspapers and magazines are rich sources for topics to accommodate the interests of everyone in the classroom. Questions on fashion, sports, furnishing a bedroom, eating, stamps, foreign currency, costs of accommodation and job wages can all be derived or created using these publications. Thus, the teacher has many resources for demonstrating that mathematics is indeed useful in everyday life.

Some Multicultural Activities

Historical accounts and studies of the mathematics developed in various parts of the world are useful strategies in teaching mathematics in a multicultural classroom. *The Thirty-first Yearbook of the N.C.T.M.* (Hallerberg *et al.*, 1979) not only provides capsule topics as starting points but gives many helpful hints for using these topics in the classroom. Menninger (1970), Zaslavsly (1973) and Jacobs (1970) also provide a wealth of interesting information. These topics facilitate the understanding of the content and nature of mathematics, and also illustrate to students the contributions to mathematics made by various cultures around the world.

Many mathematical concepts can be learned and developed by using games in the classroom. Russell (1981) has collected many multicultural games and activities which can be used in schools. The first part of her book describes twenty native Canadian games and activities such as Paquesson, Bone Dice, Onestch and Cheekahkwang, as well as twenty native Canadian recipes. In the second part of the book she describes games and activities from other parts of the world. However, although games are an effective and fun way of learning mathematics, care should be taken to ensure that individual children are not excluded from the activities. Games of chance (for example, dice) give all children a chance of winning. Cooperative games, too, can have a positive effect on learning.

The N.C.T.M. distributes a useful kit entitled *Multicultural Mathematics Posters and Activities* (Peterson, 1984), developed by the Seattle public schools. It consists of bulletin board posters and a booklet of ideas and activities for the teacher. One of the posters, entitled

"Geometry with Meaning", illustrates Arapaho symbolism in various embroidered and painted designs. Several suggested follow-up activities involve star designs, such as Arabic geometrical patterns, which thus integrate geometry and art. Students are invited to investigate these structures with rulers and compasses. They can also be studied using microcomputers and the LOGO language.

Other activities the kit contains are a "Calculator Ancestors" section, a section on numeration and some interesting background information on Pascal's triangle. The Calculator Ancestors" section shows the contributions of various countries to the creation of the calculator – the Roman Abacus, the Chinese Suan Pan, the Japanese Soraban and Napier's rods. These devices are helpful in explaining place value and the need for numeration systems and accurate computation. The activity on numeration systems provides students with an opportunity to observe the ingenious methods used by various civilizations in operating with numbers. Learning about these systems, for example, the number bases used by the Mayans, Inuit, Babylonians and Koreans, can provide insights into the structure of the modern base ten system. In the section devoted to Pascal's triangle, students learn that a similar structure was used in China in 1300 A.D.

Such information helps students to put their learning into a historical perspective. Topics such as these are sources of stimulating and interesting activities which can help to motivate and lead all students to a better comprehension and enjoyment of mathematics.

Some Suggestions for the Classroom

To provide for differences in the learning styles of students, the teacher should develop various strategies for presenting the content. In the early grades children should be provided with manipulative materials, such as blocks, toys, buttons and shells, for free exploration (Lorton, 1972; 1976). Various activity centres should be set up so that children can investigate in groups or alone. Open-ended questions using activity cards can be assigned so that children can approach problems in a variety of ways and come up with a variety of answers (Biggs and MacLean, 1969).

Integrative studies, such as mathematics at the market or at the corner store, can stimulate interest in learning for many children. Older students might become involved in mathematics projects, fairs, clubs and field trips.

Another promising mode of learning is the use of microcomputers.

Dugdale (1984) describes a software program that teaches the graphing of lines, circles, ellipses, parabolas and hyperbolae by a game called Green Globs. By using the LOGO language, children in even the primary grades can develop many mathematical skills. In giving instructions to the computer, they learn to construct various geometric shapes and at the same time develop many programming and problem-solving skills (Papert, 1980).

Some Suggestions for Problem Solving

Undoubtedly, a primary goal of mathematics is to develop in students the ability to solve problems. In fact, the first recommendation of *An Agenda for Action* (Hill *et al.*, 1980) is that "problem-solving (should) be the focus of school mathematics in the 1980's."

Attitudes towards a subject can greatly influence a student's participation and success. Unlike simple operations and algorithms, the complexity of solving problems often leads to fear and anxiety. What is particularly unfortunate is that students often blame themselves for their lack of success and begin to develop a poor self-image. Because they feel they cannot cope with the subject, they often avoid it.

The *Survive and Succeed* (Wiggan *et al.*, 1983) booklet, developed by the Toronto Board of Education, has many suggestions for helping students who feel insecure in the mathematics class. One of them is to have students write "Dear Abby" letters to describe how they feel about mathematics. The answers from "Abby" provide reassurance that they "are not alone," and go on to discuss the positive and negative aspects of anxiety. The booklet also gives advice to students on how to improve in their studies.It illustrates why they should continue studying mathematics by listing the many careers that require the subject.

Another attitude problem may result from the kinds of questions that students are asked to solve. If the problems are little more than a drill in words, students may not feel challenged and become quickly bored as a result. These questions are sometimes called "non-problems," since all the information is given and the needed operations are obvious. Some students may dislike these exercises which they perceive to be artificial and unrelated to their interests. Often, this situation may be remedied by using interesting problems derived from the real world, as we discussed in the previous section.

Writing applied mathematics problems is a time-consuming task for classroom teachers. To assist them, the N.C.T.M. has published two books which contain many diverse applications which can be incorporated into class lessons. The 1979 *Yearbook* (Sharron and Reys, 1979) includes chapters about the capture-recapture method of determining animal populations, the mathematics of music, of borrowing money, of human variability, and that which can be integrated with art, language and social studies.*A Sourcebook of Applications of School Mathematics* (Bushaw *et al.*, 1980) discusses the process of applying mathematics (Pollack, 1980), provides criteria for selecting good application problems (Bell *et al.*, 1980), and presents over three hundred pages of questions related to the various branches of mathematics.

Problems presented to math students should be challenging, yet not so complex that they become frustrated. It is important that they be informed of the goals of the lessons and be led to realize that they will become better problem-solvers by developing many different problem-solving strategies. Class discussion on this aspect of mathematics may help them to clarify these goals. They will come to see that problem-solving is a prime ingredient of mathematics and that much of the mechanical work they devoted so much time to is, for the most part, merely a means to an end. This type of discussion can be a very successful way of motivating students to look forward to problem-solving situations.

Cooperative problem-solving has several advantages. For one thing, sharing ideas in a small group may help to bolster self-confidence and reduce anxiety among shy students, who may seldom respond in a large group setting but will readily contribute in a small group. Group discussions also help students to realize that problem-solving often follows blind alleys; and enables them to isolate these difficulties. To further encourage a focus on the process rather than on just the answer, problems could be assigned where a final answer is not obtainable.

With careful planning the classroom teacher can help students develop problem-solving strategies that apply not only to mathematics but to other areas of study as well. To help develop positive feelings about problem-solving, many problems should be drawn from practical situations and students should frequently solve problems in small groups.

Fortunately for the teacher, many kits and books have recently been produced that help teach problem-solving. One of the most helpful is the N.C.T.M. yearbook for 1980, entitled *Problem Solving in School Mathematics* (Krulik and Reys, 1980). A suggested sequence of study might consist of the following elements:

1) Solving problems from the textbook.
2) Solving application problems from beyond the textbook.

3) Solving problems resulting from the correlation of mathematics with some other subject area such as science or music. For other suggestions, see *Mathematics in Science and Society* (Hoffer, 1977).
4) Solving problems related to classroom situations (e.g., how to raise money for a field trip or class party).
5) Solving problems involving school situations (e.g., equipping the track team or supplying instruments for the school band).
6) Solving problems concerning community problems (e.g., finding solutions to traffic problems, local pollution or the deterioration of the city core).
7) Solving problems of global concern (e.g., pollution, world poverty, inequality of resources).

Students should come to realize that problems such as these are worth investigating – and that they are problems that need to be solved if the world is to survive. They should also learn and appreciate the value of discussions as a means of creating a climate of cooperation and concern. Many of these problems will not involve numerical data. However, such data can be readily found in UNESCO publications and various geography books, such as *World Environmental Problems* (MacLean and Thomson, 1981).

Problems with global consequences require a special kind of thinking. Usually, they are problems without ideal solutions or complete answers, so that students need to develop a different mind-set when considering issues of this kind and magnitude. Often, they will have to deal with unconventional approaches and uncertain information, which may make some students uneasy when they are able to obtain only partial or unsatisfying solutions. These issues go far beyond the traditional problems requiring problem-solving in most mathematics texts, but they are the kinds of problems the world is faced with today.

To encourage participation by everyone, students may be coached in brainstorming techniques. Providing a safe environment where all answers are considered will help to ensure that shy students or those with language comprehension difficulties will feel free to offer solutions.

Using such books as *Mindbenders* (Harnadek, 1978) and *Critical Thinking* (Harnadek, 1976), the teacher can introduce students to the various facets of the thinking process. They can learn for themselves the role of logic, the many pitfalls of faulty reasoning, how propaganda techniques influence a person's thinking, the psychological tricks of advertising, the the deleterious effects of prejudice in our world.

214

Equity for all students in mathematics education is not a distant ideal but a reasonable goal that is in our reach. For this goal to be attainable, educators must:

1) understand the special needs of ethnic minorities in the classroom;
2) implement appropriate intervention strategies so that students can see the importance of mathematics in their lives;
3) offer appropriate classroom instruction to ensure success in the subject.

If these conditions are met, not only will students' learning of mathematics improve, but their understanding of its relevance and relationship to all other aspects of learning will be greatly enhanced.

References

Bell, M. *et al.* (Eds.). (1980). Preface. In *A sourcebook of applications of school mathematics*. Reston, Virginia: National Council of Teachers of Mathematics, 5-9.

Biggs, E. and MacLean, J. (1969). *Freedom to learn: an active learning approach to mathematics*. Don Mills: Addison-Wesley (Canada) Ltd.

Birmingham, D. (1984). Math bridge program. In H. Cheek (Ed.), *Handbook for conducting equity activities in mathematics education*. Reston, Virginia: National Council of Teachers of Mathematics.

Bradley, C. (1984). Issues in mathematics education for Native Americans and directions for research. In *Journal for Research in Mathematics Education*, *4*(2).

Cheek, H. (1984). Increasing the participation of Native Americans in mathematics. In *Journal for Research in Mathematics Education*, *4*(2).

Cuevas, G. (1984). Mathematics learning in English as a second language. In *Journal for Research in Mathematics Education*, *15*(2).

Hallerberg, A. *et al.*, (Eds.). (1969). *Historical topics for the mathematics classroom. Thirty-first Yearbook*. Washington, D.C.: National Council for Teachers of Mathematics.

Hansen, V. and Zweng, M. (Eds.). (1984). *Computers in mathematics education: 1984 Yearbook*. Reston, Virginia: National Council of Teachers of Mathematics.

Harnadek, A. (1976). *Critical thinking: Book 1*. Pacific Grove, CA.: Midwest Publications Company Inc.

Harnadek, A. (1978). *Mind benders – Al: deductive thinking skills*. Pacific Grove, CA.: Midwest Publications Company Inc.

Hoffer, A. (1977). *Mathematics in science and society*. Eugene, Oregon: University of Oregon.

Jacobs, H. (1982). *Mathematics: a human endeavor*. New York: W.H. Freeman and Company.

Johnson, M. (1984). Blacks in mathematics: a status report. In *Journal for Research in Mathematics Education*, *15*(2).

Krulik, S. and Reys, R. (1980). *Problem solving in school mathematics. 1980 Yearbook*. Reston, Virginia: National Council of Teachers of Mathematics.

Lorton, M. (1972). *Workjobs: activity-centered learning for early childhood education*. Don Mills: Addison-Wesley (Canada) Ltd.

Lorton, M. (1976). *Mathematics their way*. Don Mills: Addison-Wesley (Canada) Ltd.

215

MacLean, K. and Thomson, N. (1981). *World environmental problems*. Edinburgh: John Bartholomew and Sons Ltd. and Holmes McDougall Ltd.

Matthews, W. (1983). Coloring the equation: minorities and mathematics. In *Journal for Research in Mathematics Education*, *14*(1).

Matthews, W. (1984). Influences on the learning and participation of minorities in mathematics. In *Journal for Research in Mathematics Education*, *4*(2).

Matthews, W., Carpenter, T., Lindquist, M. and Silver, E. (1984). The third national assessment: minorities in mathematics. In *Journal for Research in Mathematics Education*, *15*(2).

Menninger, K. (1969). *Number words and number symbols*. Cambridge, Mass.: The M.I.T. Press.

Papert, S. (1980). *Mindstorms, children, computers, and powerful ideas*. New York: Basic Books Inc.

Peterson, W. (1984). *Multicultural mathematics posters and activities*. Reston, Virginia: National Council of Teachers of Mathematics.

Pollak, H. (1980). The process of applying mathematics. In M. Bell et al., (Eds.), *A sourcebook of applications of school mathematics*. Reston, Virginia: National Council of Teachers of Mathematics.

Preston, V. (1984). Mayan mathematics in the classroom. In H. Cheek (Ed.), *Handbook for conducting equity activities in mathematics education*. Reston, Virginia: National Council of Teachers of Mathematics.

Ripley, R. (1981). Attitudes of prospective elementary school teachers towards mathematics. Paper presented at the 23rd Annual Conference of the Ontario Educational Research Council, December 4, 1981, Toronto.

Russell, A. (1981). *Game for anything: multicultural games and activities for children*. Edmonton, Alberta: The Faculty of Education, University of Alberta.

Sharron, S. and Reys, R. (1979). *Applications in school* mathematics: 1979 Yearbook. Reston, Virginia: National Council of Teachers of Mathematics.

Tsang, S. (1984). The mathematics education of Asian Americans. In *Journal for Research in Mathematics Education*, *4*(2).

Turner, S. (1984). AAA Math Program.In H. Cheek (Ed.), *Handbook for conducting equity activities in mathematics education*. Reston, Virginia: National Council of Teachers of Mathematics.

Valverde, L. (1984). Underachievement and underrepresentation of Hispanics in mathematics and mathematics-related careers. In *Journal for Research in Mathematics Education*, *15*(2).

Wiggan, L., Kryger, R. and Morris, M. (1983). *Survive and succeed in math*. A Resource for Mathematics: The Invisible Filter. Toronto: The Toronto Board of Education, Mathematics Department.

Witthuhn, J. (1984). Assessing for educational equity. In H. Cheek (Ed.), *Handbook for conducting equity activities in mathematics education*. Reston, Virginia: National Council of Teachers of Mathematics.

Zaslavsky, C. (1973). *Africa counts*. Boston: Houghton.

An English Teacher Faces Multiculturalism

Gary Kellway

W ho in the dim past ever thought of having a multicultural class? Certainly not this teacher of English, nor did his mentors consider the possibility – much less the inevitability – of every English class being multicultural: hence, no training nor preparation was offered.One culture is difficult enough, if not impossible, to deal with. And now, like it or not, this same English teacher faces a multicultural group of students. A typical grade nine general level class may comprise, say, one recent arrival from Germany, two boys who speak Greek at home, one or two French-Canadians, two or three black students and a quarter of the class of British background. This class is not just in Toronto but in any town or city in Ontario. This multicultural class is not only urban but found in schools in suburbs and country districts, where there are no ghettos, no ethnic centres, no national gatherings. There are only people of differing backgrounds, living together and holding onto a private racial or national heritage.

Has the teacher noticed that the general or basic classes usually contain a greater multicultural mix than the advanced groups? Is it possible that this difference is due not to ability but to a cultural or language difference? Hence, the English teacher with a multicultural outlook should first consider the selection process and then, if necessary, work to change or beat the present form of classification.

What can the teacher do? All classes are diverse, composed of individual children who come together to learn, yet manage to retain their personal identity. The teacher who is worth his or her salt knows this. Therefore, he or she must first of all be keenly and conscientiously aware that every class today is multicultural, some more than others. Perhaps that is all the teacher needs to do: to be aware.

The teacher should remember the old practitioner who distilled pedagogy into one rule: "Get to know your kids!" The English teacher gets to know his or her kids by establishing a climate of trust: what you write, I will read with respect and confidentiality; what you say, I will listen to and consider; what you believe, I will honour. This particular teacher feels that this traditional paradigm for teaching English is not enough. The boy who speaks Greek as mother tongue develops his taste and acquires some knowledge of the literature; but he does this after he has become comfortable in his English course and confident of his ability to be successful in it. This can happen if his English teacher possesses a multicultural approach to the relationship between student and teacher. That role is, as Livingstone described it, "to develop the individual excellence of each child." While trying to do so, the teacher of English may also consider what David Holbrook said:

> English is no subject but a means to personal order, balance and effectiveness in living. To give children adequate verbal capacities is at one with giving them relief from inward turmoil, a degree of self-respect and self-possession and the ability to employ their potentialities not only in English and other subjects or at work, but as lovers, parents, friends, members of the community and creatures of God.

If the teacher can approach this ideal, then multiculturalism will be cherished and protected in the English class, just as self-esteem, or respect for the right word or an enjoyment of poems are not taught. All these qualities are indirect benefits of the atmosphere of the class and a result of the activities that the student engage in.

The motto of one English department is: "Be active; be creative; be compassionate; and, finally, if you must, be intellectual." This is surely a multicultural approach as much as a multi-individual approach.

The English class is one place where a child can be made to "feel good" about himself or herself and also about the subject. The child can know that his or her feelings, thoughts and language have validity; and can gain the confidence to express feelings and ideas in his or her own growing language. The opposite can also happen; that is, "single-culturalism." To avoid this, the English teacher must not promote traditional conventions of language, rules or grammars, but believe that free expression in any form of language available is the first step towards achieving the broad aims of the class, including fluency with English words.

The multicultural English classroom should be non-threatening. Nor should be the English curriculum: it must allow for a variety of activities and an evaluation based on where a child "begins," and then assess the growth and creative expression of the child's thoughts. Anything that has to be touched up by proofreading is not "English" and should not be assessed.

The multicultural teacher should change outworn evaluation methods, since the English class is as much a social occasion as it is a learning occasion. Students who are expected to read together, to share their written or spoken experiences and thoughts, and to find a common idea by discussion cannot be strangers. They must know one another which the teacher sees to.They must respect one another, which the teacher encourages by example. Respect and consideration is the beginning of mutual interest and concern. And, just as Emerson instructs, "You must first stop off his nonsense," the teacher must first stop off all insulting or racist words. Such expressions, even in jest, have no place in a humane classroom.

The multicultural class encourages children of many backgrounds to work in harmony. This harmony can be nurtured in the English class by drawing upon these various backgrounds. Grammar can be made comparative: ask a child whose other culture is German for another word for "father" or "dog"; then ask the same of the Italian child, the Finnish child and the Chinese child. Ask for an Indian song, a French poem. Collect songs and poems that are not in the class textbook and read them together. In the multicultural English classroom, the book is not the highest good; the child and his or her growth and learning are. The textbook serves to develop excellence in the individual and harmony in the group. The choice of book must be wise; *Huckleberry Finn*, for instance, should perhaps go. The use of the word "nigger" in the book can be explained, but why spend the time making explanations when another – albeit sometimes lesser – novel can promote harmony? And tired, old, white supremacist novels, such as *The Thirty-Nine Steps*, should be dropped. A West Indian author, Naipaul for example, or an African tale, such as *Things Fall Apart*, are more appropriate. Why not stress drama? The reading and acting out of a play promotes harmony; the children have to take roles; and if the roles are those of, say, Inuit or Native peoples, the student walks a little distance in another's moccasins. *Rita Joe* may work as effectively as *King Lear* to awaken awareness and compassion – even to develop skills. And the classroom should be filled with newspapers and magazines that inform students about a wider world.

Finally, a private activity in the English classroom that may encourage the harmony of diversity that is multiculturalism is the personal journal which grows as the child grows. This journal should be read only by the teacher, unless special permission is given. The teacher reads, not to correct or to assess, but to share and to praise honest, sincere efforts to express the vague longings, sorrows and joys that a child experiences. If the young writer knows that he or she can write in the journal without fear of censure or criticism, the teacher will probably read the best writing ever done by students, better than that produced by lessons or exercises. And it will also be the most interesting writing because in it the student is free to express feelings about his or her own multiculturalism.

The Role of Professional Multicultural Support Services in the School and Community

Beverley Nann

I n introducing the multicultural policy of 1971, Prime Minister Trudeau committed the federal government to a policy of cultural pluralism. Thirteen years later, the Special Parliamentary Committee on Visible Minorities in Canadian Society (*Equality Now*, 1984) finds most minorities still do not have full access to Canadian society.

The current thrust of the federal government is to "mainstream" multiculturalism into the fabric of Canadian life. However, the basic institutions in our society have failed to make the necessary ideological and policy shifts to realize multicultural goals which will reflect the needs and aspirations of Canada's culturally diverse population. There is also a need for specialized services to help translate the federal Multi-cultural Policy into culturally sensitive programs and services.

Hall's research (1966) on culture highlights the issue involved in developing culturally or ethnically sensitive services:

> People reared in different cultures live in different sensory worlds... The patterning of perceptual worlds is a function not only of culture but of relationship, activity and emotion. Therefore, people from different cultures, when interpreting each other's behaviours, often misinterpret the relationship, the activity or the emotions. This leads to alienation in encounters or distorted communications.

Hall (1976) proposes "contexting" as a concept for understanding cultural differences. He suggests cultures can be viewed from the perspective of a continuum, between high-context and low-context situations. A high-context (HC) communication or message is one in which most of the information is either in the physical context or internalized in the person, while very little is in the coded, explicit, transmitted part of the message. A low-context (LC) communication is just the opposite, i.e., the mass of the information is vested in the explicit code. Although no culture exists exclusively at one end of the scale, some are high while others are low. American culture, while not on the bottom, is toward the lower end of the scale. China, the possessor of a great and complex culture, is on the high-context end of the scale.

The Canadian population can also be placed on a continuum between high and low-context situations. Immigrant cultures tend to be highly structured and high-context, while Canadian society, generally, tends to be loosely structured and low-context.

Ethnic relations can also be viewed from dual perspectives (Schermerhorn, 1970) – a mainstream majority perspective, which views society from a more comprehensive macro-perspective; and a minority ethnic group perspective, which looks at society from the more restrictive micro-perspective of an "embattled group, fighting for its life and identity".

Given these views of ethnic relations, the implementation of a multicultural policy requires the development of ethnic-sensitive support services to connect and bridge the cultural gaps between cultural communities. Ethnic-sensitive services can provide a "psychic shelter" (Porter, 1976; Nann and To, 1982) for minorities, especially the immigrant population. A familiar protective structure to buffer hostility and rejection or what may be perceived as hostility and rejection from the general community. These services can also assist in diffusing problems, and discourage the formation of unrealistic fears and/or expectations on the part of both the minorities and the larger society.

Barth (1969) describes work with diverse cultural groups as involving the negotiating and manipulating of boundaries. Green (1982) defines four major modes of intervention for practitioners working with minorities in mediating cultural boundaries:

1) *Group Advocate* – the practitioner is an advocate for an ethnic or minority community with the larger society.
2) *Counsellor* – the practitioner plays a counselling role. The target of change is the client as the problems are not expected to go away.
3) *Regulator* – the practitioner is an extension of the larger society, regulating and resocializing on behalf of society.
4) *Broker* – the practitioner is an intermediary between the client and the larger society, with responsibility to both parties.

Professionally trained minorities have a unique cultural brokerage role to play as they occupy the middle ground between their own ethnic community and the larger society. Combining technical training with sensitivity to the traditions, aspirations, concerns and strengths of their own ethnic communities, minority professionals "can serve as buffers; modifying the impact of administrative decisions and procedures on ethnic constituencies ... and provide a mechanism of diffusion for new ideas that may modify the practices of those who hold power" (Green, 1982).

The need for such a role in the field of education has been documented by way of recent experiences with the school systems in the communities of Vancouver (1979 Research Study, Vancouver School Board), and Burnaby (1983 Survey, Burnaby School Board).

Although this writer has been involved with both the Vancouver and Burnaby models of multicultural services, this paper will focus on the development of the Burnaby service which is currently in its initial demonstration phase. There are many similarities in the two models of multicultural services, but also some major differences in the program developed.

The Development of Ethnic-Sensitive Services in the School System: A Partnership Between the Burnaby School District and the Community

> Multiculturalism is now a part of the Canadian way of life. Unfortunately, not all Canadians understand or accept that this significant change has and is taking place in Canada. Some view the changing cultural diversity of Canada as a threat, and therefore, as something to be vigorously opposed. It is a task of education to play a major role in overcoming such regressive attitudes and aspirations. The goal of this challenge is to have all Canadians accept and understand that the concept of multiculturalism provides an accurate description of Canadian society and the way Canadians live.
>
> (Multicultural Directorate, 1984)

The past decade in Burnaby has been marked by the immigration of people of many cultural, racial and language backgrounds. Over 30 percent of Burnaby students have English as a second language (B.C. Ministry of Education, 1983). Immigrant students and their families experience a variety of problems in adjusting to their new country. There may be difficulties based on a lack of language ability, a lack of understanding or misunderstanding of the school system and its expectations, pressures on the children because of different expectations of school and home, a lack of understanding by families of the helping services within the school system or other institutions in the community.

It is not surprising that Burnaby educators, confronted daily with the special adaptation problems of their immigrant students, should be the first group in the community to voice concern over the lack of resources to deal with the unique needs of this growing student population. They recognize that specialized multicultural support services are essential in order for these students to access the educational services offered by the school system and to foster the integration of these students into a newly-evolving multicultural "mainstream" society.

Burnaby, like other Canadian suburban communities adjoining large urban centres, relies on Vancouver-based services to meet emergency multicultural needs. The major ethno-cultural service organizations, ostensibly, with a Greater Vancouver Mandate, are situated in Vancouver. In reality, especially during present recessionary times, these agencies find it difficult to fulfill even their Vancouver mandate, with the result that surrounding suburban communities find themselves poorly served by these organizations.

The Burnaby Teachers' Association Racism Committee, successfully lobbied their school board to support the concept of special ethnic-sensitive services for the English as a Second Language (ESL) population. After five years of effort by this association failed to generate resources to establish a multicultural service in the school district, the multicultural consultant for the Vancouver School Board was approached for assistance. Action was immediately undertaken to broaden committee representation to include special interest groups, such as established ethnic organizations, local health and welfare agencies, a liaison school trustee and a senior administrator from the school board. Originally initiated in response to the special settlement needs of English as a Second Language students, this specialized program for immigrant families quickly developed into a service focusing on broader multicultural goals. A sympathetic and receptive school district and community encouraged the expansion of this service concept.

The special needs of other minority students, especially the visible minorities, also became a priority concern. The relationship between academic success and a healthy self-concept is well understood by educators. An Anglo-dominated educational system failed to affirm the ethnicity of minority students and to reflect the cultural diversity represented in their student population in the curriculum and other school activities.

In this larger conceptualization of the service, immigrant adaptation becomes a sub-part of a broader multicultural focus and the goals of the project expanded to include two major components: (1) the orientation and adaptation of immigrant students and families into the school system; (2) the promotion and "mainstreaming of multiculturalism" into the school and general community. This latter focus views the project as a concrete example of the implementation of the Federal Multicultural Policy and extends project activities into social justice and social equality issues such as racism, intercultural relations, access, cultural retention.

Working with the School System

Owens (1981) cites six special properties of organization (as identified by Fullan, Miles and Taylor) to consider when planning change in schools:

1) Their goals are diffuse, usually stated in general, even abstract terms, with effectiveness measurement difficult and uncertain.
2) Their technical capability is low, with a weak specific scientific base underlying educational practice.
3) They are loosely coupled systems, which gives rise to coordination problems: activities are not always clearly connected to goals, and control (for example, accountability) is difficult to establish. This organizational feature of schools is not necessarily entirely negative: it also can be a source of flexibility and adaptability.
4) Boundary management is difficult in as much as "the skin" of the organization seems overly thin, over-permeable to dissatisfied stakeholders.
5) Schools are "domesticated" organizations, non-competitive, surviving in a relatively protected environment, and with little incentive for significant change.
6) Schools are part of a constrained decentralized system: (each) school district ... nominally autonomous, yet with many constraints (for example, textbook market, accreditation and certification requirements. ...)

In this environment, a "contingency approach" to organization, that is, "a flexibly structured organization that emphasizes team work, collaboration, participation and integrated effort" is best. This type of administrative style tends to characterize the leadership of the Burnaby School Board.

From its inception, the board agreed to provide administrative resources for the project. A sympathetic and supportive senior administrative staff facilitated the introduction of the new service into the school system. The goal to "mainstream multiculturalism" into the school system implied institutional change, a basic shift in orientation from an Anglo-dominated focus to a multicultural focus. The coordinating committee's request to the school board to assume financial responsibility for the project service, at the end of the two-year demonstration period, challenged the board to reorder its priorities and shift resources to integrate multicultural services into the ongoing operating budget.

The board was seen as a collaborator in this common venture with concerned community groups and shared ownership of the problem. In this collaborative relationship, the school board and the project was viewed as a part of the municipal political structure, and not isolated, divorced or immune from the influence of the larger political community (particularly in a suburban community). Wide community support was sought from key individuals and groups in Burnaby to influence school board decision-making. Prominent citizens and representatives of ethnic and general community agencies were organized as required to support actions to secure resources or to support briefs to the board. Open and frequent communication was maintained between groups as a basic strategy to keep all interest groups informed and involved.

The Administrative Structure

The Coordinating Committee is responsible for the translation of multicultural needs into specific goals and objectives; the securing of resources to meet these needs; the overall development and direction of the project. This Coordinating Management Committee includes board and staff representatives from the following organizations: school trustees, superintendent's office, professional teachers' association, public health and welfare departments, ethnic organizations, parents and independent community citizens.

The committee set itself two immediate goals: (1) demonstrate the need for multicultural workers to meet the special settlement needs of immigrant families within the Burnaby School District; (2) secure funding and resources to develop this service.

The following initial program objectives were outlined: (1) assisting non-English speaking families within the Burnaby community towards a full and active participation in the educational life of their children in a Canadian context; (2) enabling these children and their families to make a viable personal adjustment to Canadian society; (3) promoting social and cultural interchange and understanding between these parents' children, school personnel and the community; (4) providing a referral and liaison service for these children and their families in order to link them with the wider network of helping agencies; (5) responding to the social and educational needs of the local minority communities, especially newcomers.

The Professional Advisory Committee membership includes senior management staff representing major sectors of the school system and the project coordinator. This high level committee ensures equal access to the multicultural services by all sectors of the educational community and facilitates the entry of project services into the school system.

The Program Advisory Committee, comprising principals, teachers, professional development staff and the project coordinator, allows for input into the development of the multicultural services from those directly involved in the delivery of educational services to ensure that services are sensitive to and compatible with school needs and services. This committee advises on program needs and develops implementation strategies to meet needs.

The Curriculum Resource Committee, consisting of teachers, parents, and multicultural workers, gathers, identifies, and reviews materials and advises on the purchase of multicultural materials for the school district.

The Multicultural Staff Team works in close cooperation with the Coordinating Committee and the school board. The project coordinator assumes a strong leadership role, gathering facts, developing strategies and programs, and introducing other individuals and resources as required to support goals, programs and actions.

Fundamental to the success of any human service is the staff. Minority practitioners who service the project come from the same cultural background as the minority families they serve. These professionals are carefully selected to ensure that all factions in the ethnic community can be served. At the same time, they must be sensitive to the needs of the school system if they are to be effective as a cultural broker between these two sectors of the community. These minority professionals are also successful role models for the minority students and families. They work in close cooperation with their own cultural community to establish a communication and resource network between the school system and their minority community.

The introduction of a professional multicultural resource team can pose a threat to educators. For example, counsellors may be concerned about their position being usurped by the multicultural worker. To avoid misunderstanding, careful introduction of the multicultural staff team as a cultural resource to culturally sensitize and enhance, not to replace existing services is essential. In this new field of service, a multidimensional approach is used by this culturally diverse professional staff team to create and test new multicultural ideas and strategies for implementation into schools and the community.

During the past two years, a team of four multicultural workers has been employed by this project to serve multicultural needs within the school system. The workers function as a cultural resource, and provide a vital communication link between school personnel, the immigrant families, and other contacts in the community. Extensive volunteer assistance has extended staff services. Over one hundred community volunteers, mainly from the minority communities, have contributed over 1000 hours of volunteer service to enrich project activities. The services of a coordinator of volunteers would further strengthen the volunteer component program.

The Development of a Program to Meet Multicultural Needs

A broad interpretation of the multicultural mandate permits great flexibility in the development of the multicultural program service. The multicultural staff team has initiated and responded to requests from all sectors of the educational system: the trustees, administrators, teachers and the community (including students, parents and the minority and general community).

A major focus of the service is to bridge the gap between the immigrant home and school, and between home and community. It is often the case that a multicultural worker first makes contact with a family at the request of a school official, such as a teacher or a psychologist who is unable to help a student with a problem because of language or cultural barriers. As families find themselves helped in this way with school problems, they subsequently take the initiative in turning to the workers with problems beyond the school.

The range of services provided by the multicultural workers related to this area of service may involve one or a combination of the following: orientation to school and community for students and parents; prekindergarten orientation services; short-term student or parent counselling; referral to community services; encouragement of parent involvement in the school and in community activities; adult education on topics such as English instruction, and parenting; cultural enrichment; social adjustment and ethnic-identification groups for students.

The broader goal of promoting and "mainstreaming" multiculturalism into the school system leads the staff team into activities such as educational workshops for teachers to further understanding of minority cultures and to assist with the task of incorporating a multicultural focus into school activities; initiating of cultural heritage language classes; working on a Multicultural and Race Relations Policy with trustees; developing programs to promote positive intercultural relations amongst students.

In the process of establishing this ethnic-sensitive school service in Burnaby, other multicultural needs have emerged. As the sole service in Burnaby with a primary multicultural focus, staff have responded to calls from such diverse agencies as the RCMP, fire department, health department and library service. In view of the overwhelming multicultural needs in Burnaby, the Project Coordinating Committee established a private society, the Burnaby Multicultural Society, to begin to address multicultural priorities throughout the municipality.

Summary

The educational sector of Canadian society is identified as a key actor in the "mainstreaming" of multiculturalism. The *Equality Now* report highlights the educational issues requiring attention: race relations policy at the board and school level; accommodating school practices to cultural diversity; relations between the home and school; student leadership programs; methods for responding to racial harrassment; assessment of students for placement; the evaluation of textbooks for bias; materials for developing more positive student attitudes; improving teacher education; early childhood education; and post-secondary education. Most of these priorities are being addressed by the Burnaby Multicultural Services Project.

An independent survey (May, 1984) of multicultural services carried out by the Burnaby School Board confirms the effectiveness of multicultural services in bridging the cultural gap between the school and minority communities and indicates the broad acceptance of the service throughout the school system and other community agencies.

The school system provides a strong base to initiate and launch multicultural services for the general community. As schools extend into every segment of the Burnaby community, a school-based service is in a unique position to reach out to assess and respond to the special needs of a community. Schools are perceived as a positive force by all cultures and as vital, neutral, and non-threatening institutions by all sectors of the community. Minority families will readily accept services offered through schools yet may shy away from services provided by other government or private agencies. Some may even refuse to turn to their own ethnic organizations for help for fear of losing face within their own ethnic community. Minority workers are called upon to assist with a wide range of problems. They are in a unique and influential position to link immigrant famiiies to other community services and to orient, encourage and support the integration of this population into the Canadian community.

The high level of cooperation from the school board and community has enabled the project to exceed its original goals and expectations. As a result of our activities with the school district as well as the Interagency Council, a coordinating body for health and social service in Burnaby, there is a growing consciousness throughout the municipality of a need for services to reflect the multiethnic population in Burnaby. To meet some of these needs, Burnaby community organizations are being encouraged and assisted to develop their own multicultural resources. To begin to seriously address multicultural priorities throughout the municipality, the newly-incorporated Burnaby Multicultural Society, as its first community endeavour, is organizing an interface between the minority community leaders and the leaders of the major institutions in Burnaby, that is, the policy makers, to consider the recommendations in the *Equality Now* report.

Cultural minorities add a dynamic quality to Canadian society and are an important feature of continued pluralism. Immigrants replenish the old ethnic stock and contribute to its change.

Naisbitt in *Megatrends* credits immigrants for the vitality and strength of today's culturally diverse U.S. society – a society offering "multiple options" in foods, religions, lifestyles, family, etc. Although this "multiple option society represents uncertainty it also presents a wide range of choices where almost anything is possible" – one which will best prepare citizens for dealing with a fast changing world which will require flexible, new structures. In a multiple option society "ethnics are not so much noticed as different as they are in tune with the country's mood and values" (Naisbitt, 1982).

The cross-cultural fertilization of ideas which naturally occurs in working with a culturally diverse staff team has generated many exciting and innovative approaches for the delivery of multicultural school services in Burnaby, thus confirming Naisbitt's conclusions.

Canada's major institutions have been slow to "multiculturalize" their service delivery system to reflect the needs and aspirations of a culturally diverse population. The experience in Burnaby (and Vancouver) points to the value of and need for culturally sensitive bridging services to assist in implementing the goals of a multicultural society. The school-based, ethnic-sensitive models developed in Burnaby and Vancouver have provided an effective vehicle for realizing the goals of promoting and "mainstreaming" multiculturalism in both schools and the community.

References

Burnaby School Board. (1984). *Burnaby multicultural services*. Report on Evaluation Questionnaire.

Canada. (1984). *Equality now*. Ottawa: Report of the Special Committee on Visible Minorities in Canadian Society.

Canada, Multicultural Directorate. (1984). *Mainstreaming multiculturalism in Canada*. Ottawa.

Canadian Education Association. (1984). *Multiculturalism, racism and the school system*. Toronto: CEA Seminar.

Dluhy, M. (1981). Policy advice-givers: Advocates? Technicians? Pragmatists?*New strategic perspectives on social policy*. New York: Pergamon Press.

Green, J. (1982). *Cultural awareness in the human services*. Englewood Cliffs, N.J.: Prentice-Hall.

Hall, E. (1977). *Beyond culture*. New York: Anchor Press/Doubleday.

Hall, E. (1966). *The hidden dimension*. Garden City, New York: Doubleday.

Naisbitt, J. (1982). *Megatrends*. New York: Warner Books Inc.

Nann, B. (1982). Settlement programs for immigrant women and families. *Uprooting and surviving*. Dordrecht, Holland: D. Reidel Publishing Company.

Nann, R. (1977). Ethnic cultures and communities in North America. *People and places: Social work education and human settlements*. New York: International Association of Schools of Social Work.

Nann, R. and To, L. (1982). Experiences of Chinese immigrants in Canada: Building an indigenous support system. *Uprooting and surviving*. Dordrecht, Holland: D. Reidel Publishing Company.

Novak, M. (1971). *The rise of the unmeltable ethnics: Politics and culture in the seventies*. New York: MacMillan Company.

Owens, R. (1981). *Organizational behaviour in education*. New Jersey: Prentice-Hall.

Peters, T. and Waterman Jr., R. (1982). *In search of excellence*. New York: Harper and Row.

Porter, J. (1975). Ethnic pluralism in Canada. *Ethnicity, theory and experience*. Glazer,

232

Nathan and Moynihan, D.P. (Eds.). Cambridge, Mass.: Harvard University Press.

Rothman, J. (1970). Three models of community organization practice. *Strategies of community organization: A book of readings.* Illinois: F.E. Peacock Publishers.

Schermeerhorn, R. (1970). *Comparative ethnic relations: A framework for theory and research.* New York: Random House.

Seebaran, R. (1983). Preparation for practice in a multicultural society. *Social work and multicultural concerns.* Vancouver: BCASW.

Vancouver School Board. (1979). *The multicultural home school workers' project.* Vancouver: Report of Research and Evaluation Services.

PART V:

Program Guidelines

Implementing Multiculturalism Through Leadership Camps

Robert Harrison

T he climate for implementing multiculturalism through leadership camps is a positive one at the present time. The document, *Equality Now* has, as one of its recommendations: "The Canadian School Trustees' Association should encourage all Canadian school boards to develop multicultural programs for their students" (p. 122). Since 1979, the Ontario Ministry of Education has expressed their support for the concept of multiculturalism in their document, "Special Populations in Education". The policy is expressed in this way:

> It has been recognized that the responsibility for preparing all Ontario students to live in Canada's multicultural society has significant implications in terms of general approaches to education, as well as in provision for special populations. In meeting the common needs of all students, publicly provided education has the task of encouraging general system sensitivity, while ensuring that individual group needs are met in a way that will facilitate full participation by all students. ...
>
> (Ontario Ministry of Education, 1979, p. 23).

However, it was a year before this document was released that the Ontario Ministry of Education became active in implementing multiculturalism. The Heritage Language Program was officially initiated in 1978 with the Ministry directive to all Ontario boards that languages other than French or English could be taught by extending school hours or after school hours (Ontario Ministry of Education Memorandum, 1978). Moreover, it was in the same year that the Ministry decided to expand its leadership program from athletics, music, and students' council to embrace the concept of multicultural/multiracial leadership programs. The Ontario Ministry of Education and the Ontario Human

Rights Commission co-sponsored the first multicultural/multiracial leadership program at Longford, Ontario. Each year, 96 teenage boys and girls with selected staff members are invited to attend a five-day program. The purpose of the program is to develop leadership skills, communication skills, organizing skills, self-confidence, as well as cooperative and responsible attitudes (Ontario Ministry of Education Handbook, 1983).

During its seven years of successful operation, the program has been emulated by other boards of education. The facilitators and students who participate in the program are trained to design and implement a part or all of the Ministry's program. A number of boards have structured and implemented similar multicultural programs, for example, the North York Board of Education (1981), the Toronto Board of Education (1982), the Vancouver Board of Education (1982), and the Eastern Ontario Boards of Education (Frontenac, Ottawa, Renfrew, Stormont, Dundas and Glengarry) (1984).

The climate is certainly appropriate for individual boards to initiate similar multicultural leadership programs for staff and/or students. With federal and provincial endorsement of these programs, many boards have established multicultural programs unique to their needs. Their programs combine certain elements that provide for the promotion of interethnic attitudes by utilizing a "multidimensional approach". The approach is based on an experimental program with emphasis on cross-cultural similarities and role-playing, within a trusting atmosphere (Ijaz, p. 134). With this in mind, other boards may want to mount their own programs. Therefore, the remainder of the paper deals with the key components that are required in implementing a multicultural leadership program.

Components for a Multicultural Leadership Program

The description below outlines the key components for the implementation of a leadership program. The steering committee is the one component that threads its way through the other components. The steering committee re-cycles the data from the evaluation stage back into the other components so that appropriate changes can be made. Any one component can be altered when necessary during and after the implementation of the program.

Steering Committee

The membership of the steering committee must represent the different levels in the hierarchy of the educational system, and, if applicable, the agencies and organizations in the community that have a direct bearing on the development of the program. The success of the implementation depends upon the office and the commitment of the officer. The officer provides resources and approval for the concept of multiculturalism through a leadership program. A model for this committee is the Eastern Ontario Leadership Program, the members of which are:–

– Ministry of Education (Eastern Ontario Regional Office)
– Ontario Human Rights Commission (Race Relations Division)
– National Capital Alliance on Race Relations
– Ottawa-Carleton Immigrant Services Organization
– Frontenac Board of Education
– Ottawa Board of Education
– Renfrew Board of Education
  – Stormont Dundas and Glengarry Board of Education
– Students

(Eastern Ontario Handbook, 1984).

The individual members come from the ranks of educational officers, superintendents, coordinators, consultants, teachers, and students. Their input and direction mould a leadership program that is unique to the area, and, therefore, acceptable to their boards and organizations.

Goals

The goals are based on statements from the documents that are released at the federal, provincial and board levels. The goals are general statements, such as:the goals of the program are to provide an opportunity for students to become more aware of themselves as individuals and to recognize and to respect the differences of other individuals.

Objectives

The objectives for the leadership program should be tailored to meet the needs of the participating boards. A composite list of objectives from the programs that have been implemented is provided below:
– To have students become more aware of the realities of multicultural schools and society.

- To develop skills in communication and problem-solving which may lead to building of self-confidence and group cooperation.
- To develop trust in and empathy for other students.
- To achieve a sense of multicultural harmony and understanding through a positive emphasis on similarities in belief systems, customs, and personal experiences.
- To introduce self-insight through moral awareness development and through appeals to empathy gained by role reversal and personal experience sharing.
- To learn problem-identification and problem-solving skills which can be utilized in the student's school and community environment.
- To help students identify the leadership role they can play.
- To build teams in schools and a supportive network in the system.

From *Equality Now*, pp. 121-122.

The camp program is organized on the concept of "family". It is within this framework that an atmosphere of trust and respect for the individual's ethnicity is developed so that intercultural communication takes place. Each individual in the family has an opportunity to examine their own attitudes, their attitudes towards their own ethnic groups, and their attitudes towards other ethnic groups (Berry, p. 104).

The criteria for structuring each family are:

- 8, 12, or 16 students;
- equal number of males and females;
- equal number of students from different schools;
- a cross-section of ethnic identities.

(Eastern Ontario Handbook)

Each family has one or more facilitators depending on the size of the family group. Most of the activities and games are performed within the family, but some sessions are structured so that all families share their experiences with the whole camp (community). It is on these occasions that the administrators become the facilitators.

Intercultural communication is handled so that the family is highly profiled. The coordinator and the facilitators disseminate information through the participation of the students.

Orientation

Orientation occurs at all levels. The process of structuring the steering committee initiates the orientation of the educational system to the concept of the leadership program. Once the committee has been established, orientation of the goals, objectives and other components for the program continues throughout the board.

Student Selection

The orientation to the program at the school level can be accomplished through a selection process. A selection panel, composed of respected staff members of the school, develops an open competition for all students. The criteria itself attracts certain students, and, therefore, a respectability for the program is developed.
The criteria may include:

- equal number of males and females;
- students from grades 10 or 11;
- ethnic representation of the student body;
- satisfactory academic qualification;
- acceptable level of language proficiency.

(Vancouver School Board, p.5)

Student Awareness

The selected students are given limited information about the program. The goals, objectives, location, dates, transportation, personal belongings, as well as a few "don'ts" about the program are described in a handout. In addition, all students are requested to complete a short questionnaire on their expectations for the program. This completed sheet is then placed in an envelope that is sealed. The envelope is to be opened by the student on the last camp day.

Facilitator Awareness

A special orientation session that should be held at the actual camp site is a requirement. The purpose is to provide an opportunity for the teachers to acquire the skills of a facilitator. The role of the facilitators is multilevel. The facilitators are the ones who on the one hand stimulate discussion, devise strategies, promote healthy feedback, and on the other hand, assess the tone of the family and observes problems. At all times the facilitators use their authority only to provide a positive direction for the family and become totally involved with the students (Borough of East York, p.17).

The orientation session not only assists the teachers in acquiring skills of a facilitator, but also provides an opportunity for the teachers to acquire ownership of the multicultural program. The day-to-day agenda has to be moulded around their expertise and experiences. Therefore, the appropriate teacher selection is vital to the success of the camp.

Parental Awareness

The parents become aware of the program through their endorsement of their child's application and registration in the camp. A parental package may include:
– an information letter outlining the rationale, goals, objectives, location, dates, times,....;
– a selection process of students and teachers;
– a permission form;
– health and dietary forms;
– student contract.

(Eastern Ontario Handbook)

The Camp Program

The program at the camp is based upon three premises:

1) the activities provide for active, intellectual, emotional, and physical participation;
2) sessions provide background information on specific cultural groups with explanations for cultural differences;
3) the focus is on the cross-cultural similarities and values common to all human beings.

(Ijaz, p.134)

The structured experimental content, based on the above premises, creates opportunities for the students to become involved with the result that growth and learning can occur in each participant. Sensitive and personal aspects such as values, prejudice, discrimination, power, and socio-economic status can be discussed in an open and direct way. This means that the content of the program has to be carefully applied and sequenced (Sawyer and Green, p. 6). Moreover, the process the students experience from the moment they arrive and depart from the camp, determines the success of the program. The process is where learning starts to take place. What has to be observed is how the students relate to the activity and to the other participants while they are actively engaged. The dynamics that come from the content (activities, games) determine the morale, feelings, influence, participation, conflicts, competition, and determine the significant impact on students' attitudes. The formation of positive attitudes is the basis for future experiences.

The process is outlined by Pfeiffer and Jones. The five phases that the students experience from the administration to the debriefing phases for each activity and from the initiation to the conclusion of the program are:

1) the experimental phase is when the students experience the activity;
2) the sharing phase is when the students share their observations and feelings;
3) the processing phase is when general patterns and principles are discussed;
4) the generalizing phase is when patterns are linked to the real world; and,
5) the application phase is when participants link their experiences to their personal lives by initiating an activity for their schools.

An application of the content and the process is outlined in a three-and-a-half day program.

Day 1

1) Group identification, family groups.
2) Individual information sharing and group development through various exercises; (i.e. Paired Conversations, Name Whip, Apple Network).
3) Students begin to develop diaries.

Day 2

1) Sessions: Leadership Skills and Styles; Problem Solving Techniques; Group Cooperation Techniques; Personal Inventory of Values.

2) Viewing of film – *Myself Yourself*
3) Discussion and clarification of discrimination, stereotype, racism, by role playing, role reversals, etc.
4) Group tasks and group challenges by rope orienting exercises, group songs and flags, etc.

Day 3

1) Case studies showing racial discrimination
2) Personal experiences of discrimination
3) Seminar Groups:
   i) *Role Play*: B'nai B'rith League of Human Rights
   ii) *Blue Canadian Sky:* immigration to racism and discrimination
   iii) *The Wall*: Group cooperation challenge
4) Family Group Presentations: "What kind of world do we want?"

Day 4

1) Identification of problems in school and community (racism and discrimination)
2) Developing a school project or program to combat problems
3) Evaluation of program.

Evaluation

Kehoe states that "No important outcome is intangible. To be important, it must make an observable difference, and all that measurement requires is the observation of differences... Any complex outcome that has been defined clearly enough to be taught effectively can be tested effectively" ("Achieving the Goals of Multicultural Education in the Classroom," p. 145). Since the multicultural leadership program has defined objectives, they should be evaluated. The evaluation should be of the students themselves and of the program as a whole.

What is to be measured is the students' attitudinal shift as a result of the program. One method is the more informal approach. The students can be observed before and after the program to ascertain if the quantity and quality of their activities are directed towards the concept of multiculturalism. Such activities as organizing multicultural clubs, classroom presentations on human rights issues (apartheid) in the post camp follow-up, are indicators of significant changes. Another method, of course, is for the students to open their sealed envelopes and re-evaluate their expectations. A third, and a more formal method, is to apply an attitudinal measuring device. One of the attitudinal tests that has been applied with success, in measuring cross-group and cross-cultural verification, is the semantic differential (Clifton and Perry, p. 80).

The other evaluation level is aimed at the program itself. The staff and students should have an opportunity of analyzing the positive/negative aspects of the entire multicultural leadership program from the first time they are invited to attend the camp until six months after the program ends. This means that formal and informal devices need to be applied.

The net result of gathering information on attitudinal shifts and content analysis of the program is its re-cycling effects. The data have to be applied so that changes can be made for the new program.

A Word of Caution

Funding naturally places constraints on the type and the in-depth activities that can occur during the entire program. Moreover, the people who participate in the program are eager to share their experiences and initiate action plans in the school. However, they are surrounded by students and staff who perceive different priorities. In many instances, the students have to "catch- up" on their homework. Thus the spirit of the camp may soon wane as the reality of school life impacts upon the students. Sometimes the staff teacher who atends the program has to become a coordinating force in implementing an action plan(s).

Does the Leadership Program Work?

A number of indicators support the concept of leadership programs as an effective means of implementing multiculturalism. As mentioned in the above, many boards of education have initiated their own programs since 1978. The growth of leadership programs in Ontario and British Columbia is evidence that educators believe that a "camp" approach is an effective vehicle for implementing multiculturalism. A comment from a principal of a secondary school illustrates the type of change that can be effected by the program:

In previous years we had difficulties between black students and white students. In the space of one year the behaviour of some of the students was 180 degrees opposite. Some who had been involved in violence, just one year later prevented violence. ... (*Equality Now*, p. 122).

Finally, there is the formal evaluation indicator that measures the impact of the leadership program. This measurement device provides a more objective observation of the strengths and weaknesses of the program. The evaluation of the Eastern Ontario Leadership Program is more of a descriptive and not a statistical report (Megalokonomos, #84-11). However, the report does show that the students and staff have had a valuable experience; that the students and staff have acquired a higher degree of awareness; that the students will convey what they learned to their school environment; and, that the program for future camps should be altered (Megalokonomos, 1984). It appears that the multicultural/multiracial leadership programs are an effective means of implementing multiculturalism in the school and its community. However, more research and follow-up have to be developed so that the quality of the action plans is measured.

References

Berry, J. (1984). Multicultural attitudes and education. In R. Samuda, J. Berry and M. Laferriere (Eds.), *Multiculturalism in Canada: Social and educational perspectives*. Toronto: Allyn and Bacon.

Board of Education for the Borough of East York. (1982). *Multicultural leadership program: Resource book*. Toronto: Board of Education for East York.

Casse, P. (1981). *Training for the cross-cultural mind*. Washington, D.C.: SIETAR.

Clifton, R. and Perry, R. (1983). Two techniques for evaluating multicultural programs. *The History and Social Science Teacher, 19*(2). Toronto: University Microfilms International.

Eastern Ontario Boards of Education. (1983). *Multicultural leadership program: A handbook*. Ottawa: Ottawa Board of Education.

House of Commons. (1984). *Equality now*. Ottawa: House of Commons.

Ijaz, A.(1984). Ethnic attitude change: A multidimensional approach. In R. Samuda, J. Berry and M. Laferriere (Eds.), *Multiculturalism in Canada: Social and educational perspectives*. Toronto: Allyn and Bacon.

Kehoe, J. (1984). Achieving the goals of multicultural education in the classroom. In R. Samuda, J. Berry and M. Laferriere (Eds.), *Multiculturalism in Canada: Social and educational perspectives*. Toronto: Allyn and Bacon.

Kehoe, J. (1983). Enhancing the multicultural climate of the school. *The History and Social Science Teacher, 19*(2). Toronto: University Microfilms International.

Megalokonomos, T. (1984). *Evaluation of Eastern Ontario multiracial/multicultural leadership program*. Ottawa: Ottawa Board of Education, Research Report #84-11.

Ontario Ministry of Education. (1978). *Heritage language*. Policy Program Memorandum: 40.

Ontario Ministry of Education. (1979). Special populations in education. *Review and Evaluation Bulletins*. Toronto: Ministry of Education: 1(3).

Pfeiffer, J. and Jones, J. (1972). *The 1972 annual handbook for group facilitators*. Iowa City: University Associates. Sawyer, D. and Green, H. (1984). *The NESA activities handbook for native and multicultural classrooms*. Vancouver: The Tillacum Library.

Vancouver School Board. (1984). *The race relations and multicultural leadership camp: A handbook*. Vancouver: Vancouver School Board.

Guidelines for Training Students in Race Relations

Inez Elliston and Trevor Ludski

Introduction

Residential multicultural leadership training camps are receiving increased interest by school boards across Ontario. This came about as a result of leadership initiative by the Ontario Ministry of Education in 1976. To our knowledge, there is no empirical data about programs of this nature. There are, however, a number of reports such as the Cartaret Story (*Phi Delta Kappan*, November 1978, Volume 60, No. 3), which attests to the success of similar types of programs in promoting positive attitudes towards other cultures and races.

A number of school boards in the Toronto area, such as the Scarborough, Metropolitan Toronto, East York and Etobicoke boards have multicultural leadership programs in place. Some school boards have had variations of the multicultural leadership program ongoing for four or five years. The programs have also received federal support. *Equality Now*, the 1983 federal task force document on visible minorities in Canadian society (Recommendation 71), states that school boards should be encouraged to develop multicultural leadership programs to assist staff and students in developing skills and positive attitudes towards the acceptance of human diversity in Canada.

Evaluations are usually completed by all participants at the conclusion of their programs. None of the boards, however, has evaluated the program in terms of both process and outcome goals. Nevertheless, the results of these programs have been sufficiently encouraging to engender confidence in the conclusion that they have been fulfilling a need.

The Scarborough Initiative

The Graduate Race Relations Awareness and Community Experience program (GRACE) exemplifies a year of endeavours aimed at the development of an advanced leadership training module for students in Scarborough who were graduates of the board's multicultural leadership training activities. The focus of this additional program was on race relations. There were two major reasons for the creation of this program. Firstly, written evaluations of the Scarborough Multicultural Inter-school Leadership Experience (SMILE) strongly indicated that students wanted more in-depth discussions. Secondly, a perception was shared by the majority of the volunteer leaders that these young people were deeply concerned about the quality of life for themselves and their families as they strove to establish themselves as Canadians. This concern expressed itself in the students' willingness to explore racial incidents, in their ability to objectively examine issues of racial conflict in the school and the community, and finally, in an articulated wish for more on-going opportunities to air their concerns and to consider solutions. While situationally defined issues suggest a focus for the content of such programs, the literature provides further information about programs and materials dealing specifically with race relations awareness training (Casse, 1979; Fromkin and Sherwood, 1976; Katz, 1978; Kehoe, 1980; and Thomas and Novogrodsky, 1983).

Description of the GRACE Program

The objectives for the GRACE camp experience were:

1) to address issues in interpersonal and race relations which were identified by students and related to school and community life;
2) to provide an out-of-school learning experience that would enable students to practise skills needed for:
   a) problem-analysis, problem-solving and decision making;
   b) conflict management;
   c) self-management, that is, coping with stress and using time effectively;
3) to develop an awareness of options as an important aspect of interpersonal relationships and life management;
4) to expand participants' knowledge of community resources and how to access them when dealing with race-related issues;

5) to encourage community involvement by the participants in the solution of personal and institutional problems.

Student participants were graduates of either or both the Scarborough Board of Education or the Ministry of Education leadership camps. In general, the students were individuals who had taken an interest in multicultural activities or had been identified by their schools as having positive leadership qualities. Collegiate institutes involved in past multicultural leadership programs in the past were invited to send student participants. Initially, thirty-five students from nine collegiate institutes attended.

These students were taken from grades 10 to 13 and to some extent reflected the multicultural mix of their schools and of the city of Scarborough in general. There were participants those of South Asian heritage (13), West Indian (15), Anglo-Canadian (4), Central and Southern European (2), and Oriental (1). There were nineteen female students and sixteen male students.

A staff of fourteen full-time and part-time persons included representatives from both the Program Department and Student and Community Services. The staff consisted of eight teachers, five Student and Community Services staff members (social workers, psychologists and multicultural community liaison officers and two Program Department consultants (in values education and physical and health education).

Program Design

The overall design of the program consisted of two modules.

A. *Problem Identification and Analysis*
Activities were directed at:

a) the identification of issues and incidents in race relations;
b) strategies that could be used in dealing with race-related incidents or problems.

B. *Skills Building/Personal Growth – Leadership Role in the school and community*
Activities for personal growth and development:
a) developing leadership skills; and
b) planning projects that could be implemented when the students returned to their schools and communities.

An outline of the program is given on the next page. A training manual with details of events for each day is available from the Scarborough Board of Education.

Participants were placed in one of three heterogeneous groups and facilitators were assigned to each group. Students were periodically reassigned for specific activities. This arrangement allowed for both stability in group building relationships and mixing among participants.

Facilitator Training

A total of forty potential teacher-facilitators were invited to a one and one-half day facilitators' training workshop. The workshop sessions dealt with the rationale for the camp, program design, the content of the materials and the strategies that would be used for the activities outlined above. The main focus was to design a program that would make participants comfortable in examining race relations issues and to encourage them to develop skills to deal with racial conflict.

GRADUATE RACE RELATIONS AWARENESS AND COMMUNITY EXPERIENCE

Program Implementation

In a pre-orientation session, students were encouraged to reflect on the issues and were provided with questions as a means of stimulating thought and later discussion. A list of the questions is given below.

1) Think of ideas that have come up in your school or community that lead positively to the promotion of racial tolerance and under-standing.
2) Identify and bring to the attention of the group any examples of successful activities that have promoted good race relations among people of different racial backgrounds in your school or community.
3) Be prepared to recommend programs that you think would promote racial understanding, tolerance and harmony in your school and community.

The first day's events included group building exercises like "Getting to know one another" and "They are all alike," and the identification of school-community related issues. In this part of the program, the film "Myself Yourself" proved very useful as a focal point for looking at racial incidents and labels. Participants were guided in their viewing by being given quotations from the film in advance. The intention was to enable participants to be able to distinguish differences in labelling through the examination and analysis of life experiences in context. Below are examples of terms that were defined and discussed in conjunction with the viewing of the film.

Race: racism, discrimination, systemic discrimination, equal rights, equal opportunity, affirmative action.

Culture: cultural pluralism, culture shock, integration, constitutional rights, assimilation.

Examples looked for in the film

- racial discrimination
- systemic discrimination
- discriminatory treatment
- ethnocentricism
- prejudice
- attitudes and/or values that exemplify specific cultural values
- situations suggesting pressure to duplicate the melting pot theory in Canada
- culture shock

The well-known social attitude/social action model of analyzing race relations was used.

Social Attitudes

Systemic Racism

Discrimination

Prejudice

Stereotyping

Social Action

This was followed by an analysis of multicultural interactions, especially of situations dealing with ambiguities.

Each day began with a warm-up exercise that was directly related to the previous day's discussion or that provided an appropriate starting point for the day's theme.

On Day Two, the focus was on problem analysis and strategies for problem-solving. The main approach was to use case studies, which illustrated concepts associated with intercultural communication and equal status interaction, as a strategy for reducing prejudice. Participants examined situations in the community that would allow equal status interaction among individuals, that would encourage institutional support, and that would foster contact with high status individuals in ethnic minority groups. Activities involving superordinate goals and intergroup cooperation were also studied.

In the case studies, specific incidents were analyzed and solutions posed. The steps below illustrate the process.

Program Analysis

WHO is involved?
WHAT actually happened? WHAT went wrong?
WHERE did it occur?
WHEN did it happen?
WHY were these people involved?

Problem Solution

WHO cares during the conflict?
WHAT is the next step?
WHERE can we get help? WHERE can we start?
WHEN can help be expected? WHEN is an answer needed?
WHY is it important to solve the problem?
HOW else can we help? HOW can we involve others? HOW much will it cost?

Participants also had an opportunity to hear from multicultural community liaison officers about their role and function in the ethnic community and the wider community respectively.

A central aim of the five-day training session was to give participants information to provide them with opportunities to: (a) problem solve and (b) take action on their own behalf and on behalf of the community of home, school and neighbourhood when problems in intercultural living occur.

On Day Three, representatives from a number of key organizations and institutions were invited to the camp. These institutions included:

Ontario Human Rights Commission
Office of the Ombudsman of Ontario
Urban Alliance on Race Relations
Ethnic Relations Unit of the Metropolitan Toronto Police Force
Office of Civil Liberties Association
B'nai B'rith Association of Metropolitan Toronto
Canadian Council of Christians and Jews

In order to ensure maximum exposure and participation, a cooperative learning strategy, the jigsaw classroom, was employed. This enabled the community resource people to interact with small groups of students. The students then formed cross-groups and shared their newly-gained expertise with each other.

At the end of the session the panel of visitors answered questions or clarified points raised in the small group sessions. Apart from expanding the participants' knowledge of community resources, this activity provided a good example of the importance and value of networking, a concept that was introduced in a subsequent activity session.

During the final two days of the program, emphasis focussed on re-entry into the home, school and community environments. Participants were asked to consider the feelings of family members who had not shared their unique experience. A further consideration was how they could be most effective in communicating their ideas on their return. A variety of activities were introduced in the session that followed. Included were: a) opportunities for youth to volunteer their services (youth clubs, senior citizens); b) opportunities to travel (Kitimavik, Young Canada); c) opportunities to engage in community building projects.Guidelines for proposal writing were provided and specific ideas related to projects such as International Youth Year, local community issues and youth programs were explored. Self-management skills, such as time and stress management, goal-setting and self-contracting for task completion, were emphasized.

Unique Features of Program Design and Program Process

The GRACE program contained some unique features. Among these were:

1) Program flexibility;
2) A deliberate attempt to prepare participants
   a) for re-entry into the community of home, school and neighbourhood,
   b) for the transition from the role of student to other life roles, and
   c) for participation in community life.

Program Flexibility

The program was designed with the expectation that administrators and facilitators would be flexible in their planning, and that they would implement the program in a way that would allow input from all participants.

As was noted earlier, a pre-camp orientation session was held. This allowed for specification of the objectives of the camp and a general description of the camp program outline. The idea of a cultural evening was also raised, to which the students responded enthusiastically. The result was a very satisfying experience in which staff and students exchanged or wore clothes from various cultures and partook of different foods.

An interesting feature of this latter experience was the anxiety that surfaced among some participants at the prospect of appearing different (that is, altered in appearance as a result of wearing different clothes). Many participants revealed that wearing clothes that might be regarded as unusual presented a threat to their self-perception. However, in the non-threatening atmosphere of the camp, people were able to cross cultural distances. In other words, they could risk taking on another identity. This spirit of adventure and, more importantly, of acceptance of differences was manifested in the eagerness of participants to join in national dances and other cultural expressions.

The success of any endeavour can be gauged by some of the unanticipated events and outcomes. As emphasized above, the central thrust of the camp was to encourage participants to manage their own lives, and to expand their awareness of issues, needs and opportunities to bring about change. Many of the responses to the activities in the camp demonstrated that program objectives were being realized. For example, participants were able to respond to the interest of a group of senior citizens who were sharing adjoining accommodation. The seniors were invited to the young participants' social evening and were encouraged to take part in the activities which they did with enthusiasm. It is safe to say that the objective of expanding the participants' awareness and receptivity to the point of viewpoints and needs of others contributed creating a climate of acceptance that bridged the age and interest gaps and enabled the young and old to mingle and enjoy one another's presence.

Program flexibility also allowed changes to be made in the tempo of activities in response to the needs of the participants. For example, though the week was planned to allow enough time for rest and outdoor activities (cooperative games), halfway through the week's session it became obvious that a break in the flow of events was necessary to take a "time out" from the intense involvement with the various activities. Flexible scheduling allowed for this change of pace, as well as for the possibility of bridging activities without disrupting the shape and rhythm of the sequence of events.

Preparation for Re-entry into the Community of Home, School and Neighbourhood

The activity, "Designing a school that does not work," allowed participants to express ideas and feelings about the conditions they had left behind and those they considered unsatisfactory. As they deliberated, it became evident that they were becoming more conscious of things that they would like to change. Possible roles they could take in the change process also became obvious. This led to an examination of how prepared they were to assume new roles and of where they could find support.

The Transition from Student to Other Life Roles

While the program did not stress life planning, the discussions, activities and tasks had the effect of leading the participants to speculate about the future roles each person could or might be required to play in various life situations. It was obvious that the students took their assignments seriously and were occupied with the nature of the transition from student to other roles. Life-management skills, such as time management, coping with stress and being self-aware, were some of the transition skills that were emphasized.

Participation in Community Life

A consideration in the planning of the program was how to ensure that the excitement and interest generated by the camp would not be lost but would be translated into action. It was felt that the program design should incorporate tasks that would encourage involvement in the community when the students returned home.

Several activities in particular were particularly directed to this objective. These were: the visit of community resource people to the camp who would be valuable contacts in the post-camp period; teaching the skills of networking; providing information on opportunities for project development; having participants brainstorm ideas for workable projects; and providing guidelines for developing project proposals.

As the evaluation revealed, each participant was able to return home with at least two ideas he or she could attempt. Translating these ideas into workable activities has provided these youngsters with challenging post-camp experiences.

Evaluation

The evaluation of the camp experience can be viewed in terms of 1) the general results; 2) achievement of the objectives; and 3) any significant impact. Various strategies were employed in the collection of data for the assessment of this program outcome. The result provided a wealth of information on various aspects of the program. The overall impression was that participants benefitted greatly from the experience in terms of knowledge, skills, attitudes and perception of their own worth and of their ability to influence change.

Considerations for Program Implementation

The nature of the week-long events at the GRACE program, the response of the young people to the issues and their expressed desires indicated clearly and unequivocally that there is a need to directly address issues of race relations and that strategies and procedures to do so should be in place. This perception along with a strong commitment to the process of effective cross-cultural dialogue, led to two main considerations for program implementation.

Program Needs

It is important that programs of this nature are seen as one aspect of an overall strategy that recognizes the multicultural reality of the community and that takes measures to ensure that there is a purposeful and meaningful attempt at cultural integration and citizenship education throughout the system. The amount of time and energy required to plan and implement an effective program is immense, especially considering it is usually done on a voluntary basis. Under these circumstances, it is necessary to consider under these circumstances how much is possible and what is the most effective procedure for program delivery.

One of the advantages of the GRACE program design is the manageable size of the group (35 students and 14 staff) located together in one area. Because of this, it was relatively simple to build group cohesiveness, and some of the logistical problems in program organization were easily overcome. Consideration should therefore be given to the number of participants in this type of program, ideally a number not exceeding 45 students, with an appropriate number of staff persons.

The question of leadership qualities in student participation was intensely debated prior to the camp program. Opinions were varied as to whether multicultural leadership graduates only should be accepted. The main assumption was that previous multicultural training experience, as provided by the Board of Education or by the ministry's program, was a necessary and sufficient condition for the understanding of race relations issues. Another view was that all life experiences are valid in terms of learning and that leadership qualities can emerge or be fostered in the context of involvement in other aspects of school or community life. The results of the program suggest that the selection of students should be guided by criteria that define leadership qualities and expectations.

While the general response to the program has been favourable, the evaluation reports reveal some gaps in the content.In particular, students expressed a strong wish that more opportunity had been provided for discussing the racial and cultural backgrounds of participants.

Policy Initiatives

It is advisable that a system-wide training program in race relations awareness be provided as part of professional development activities and this initiative should include discussions of racism, prejudice and discrimination, activities and strategies for dealing with racial incidents, and skills in effective cross-cultural dialogue and conflict management.

Conclusion

In the last decade we have made remarkable strides in understanding the process of cultural adaptation. This has led to a re-evaluation of the value of cultural assimilation and the articulation of a policy of multiculturalism. The underlying thrust is that only inasmuch as people have a sense of their own culture (roots) are they able to truly appreciate and embrace the culture of others. Young people growing up in Canada today want to be first and foremost Canadians. This means being seen as such accepted as such, and given access to all the rights and responsibilities of citizenship.

Multicultural programs provide young people with the opportunity to explore, in a non-threatening environment and under supervised conditions, their fears of multiculturalism, to exorcise their hostilities and their misconceptions, and to formulate positive action plans for citizenship participation. Programs such as the GRACE program can provide precisely that opportunity. In the words of one participant:

> After a week my expectations of this camp have been fulfilled and greatly developed. I have learned more about being active in society, also it has helped my self-image to grow, making me secure and more Canadian.

References

Canada House of Commons. (1984). *Equality now! Report of the Special Committee on Visible Minorities in Canadian Society*. Ottawa: House of Commons, Issue #4.

Casse, P. (1979). *Training for the cross-cultural mind: A handbook for cross-cultural trainers and consultants*. Washington: SIETAR.

Fromkin, H. and Sherwood, J. (Eds.) (1976). *Intergroup and minority relations: An experiential handbook*. La Jolla, Calif.: University Associates.

Katz, J. (1979). *White awareness: Handbook for anti-racism training*. Oklahoma: University of Oklahoma Press.

Kehoe, J. (1980). *Ethnic prejudice and the role of the school*.

Thomas, B. and Novogrodsky, C. (1983). *Combatting racism in the workplace: A course for workers*. Toronto: Cross-Cultural Communication Centre.

Some Guidelines for Developing a Student Interchange Model

Raymond Pavlove

This chapter deals with the World Interchange Project, an integrated classroom project of sharing items and information with classrooms around the world. It is a project which creates a familiarity with other countries and cultures, and which enables young people to recognize common problems and the shared value of all the world's people. It is a project which informs, sensitizes and enlightens young people so that they can better understand themselves and the complex multicultural world in which they live. It is a project which develops international understanding through communication at the personal level.

The sharing of information, the appreciation of new knowledge, and the formulation of attitudes and patterns of behavior that enhance the values of our pluralistic society form a cornerstone of the education system. It is incumbent upon educators at all levels to provide integrated programs that will give each child an opportunity to "develop or retain a personal identity by becoming acquainted with the historical roots of the community and culture of his or her origin, and by developing a sense of continuity with the past, begin to understand and appreciate the points of view of ethnic and cultural groups other than his or her own; and at the same time to develop an understanding of such concepts as community, conflict, culture, and interdependence; learn the social skills and attitudes upon which effective and responsible cooperation and participation depend" (Breithaupt, Burke, Kane and Michalski, 1977).

The World Interchange Project has been sensitive to these program objectives, and invites teachers to participate in similar projects of sharing our multicultural identity with others.

The guidelines for the World Interchange Project model focus on the middle grades of elementary school. However, adaptations can easily be made that will allow students from kindergarten to grade 13 to communicate successfully with other classes in all corners of the world.

> Many of the fundamental attitudes are moulded during the first years in life. The elementary school should therefore devote greater attention to instilling open and positive international attitudes. It is in respect of affective goals that the primary school can perform its big mission – a feeling of tolerance, learning how to work together with others, a sense of individual and collective responsibility. Further, children should be introduced to international subject matter in games, songs, stories, books, pictures, and films. Portrayals of children and families from other countries should stress the elements shared in common and not the disparities. The trumpet should not be blown for the homeland in terms that tend to belittle other peoples and cultures.
> (Prueter, 1976).

A Commitment to Sharing Information

The key to a successful interchange is to have a realistic vision coupled with an enthusiastic commitment to developing positive attitudes in oneself and others. The role of the teacher is crucial in creating a classroom environment that is conducive to intergroup sensitivity, understanding and respect. Speak to your principal about the idea of establishing contacts with other schools around the world. The principal's support is necessary, and he or she can provide much assistance and guidance as the project evolves in the weeks, months and years ahead.

The method of presenting the idea to your students will vary from classroom to classroom, and from teacher to teacher. Two approaches in proposing the project to your students might be: 1) to wait for an opportune time – during a reading, mathematics, or social studies lesson where the discussion can naturally lead into the possibility of an international communication with other children around the world; 2) to speak out directly and ask: "What do you think of the idea of trying to make contact with other grade 6 students in different schools in different countries of the world?"

The key is to tread slowly, so that your and the students' enthusiasm does not become overbearing or overshadow the practicality of the project. If the makeup of your classroom is multicultural, you may take advantage of this situation to discuss how interesting and fun it would be to learn more about the various ethnic countries represented.

It is best to let the idea sink in for a day or two, thus providing students with an opportunity to reflect on the project. However, before proceeding further, you must get a commitment from your students and the reassurance that they wish to become involved and are prepared to work together to plan, discuss and formulate the process necessary for a successful interchange. Once that commitment is received you are on your way.

Number of Contact Schools

The number of schools you wish to establish contact with will depend on your enthusiasm, the interest of the students and the financial resources available to you. It is suggested that 10 to 15 schools is a reasonable number to try to establish contact with in your first year.

The school year in the southern hemisphere usually begins in February and ends in early December. The school year in the northern hemisphere usually begins in September and ends in June. There is no "right" time to make contact, but the earlier in the school year, the better.

Countries to be Contacted

A brainstorming session with your students to decide on which countries to make contact with will get them involved in the project. Various criteria and procedures for selecting countries are suggested below.

1) Communicate with only those countries which are on the course of study for the grade you are teaching. For example, if the western hemisphere is on the course, try to establish contact with schools in the countries located in that area.
2) Ethnic representation in the classroom, e.g., if you have children representing a variety of countries, you may decide to establish contact with schools in those countries. Should there be more countries represented in the class than you wish to consider, be very careful not to alienate any students by not seeming to want to communicate with "their" country. If possible, try to involve all of the students in some way.
3) For a global perspective, you may decide to communicate with, say, three schools in each of the five major continents. In this way you will have a manageable number of schools and a good cross-section of the world.

4) Other options which may be suggested by students:
   – throw darts at a map;
   – appoint a small group of students decide for the class;
   – select countries which the students have never heard of before;
   – let the teacher decide;
   – select countries which the students or teacher have very little knowledge of.

Before proceeding to the next stage, it is advisable to reach a class decision on which countries to try and establish contact with and to stick to that decision.

Obtaining Addresses of Contact Schools

Once the decision has been made, the next step is to decide on methods of obtaining addresses of schools that would be willing to communicate and share information.

Once again, the procedure is to ask your students to suggest methods for obtaining addresses. These responses should be listed on the blackboard or in a flow chart.

1) Students may have friends or relatives abroad whom they can write to and ask for assistance in providing names and addresses of schools that might be willing to correspond. With the students' letters, a covering letter from the principal or superintendent, briefly outlining the project, should be included.
2) Community resources, such as churches, neighbours, ethnic organizations and service clubs, may be able to assist with a school address or two. Challenging students to seek our community resources is an excellent community awareness exercise.
3) Canadian embassies abroad or foreign embassies and consulates in Canada are very good sources. You may contact your federal Member of Parliament for the addresses and phone numbers of the embassies and consulates you wish to contact.
4) You may suggest to your students (if they do not make the suggestion first) that they may attempt to obtain addresses through national teacher organizations or ministries of education in foreign countries. For assistance in this regard, write to the Canadian Teachers' Federation, 110 Argyle Street, Ottawa, Ontario, K2P 1B4.
5) The Canadian Organization for Development through Education (CODE) is a good source for addresses of schools in developing

countries which would be willing to correspond with Canadian schools.

Do not hesitate to contact selected organizations and individuals in seeking assistance for school addresses. It is important to send these requests for information out before you start assembling your goodwill package of information and items. In this way, by the time you write to your contact and receive a reply, you will have your package prepared and ready to dispatch. Allow two to three weeks for international mail.

Preparing the Goodwill Package

Deciding on the specific information and items you wish to share with others is a challenging task for children. This stage of the interchange will provide them with many opportunities for organizing, recording ideas and information, making comparisons, extending oral and written vocabulary, and developing creative talents. The innovative teacher will be able to integrate many learning skills into the curriculum.

The students will have to recognize who they are and to come to grips with the multicultural diversity of the community in which they live. It must be learned that the communication shared between oneself and others is not absolute, but rather, a beginning towards understanding and appreciation. The multicultural society in which we live is changing and will continue to change. This diversity is difficult to express in terms of specific items and information.

One of the ways to help children decide what they wish to share about themselves, their community and their country with others is to ask: "What would we like to know about other children, their community and their country?" Listing specific questions they would like answered about another country will assist them in preparing their goodwill package. The assumption, of course, is that children throughout the world have similar interests about others. Children will probably ask questions like: "What do they eat?" "Do they have homes and what are they like?" "What is their school like?" "What are their families like?" "Where do they live?" "Do they participate in sports and hobbies?" "What colour are they?" "What language do they speak?" "Do they have any pets?"

The students will have to try to answer these questions about themselves. They will have to make sure that the information they present in the package is accurate and relevant to their experiences.

Whatever they present must reflect their level of skills and under-standing.

Items for students to include, as listed below, have evolved from questions asked earlier in this paper.

- local currency
- a brief history of the community (invite local historians to tell you about the community)
- a description of the school: size, grades, activities, subjects
- size and kind of houses
- pets: number and kinds
- foods: breakfast, lunch, supper
- hobbies or leisure activities
- favourites: books, foods, colours, television programs, cars, politi-cians, pets, subjects, toys, sports, etc.
- geography of the area
- songs about the community (written and sung by the students)
- students' names and their meanings
- a page on "Me"
- pictures of homes, people, pets, foods, school, dress
- animals, birds, flowers of the community
- seasonal activities
- holidays and their meaning
- art media: neighbourhood sounds, clay models, papier-mache, sculptures, murals, collages
- a tape cassette made by students reading stories and poems; speaking informally with friends about current topics; telling about them-selves, giving newscasts, weather reports, making strange sounds. A taped message lends a personal touch to the project. (It is not necessary to spend a great deal of time editing the tape. The more informal, the better.)
- a survey of the community to find out ethnic composition, size of families, work done by father and/or mother, number and kinds of pets, number of years lived in the area, languages written and spoken, etc. Keep surveys small and simple so that the data can be easily interpreted and presented.

Other items students may wish to include are:

- a Canadian flag. (As well, small Canada flag lapel pins may be available from your federal Member of Parliament).
- laminated leaves and flowers

- arts and crafts which reflect the multicultural composition of the community
- maple syrup, coins, stamps
- pictures of the community, community buttons, stickers and badges

The list is not all-inclusive as the students will have many more suggestions about what to include:

When the class has decided on the information and items to be included that represent itself, the school and the community, two or three more packages than required should be prepared. Items should then be collected and the written information produced. A master list numbering all the items should be made up, along with a brief description on each item. In this way, the contact school can easily identify the contents of the goodwill package. Ask for a similar list to be prepared in return.

It is important that every student in the class contribute to each package. A nice touch is to affix a photograph of a student contributing a piece of written information to his or her work. Photocopying small black-and-white photographs taken by the school photographer are appropriate for this purpose. Written information and items should be student-made whenever possible. "Homemade" is appreciated much more than "store bought."

Preparing a Budget and Seeking Financial Assistance

You will require financial assistance for your World Interchange Project. Fund-raising can be distracting and time-consuming; however, do not let this or the cost of the project deter you. Money is necessary, and fund-raising adds a realistic dimension to the project. Students are great fund-raisers if they believe in the cause and are directly involved in the process.

Introduce a ledger sheet with the basic entries of receipts and expenditures to your students. All students should keep one. You will also have to open a bank account. If your school board approves, elect a student president and secretary, who will have signing authority in addition to yourself.

Sources of funds include class fund-raising activities (bake sale, flea market, etc.); the school fund; the board of education; service clubs (Rotary, Lions, Kinsmen, Legion, Knights of Columbus); the local teachers' federation.

Money is almost invariably forthcoming when students present their project to selected organizations and ask for assistance. Do not be surprised if you receive more money than originally requested. Also, be prepared to receive anonymous donations.

Sample Budget

Expenditures: postage for letters ($20.00); postage for goodwill packages (15 at $10.00 = $150.00); photographs (5 rolls at $12.00 = $60.00); tape cassettes (15 at $1.50 = $22.50); contingency ($50.00); showcase ($100.00). Total = $402.50.
Receipts: class fundraising ($50.00); school fund ($100.00); board of education ($100.00); service clubs ($150.00).
Total = $400.00.

The costs will vary from project to project, as will the sources of financial assistance. Each class undertaking a World Interchange Project must assess their school and community to determine the activities necessary to obtain the necessary funding.

World Interchange Project Presentation

Should it be necessary to seek financial assistance from outside the school, permission should first be sought from the principal. Students can then prepare a presentation to be given to selected community organizations. It is of utmost importance that all students be directly involved with each presentation. Community organizations are usually receptive to student-oriented projects. The presentation should be well-organized, well-rehearsed and planned by the entire class. Four to six students is a manageable number to be involved in the actual presentation, with each student being responsible for one element of the project. The elements could be, for example:

1) An introduction
2) Whom the class is contacting
3) Samples of items and information being sent
4) Budget and costs, with a request for an actual amount of funds
5) Integration of the project into the curriculum

Should more than one presentation be necessary, use different student presenters, so that all students have a chance to speak on behalf of their classmates. This is a great learning experience and should not be denied to any student, regardless of level of ability or confidence.

Be sure the student presenters are given an opportunity to report their experiences to the class or at a school assembly. Remember to send a class "thank you" letter to the selected organizations.

Dispatching the World Interchange Project Package

After the letters have been sent, it will take about six to eight weeks to receive a commitment from your contact schools indicating that they are willing to correspond with you. Your goodwill World Interchange packages will be ready or very nearly ready to dispatch. It is nice to get them away as soon as possible after obtaining the addresses of the schools. In this way they will receive your package in about two to three weeks after they have written to you.

Be sure the information and items are packed securely. Check with the post office to verify the postage required. At the present time, it is less expensive to air mail two 500-gram packages than a one kg. package to the same address. Considerable savings will be realized if you are able to package in multiples at or under 500-grams. Furthermore, packages of this weight do not require customs declarations but only a customs label. If your packages weigh more than 2 kilograms each, it may be advisable to send them surface mail. Delivery time is about four to six weeks.

When stamping your package, put on as many stamps of as many different denominations as possible. Ask your contact schools to do the same. When the packages are finally ready to mail, take a group of students to the post office for a final weigh-in and brief explanation from the post master about the operation of Canada Post and international mail.

Studying Contact Countries

Strange as it may sound, neither you nor your students will be tired from all the work you have done in getting the goodwill packages together. While the class is waiting for the contact schools to reciprocate, the students can be spending some time learning more about them, the country they are in, the culture, the geography, the products of the country, etc. Several activities may be planned in this regard. Avoid superficial appraisals of other cultures and try to have students understand and appreciate them at a level commensurate with their knowledge and experience.

Receiving Packages

What a great day it will be when the first goodwill package arrives from overseas. The students and probably you yourself will immediately want to find out: "What did they send?" Take your time, and before opening the package, review the information the students have learned about the country.

Next, have the students predict what they think is in the package. List their comments on the board. When the package is opened, look for the master list of items. If it is there, analyze and discuss each item as it is taken out in chronological order. If no master list is provided, start from the top of the package and work down. Depending on its size and contents, you will proably spend half a day or longer studying and appreciating each item. Do not worry about the time as this is a very exciting event. You may wish to invite the principal to the classroom to share with the learning and enjoyment. Once all the items and information have been examined, display the entire contents of the package, with appropriate titles, in the hallway of the school.

The students should take turns opening packages when they arrive. Feel free also to send packages home with students, so that their family and neighbours can experience the joy and excitement of learning about another culture.

Follow-Up Activities

The first responsibility after receiving a package is to write back to the contact school and thank them for their goodwill package. If necessary, ask for clarification about certain items or for further information. You may wish to send some small token of appreciation and in this small way, establish a correspondence that may continue for years to come.

Other Follow-Up Activities

– A group of students or the entire class may wish to study a particular ethnic group or country further.

- Inform the individuals or organizations who generously donated money to the project that the package has been received, and invite them to your school.
- build a museum showcase in the school to display the items and information received
- invite individual students or groups of students to establish penpals in the various countries
- as the project unfolds, be prepared to present it to community groups
- consider the possibility of an exchange visit of student(s) with one of the schools contacted.

Management and Organization

With so much happening you, the teacher, will require the support and cooperation of all the students. It is suggested that responsibilities be delegated to individual students or small groups of students. Whereas the teacher is the leader and director, the students are the "executives."

Assign students to as many responsibilities as possible, some of which are listed below:

- diary keeper: responsible for recording the activities and events of the project
- class "whip": responsible for keeping track of each task, whom it was assigned to, and the date due
- keeping a photo album: take pictures of all activities, they will be a great historical record. Do not neglect captions.
- collecting stamps and coins: many stamps and coins will be received and could be organized in albums
- package organizers: responsible for monitoring the items and information as they are prepared and collected. Individual boxes for each item make the job easier.

Various other tasks will arise, requiring student involvement and monitoring.

The guidelines presented in this chapter are by no means all-encompassing. They are meant to motivate and inspire educators at all levels to become involved in multicultural and intercultural projects. It is not expected that every class which undertakes a World Interchange Project will follow exactly the same guidelines. Quite the contrary. Some classrooms may want to interchange with one school; others may wish to send the same information to many schools in the hope of establishing a longterm relationship with some of them. The strength of multicultural and intercultural education is that there is no one right way or best way to achieve success. Each school and each community in Canada's multicultural society is unique and, accordingly, the project should reflect this.

Dr. Akira Takahashi of the University of Tokyo sums it up this way. "Education liberates people from prejudice. It contributes to international understanding which forms a basis for peace. The first step is to learn about your neighbours. Promote area studies and linguistic courses. Respect the cultural identity of minority groups, and demonstrate your leadership in sharing of ethnocentric points of view" (Takahashi, p.40).

Conclusion

The World Interchange Project began in 1976 at McDougall Public School under the jurisdiction of the West Parry Sound Board of Education in Parry Sound, Ontario. In the first eight months of the project, McDougall School sent packages of twenty-two items and information representing the school and area to one hundred classrooms around the world. In a few short weeks, the school received information and items from sixty-two of the contact schools. Some schools corresponded months later, and a few never responded. Fourteen showcases now line the hallways of McDougall School, displaying hundreds of items received from all corners of the world.

The World Interchange Project has been an ongoing program at the school and has provided a variety of experiences for the students and staff. Nearly sixty presentations have been given on the project at local, provincial, national and international seminars and conventions. Students from Bermuda and Australia have visited the school as a result of the project.

Awards from Rotary International, the Ontario Public School Trustees' Organization, and Columbia Teachers' College in New York attest to the value, worth and significance of the project.

As McDougall School students say in an audio-visual presentation on the World Interchange Project:

> A great deal is still to be gained as the information and materials are received from their contacts around the world. In this way they will be more sensitive to the cultures, religions and ways of life of others. WIP has been a rewarding experience for the students at McDougall School as well as for their community. A learning and sharing of information with other countries has created a greater

awareness of the cultures that surround them. It is stimulating to know that there are many people of various colours, races and religions who share the belief that all of us can do our part, however insignificant it may seem, in developing a greater sensitivity to the world. They invite you to join them in this crusade by doing whatever you can in bringing about a unity of purpose, and turning back bigotry and prejudices in our troubled times (Brear, Frey, Green and Pavlove, 1977).

References

Brear, C., Frey, B., Green, T., and Pavlove, R. (1977). *Around the world and back: world interchange project*. Parry Sound: McDougall School, West Parry Sound Board of Education.

Breithaupt, A., Burke, M., Kane, B. and Michalski, B. (1977). *Multiculturalism in action*. Toronto: Ontario Ministry of Education, 76-77/6130.

Dixon, R. and Maude, J. (1979). *International year of the child – World interchange project*. Huntsville: Northern Ontario Public School Principals' Association, vol. 5, no. 2.

Pavlove, R. (1977). *It could be a wonderful world*. Ottawa: Communications Branch, Canadian International Development Agency.

Pavlove, R. (1979). *A "thank-you" letter: Fred L. Barttlet, memorial award winner*. Toronto: Ontario Public School Trustees' Organization.

Prueter, K. (1976). *Ideas and information for elementary and secondary schools*. Toronto: Ontario Development Education Committee, 1-4.

Reekie, G. (1978). *World interchange project*. Toronto: Ontario Association for Curriculum Development.

Shelley, S. (1976). *Development education: key to a more humane future*. Singapore: World Confederation of the Teaching Profession Annual Assembly.

Takahashi, A. (1985). Manila: unity in diversity. In *The rotarian: an international magazine, 146*(3), Evanston, Illinois.

Tracy, M. (1984). *World interchange project is an education and fun experience for McDougall students*. Parry Sound: Georgian Bay Focus.

Implementing Programs to Reduce Prejudice

Daniel McDougall

Maria Campbell, author of *Halfbreed* (1973), describes the following incident in her life:

> The school was built in Spring River when I was nine. It was three miles away, and on opening all the parents had to bring their children for registration. Because it was a mixed school, whites and halfbreeds were gathered together officially for the first time, but the whites sat down on one side of the room while the halfbreeds sat on the other. (p.45)

While this passage describes a problem in the past, it illustrates divisions that still persist, although more subtly, in Canadian society. How can educators implement programs that are designed to reduce prejudice and discrimination? To answer this question, this paper discusses approaches to the people and processes that are relevant to successful implementation.

Public Relations

Before a program designed to reduce prejudice and discrimination is implemented, people in the community where the schools are located should be informed of the program's objectives, content and procedures. Hilgard (1964) refers to this as a "strategy for innovation." There are at least two reasons for dispensing this information: first, the general public may resist the program; and second, even if they do not resist, the more information they have, the better they will be able to understand the objectives of the program. Public resistance may partially be based on the fear that teachers will be distracted from what some groups, such as the Genuine Education Movement in Vancouver, perceive as the main purpose of education: to maintain and enhance basic literacy. Efforts at increasing tolerance and understanding may be seen as a secondary educational role that may draw attention away from teaching the basics. Resistance may also be founded on ignorance of the danger that prejudice poses for society. Given the recent widespread media coverage of the Zundel and Keegstra affairs, as well as renewed interest in the treatment of Japanese Canadians during World War II, it seems unlikely that the latter objection would still be a problem. Nevertheless, public education programs can function to lower resistance to innovation.

Administrators and Teachers

Administrators and teachers need to increase their personal awareness of prejudice and discrimination. They need to understand the programs sufficiently well, and they must develop the necessary skills to carry out proper implementation. To be effective leaders and teachers, individuals must voluntarily confront their own prejudices.

Judy Katz (1976) has discussed a systematic and countergroup program for guiding participants through six stages of awareness about prejudice. *Stage 1* creates an accepting atmosphere in the group, defines fundamental terminology and examines societal inconsistencies about race. *Stage 2* confronts the issue of prejudice and discrimination in social institutions, manifested mainly in discrepancies in attitudes and behavior. *Stage 3* explores participants' feelings that arise out of the previous two stages. Feelings are shared with and supported by the group. *Stage 4* produces an understanding of cultural differences between European and Third World cultures, and examines ethnocentrism. *Stage 5* explores the meaning of being white in a white-dominated society, by focussing on the differences between personal attitudes and behavior. *Stage 6* seeks action strategies to combat prejudice. Group members consider the benefits and problems of being actively involved in reducing prejudice, compared to the possible negative results of inaction. Methodology throughout the program includes readings, guided discussions, questionnaire analyses, audio-visual displays, simulation games and role-playing. Katz found that trained individuals, as compared to untrained individuals, showed more positive attitudes and behaviors.

Most other studies of sensitivity-training show that such programs have produced greater acceptance of minority group members (see Beasely, 1972; Carkhuff and Banks, 1970; Steele and Nash, 1972). Gamez (1970) found no change in sensitization. However, the evidence is sufficiently strong to suggest that group sensitivity-training could make administrators and teachers more effective workers in ethnic relations. As part of their pre-service and in-service training, they could be sensitized to their personal prejudices and to prejudice in general.

Educators require knowledge about the history of prejudice in Western society. Educators should have knowledge of the social, economic and political background of Canada, beyond an introductory history course. Emphasis should be placed on immigration to Canada, the development of Canadian immigration policies, and majority-minority intergroup relations, including case studies of oppressed minorities such as Amerindians, Japanese Canadians, Jews and women. Problems and contributions should be studied. Placing current problems into an historical context may lead to greater understanding and perhaps more creative problem-solving.

Since social psychology is the central discipline in the study of prejudice and discrimination, its concepts and principles should be known to teachers and administrators. With an understanding of how prejudice develops and how it is maintained and altered, educators will be better able to implement strategies designed to reduce prejudice. Social psychology is the mainspring for effective action.

Studies in cultural geography of the countries of origin of the major immigrant groups support historical and social psychological foundations. Such studies produce awareness of the heterogeneity of groups such as the West Indians: Jamaicans, for example, are obviously different from Trinidadians, and their respective cultures reflect this. Teachers who are aware of such differences are better able to meet the needs of immigrant students. As the source areas of immigrants change, in-service courses will be needed to keep educators up-to-date.

Students

Most educators are aware that prejudice is most significantly a problem of the majority. As such, programs should help majority children to overcome their prejudice. Successful implementation requires that students be ready to accept the special instruction that is designed to enhance tolerance and understanding. Advanced moral development and adequate self-esteem are prerequisites for overcoming prejudice. Heightened awareness of prejudice and increased analytical skills are also helpful.

Gradations in moral thinking exist, and teachers, through values clarification exercises, can help to advance the moral thinking of students. According to Daniels, Douglas, Oliver and Wright (1978), prejudice is a moral issue. When people treat others unequally, they usually do so for irrational reasons and violate the "respect for persons" principle of morality. Values clarification enables students to see prejudice as irrational and immoral.

Frequent failure lowers self-esteem (Hamachek, 1978), and low self-esteem is often associated with aggression and hostility towards others (Coopersmith, 1967; Rosenbaum and Staners, 1961). Greater self-acceptance, on the other hand, is related to decreases in prejudice (Rubin, 1967a, 1967b).

The frustration of failure may lead to aggression such as scapegoating (Berkowitz, 1961; Cowen, Landes and Schaet, 1958; Weatherley, 1961). Under frustrating conditions, the purpose of aggression is to destroy barriers to need gratification. But because there may be a high risk of retaliation from the party in question (e.g., a feared authority figure), the aggression may be directed towards relatively powerless figures, such as minority groups, who end up being scapegoats (Simpson and Yinger, 1972).

Academic failure is punishing, and if a student anticipates success but arbitrarily fails, frustration and aggression may occur. While progressive promotion policies have reduced the number of students failing whole grades, there are still some who must repeat. Because these students lack skills and discipline, there is too much failure during daily work, with the result that self-esteem suffers.

Just as educators may increase their awareness of prejudice through sensitivity-training, so may students, in a similar program.In addition, if students were to advance their level of cognitive sophistication, even without specific consideration of prejudice, the occurrence of discrimination would probably be lowered (Glock, Wuthnow, Piliavin and Spencer, 1975).

Teaching Methods

For a curriculum aimed at enhancing tolerance and understanding to succeed, teachers must acquire different methods of instruction. For example, there are strategies that facilitate moral development and enhance self-esteem. Other strategies, such as perceptual differentiation, cooperative learning, teaching empathy, and techniques that advance students' cognitive sophistication, promote tolerance and understanding among students. Brief descriptions of these methods follow.

Moral development is promoted by various values clarification exercises. An important way to use these exercises is to place students who are at one stage of moral development with pupils who are at higher stages. When the students at the lower levels study with classmates at the higher levels, the less-developed students are more likely to move up to the higher stages (Kohlberg and Davidson, 1977). A decrease in prejudice is then more likely, because tolerance is significantly related to the higher stages of moral development (Davidson, 1977). As a means of helping teachers to promote tolerance, teacher education programs should include careful training in values clarification methodology.

When instruction is individualized, there is greater likelihood of success and enhanced self-esteem among students. Individualized teaching however, creates the need for massive amounts of preparation, careful diagnosis, detailed marking and other time-consuming tasks, all of which are often beyond the time resources of most classroom teachers. While fully developed individualized instruction demands these resources, all teachers can achieve some degree of individualization. For instance, to allow for different rates of work, teachers may assign students varying lengths of time for task completion. The more able pupils may, if they complete their assignments early, study related enrichment materials which they can correct themselves with the help of teacher-prepared keys. The slower children can proceed at their own pace and are less likely to feel frustrated and hence, belligerent.

Another impediment to implementing non-biased programs is the norm-referenced evaluation system that currently predominates. Norm-referenced grading usually exists when a student's performance is assessed in relation to a previously defined group. Through criterion-referenced grading, we can stress achievement without emphasizing competition among individuals. Criterion-referenced evaluation also lowers competition for the difficult-to-achieve high grades. In such a system, the teacher stresses mastery of the most important skills and knowledge. Desire to achieve takes the form of improving on past performances rather than of a comparison with peers. Success is defined as improvement over a student's previous performance, and increased feelings of success result in increased self-esteem.

Let us consider additional methods of instruction that reduce prejudice. Some strategies encourage students to perceive the differences among minority group members. Other strategies allow youngsters to understand each other better and to work together more harmoniously. To illustrate both strategies, a brief discussion of perceptual differentiation, cooperative learning, the teaching of empathy and methods of developing analytical thinking follows.

Perceptual differentiation of minority group members produces more positive racial attitudes. This conclusion is based on the observation that faces of other races appear more similar to each other than those of the in-group (Brigham and Barkowitz, 1978; Katz, 1973). Because of this perceived similarity, generalization of negative attitudes towards all members of a visible minority group may occur. However, children can learn to perceive facial differences among out-group members. Katz (1973) and Katz and Zalk (1978) familiarized white children with the faces of black children by encouraging the correct naming of pictures of black persons and by having the white children practise distinguishing between sets of two black faces. Perceptual differentiation of minority groups facilitates tolerance of individual differences (Cantor, 1972).

Cooperative learning exists when two or more individuals work together for their mutual benefit to reach the same end. Two broad types of cooperative learning are student tutorials, illustrated by the jigsaw technique, and the group-investigation model. Cooperative learning improves student perception of ethnically different classmates (Aronson, Blaney, Stephan, Siles and Snapp, 1978). It produces increased friendships and interactions among students from different ethnic backgrounds (DeVries, Edwards and Slavin, 1978; Slavin, 1979). Marked increases in cross-ethnic helping of peers have been recorded (Weigel, Wiser and Cook, 1975). Cooperative learning encourages students to prefer ethnically heterogeneous student groups (Aronson *et al.*, 1978; Johnson, Johnson and Scott, 1978), and may produce long term reduction of prejudice.

Empathy can be thought of as symbolically standing in the shoes of another person and approximating what that person is thinking, feeling or seeing. Empathy is associated with pro-social behaviour such as altruism, helping and cooperation. It has also been associated with decreased aggressiveness, aggression being a quality we have already associated with discrimination. Hence, enhanced empathic understanding may diminish discrimination.

There are various ways of teaching empathic understanding. One approach is to stress other-oriented rules of conduct. For example, consider the rule that we should be polite to others. Through a teacher-guided discussion, students can consider the consequences of impolite behavior. Empathy is enhanced by an explicit person-oriented rationale (Gove and Keating, 1979; Nippold, Leonard and Anastopoulos, 1982). In another approach empathy is taught directly. Adult group leaders are trained in empathic skills. They then teach the empathic skills of identification with feelings and feeling the same as others within the context of sequentially organized skill levels. Children who undergo this program show greater capacity to feel the way others feel, as compared to untrained children (Ridley, Vaughan and Wittman, 1982).

As previously stated, analytical thinking can be developed. Students can learn to distinguish between facts about group differences and the overgeneralizations which abound. Because it helps individuals to make such distinctions, the logic of inference should be taught. Glock *et al.* (1975) found that teen-agers falsely attributed the aloofness of Jewish teenagers to their "Jewishness" rather than to the diligence of this group. Explanations of the notion of causality are necessary in order to encourage students to go beyond the superficial, easy explanations. In addition, the proper analysis of evidence should be taught so that pupils will know what conclusions can be reasonably drawn from observed behaviour and what limitations exist in the available evidence. An understanding of the principle of randomness also greatly assists the assessment of whether information gathered from everyday experiences is valid or invalid. Furthermore, the study of the concept of natural justice promotes appreciation of fairness in intergroup relations.

By mastering instructional strategies such as values clarification, individualization, criterion-referencing, perceptual differentiation, cooperative learning, the teaching of empathy, and techniques that enhance logical analysis, teachers will be able to successfully implement curriculum innovations intended to reduce prejudice.

Climate

Implementation of prejudice reduction programs is most effective in schools with an appropriate climate. Innovation in the curriculum is easiest in schools that have the following attributes: 1) People who have concern for one another's welfare; 2) individuals who feel that they think similarly on important issues, i.e., the group is cohesive; 3) a recognition that personal growth is a significant goal of all people; 4) a relaxed feeling about tasks and interpersonal relations, and high morale; 5) contributions which are encouraged from all participants and which are carefully considered in decision-making; 6) participants who work well together in solving problems; 7) high self-respect in which individuals value themselves and their ideas; 8) people who trust each other to behave responsibly (Schmuck, 1980). These attributes define a school climate that is able to effectively reduce prejudice.

Well-disciplined schools produce the appropriate climate for tolerance and understanding.The Phi Delta Kappa Commission on Discipline (1982) identified the characteristics and goals of well-disciplined schools. The characteristics are as follows:

1) effective past practices are continued;
2) the school environment is designed to facilitate appropriate behaviour;
3) accomplishments are rewarded;
4) student needs are met;
5) solutions are directed at the causes of problems;
6) positive actions rather than punishments are stressed;
7) models such as teacher effectiveness training are adapted to the requirements of the school;
8) the principal's leadership is positive;
9) key administrative personnel as well as the entire staff support the principal;
10) classroom teachers handle most of their own discipline problems;
11) the teaching staff have strong links to the communities they serve; and
12) regular assessments are conducted.

Well-disciplined schools are able to achieve the following seven objectives. They:

1) encourage joint problem-solving efforts of staff and students;
2) reduce authority and status differences between individuals;
3) increase students' sense of belonging;
4) enlarge students' involvement through curriculum and instruction improvements;
5) help students and teachers with personal problems;
6) strengthen the ties between the home and the school; and
7) improve the physical and organizational aspects of the school.

These goals are achieved through various procedures systematically applied to improve discipline.

Research

For the proper development of educational innovations, both basic and applied research are needed (Hilgard, 1964). Basic researchers investigate problems without regard for practical implications. For example, a developmental psychologist may study the emotional development of young children from a theoretical standpoint rather than in relation, say, to nursery school care. Applied researchers, on the other hand, study practical problems that typically confront regular classroom teachers. In applied research, the emphasis is on answering questions, usually in a two-step process about the best way of getting things done in the classroom. First, there are tryouts in a reasonably well-controlled environment, such as a laboratory classroom with selected teachers and students. Second, the methodology is tested in a typical classroom. Using the example above, the basic research problem of how emotions develop in young children may be translated into an applied question about what is the best way to teach a particular emotion such as empathy to preschool children. The second question is important to our topic because empathic understanding is a significant characteristic underlying positive social interaction (Hoffman, 1977). When creating methodologies that are to be compared, the applied researcher uses the ideas generated by basic researchers. Hence, information from both basic and applied studies is needed to properly apply programs to reduce prejudice.

Summary

Practical programs that reduce prejudice will be successfully implemented using approaches that consider the relevant people and processes. The general public, school administrators and teachers should be informed about the objectives, content and procedures of new curricula. Innovative strategies can help overcome resistance and avoid application difficulties. Various instructional strategies can help teachers sustain and/or heighten moral development, self-esteem, tolerance of ethnically different peers, awareness of prejudice and cognitive development among majority students. The beneficial effects of novel teaching methods can be maximized in schools where an appropriate climate exists. Well-disciplined schools can help to foster a climate conducive to tolerance and understanding. With a broadly-based approach to implementation, problems similar to those that troubled Maria Campbell will be diminished.

References

Aronson, E., Blaney, N., Stephan, G., Sikes, J. and Snapp, M. (1978). *The jigsaw classroom*. Beverley Hills: Sage.

Beasely, L. (1972). A beginning attempt to eradicate racist attitudes. *Social Casework*, *53*, 9-13.

Berkowitz, L. (Ed.). (1969). *Roots of aggression*. New York: Atherton.

Brigham, J. and Barkowitz, P. (1978). Do "they all look alike?" The effects of race, sex, experience, and attitude on the ability to recognize faces. *Journal of Applied Social Psychology*, *8*, 306-318.

Campbell, M. (1973). *Halfbreed*. Toronto: McClelland and Stewart.

Cantor, G. (1972). Effects of familiarization on children's ratings of pictures of whites and blacks. *Child Development*, *43*, 1219-1229.

Carkhuff, R. and Banks, G. (1970). Training as a preferred mode of facilitating relations between races and generations. *Journal of Counselling Psychology*, *17*, 413-418.

Coopersmith, S. (1967). *The antecedents of self-esteem*. San Francisco: Freeman.

Cowen, E., Landes, J. and Schaet, D. (1958). The effects of mild frustration on the expression of prejudiced attitudes. *Journal of Abnormal Social Psychology*, *58*, 33-38.

Daniels, L., Douglas, L., Oliver, C. and Wright, I. (Eds.). (1978). *Prejudice: Teacher's manual*. Toronto: Ontario Institute for Studies in Education.

Davidson, F. (1977). Respect for persons and ethnic prejudice in childhood: A cognitive-developmental description. In M. Tumin and W. Plotch (Eds.), *Pluralism in a democratic society*. New York: Praeger.

DeVries, D., Edwards, K. and Slavin, R. (1978). Biracial learning teams and race relations in the classrooms. Four field experiments using Teams-Games-Tournament. *Journal of Educational Psychology*, *70*, 356-362.

Gamez, G. (1970). T-groups as a tool for developing trust and cooperation between Mexican-American and Anglo-American college students. *Dissertation Abstracts International*, *31*, 2305B. (University Microfilms, No. 70-18234).

Glock, C., Wuthnow, R., Piliavin, J. and Spencer, M. (1975). *Adolescent prejudice*. New York: Harper & Row.

Gove, F. and Keating, D. (1979). Empathic role-taking precursors. *Developmental Psychology*, *6*, 594-600.

Hamachek, D. (1978). *Encounters with the self (2nd edition)*. New York: Holt, Rinehart and Winston.

Hilgard, E. (1964). A perspective on the relationship between learning theory and educational practices. In E. Hilgard (Ed.), *Theories of learning and instruction: The sixty-third yearbook of the National Society for the Study of Education* (402-415). Chicago: University of Chicago Press.

Hoffman, M. (1977). Empathy, its development and prosocial implications. In H. Howe and C. Keasey (Eds.), *Nebraska symposium on motivation: Social cognitive development*, *25*, 169-217. Lincoln: University of Nebraska.

Katz, J. (1976). A systematic handbook of exercises for the re-education of white people with respect to racist attitudes and behaviors. (Doctoral dissertation, University of Massachusetts, 1975). *Dissertation Abstracts International*, *37*, 170A. (University of Microfilms No. H76-14695).

Katz, P. (1973a). Perception of racial cues in preschool children. A new look. *Developmental Psychology*, *8*, 295-299.

Katz, P. (1973b). Stimulus predifferentiation and modification of children's racial attitudes. *Child Development*, *44*, 232-237.

Katz, P. and Zalk, S. (1978). Modification of children's racial attitudes. *Developmental Psychology*, *14*, 447-461.

Kohlberg, L. and Davidson, F. (1977). Appendix B: The need for moral education to make ethnic pluralism work. In M. Tumin and W. Plotch (Eds.), *Pluralism in a democratic society*. New York: Praeger.

Nippold, M., Leonard, L. and Anastopoulos, A. (1982). *Journal of Speech and Hearing Research*, *25*, 193-202.

Phi Delta Kappa Commission on Discipline. (1982). *Handbook for developing schools with good discipline*. Bloomington, IN.: Phi Delta Kappa.

Rosenbaum, M. and Staners, R. (1961). Self-esteem, manifest hostility, and expression of hostility. *Journal of Abnormal Social Psychology*, *63*, 646-649.

Rubin, I. (1967a). Increased self-acceptance: A means reducing reducing prejudice. *Journal of Personality and Social Psychology*, *5*, 233-238.

Rubin, I. (1967b). The reduction of prejudice through laboratory training. *Journal of Applied Behavioral Science*, *3*, 29-50.

Schmuck, R. (1980). The school organization. In J. McMillan (Ed.), *The social psychology of school learning* (169-213). New York: Academic Press.

Simon, S., Howe, L. and Kirschenbaum, H. (1978). *Values clarification: A handbook of practical strategies for teachers and students* (revised edition). New York: Hart.

Simpson, G. and Yinger, J. (1972). *Racial and cultural minorities: An analysis of prejudice and discrimination* (4th edition). New York: Harper and Row.

Slavin, R. (1979). Student teams and comparison among equals: Effects on academic performance and student attitudes. *Journal of Educational Psychology*, *70*, 532-538.

Steele, R. and Nash, K. (1972). Sensitivity training and the black community. *American Journal of Orthopsychiatry*, *42*, 424-430.

Weatherley, D. (1961). Anti-semitism and the expression of fantasy aggression. *Journal of Abnormal and Social Psychology*, *62*, 454-457.

Guidelines for Implementing More Visible Partnerships in Schools

Esmaralda Thornhill

"**M**ore visible partnerships" is the theme and message I have chosen in order to expound on the notion we more commonly refer to as "community involvement."

"More visible" is a deliberate and perhaps provocative choice of terminology which attempts to unmask the euphemistic and insidious wordgame at which we have become so adept. The question it raises, of course, is: "More visible in relationship to whom?"

Convenient labels such as "visible minorities," "cultural communities," "ethnic groups" and "immigrants" are, in our collective consciousness, synonymous with the notion of non-white: "Us versus Them." These labels nicely and politely obfuscate the very real and perplexing problem of racial differences, thus cunningly reinforcing and perpetuating the very same injustice we profess a commitment to eradicating – namely, racism.

"More visible partnerships" is a theme which is at one and the same time therapeutic and diagnostic, proposing a positive solution while confronting a very real problem. For no real multicultural education can proceed without the meaningful involvement of those communities most affected and to date, community involvement most definitely has *not* been equated with partnership as it should be. Community involvement has been limited to unilateral, often patchy and tardy consultation, which is more often capricious than rigorous.

Multiculturalism represents a social, educational and political goal we seek to attain (Moore, 1984). The multicultural ideal evokes the social contract which we must re-negotiate in the name of equality and non-discrimination in a "free and democratic" society. We must re-negotiate this social contract while taking into full account an historical past where colonialism and slavery have been the lot of black and native peoples, and where, today, ours is clearly a legacy of institutional racism towards these groups (Thornhill, 1984). Yet, it is difficult to find a philosophy and practice of education that attempts not only to reflect a multicultural society, but also to combat the effects of racism (Rees, 1984). We concede, rather reluctantly, that there are victims of racism, but we fail to pinpoint the victimizers. By the same token, it is equally difficult to find in practice a community involvement predicated on a relationship of "visible partnership." Racism thus far has tainted the notion of community involvement, making it colourless and meaningless.

Accordingly, in this short essay, I shall examine the issue of "visible partnerships" within a context of multicultural education based on two premises:

1) Multicultural education, *ipso facto*, means anti-racist education.
2) Visible partnership, *ab initio*, signifies a change in our collective mind-set.

Our North American history of colonialism and slavery has bequeathed to us a legacy of institutional racism, wherein members of more visible minorities have been and still are systematically and conspicuously excluded from important decision-making levels: namely, problem-diagnosis and problem-solving; goal-setting and evaluation; policy-making; implementation; and enforcement.

More visible partnerships must be an essential ingredient in any valid, ongoing dialogue on, or initiative in, multicultural education. This is because more visible partnerships is a form of redress that will give exposure upfront to that unheard point of view – the minority perspective. Up to the present time, this minority viewpoint has been nothing more than a suppressed scream clamouring for a new order in our rapidly shrinking global village.

In addition, more visible partnerships is a concrete recognition of the special experience of people of colour. Only those who have been oppressed and repressed in a white-dominated society can ascertain whether a proposed action will really help to eliminate racism or merely allow it to continue in a new form (National Education Association Publication, 1973).

What doctor would attempt to treat a malady without first asking the patient for a complete rundown of symptoms and ailments felt? More visible minorities have, of necessity, developed over the years an acute awareness and in-depth knowledge of the problems that plague them (Head, 1975). Yet, again and again, they see consultations taking place, committees being appointed, conferences arranged, reports written, hierarchies organized (or re-organized) and spokesmen named, without involvement in the smallest way, directly or indirectly, of groups or individuals from among them. This happens, even where their interests are central to the discussion. How, they ask, can policies formulated under such circumstances possibly take proper and true account of their needs (Rampton, 1981)? It is high time that more visible minorities stop being the objects of other people's histories and studies, and start becoming subjects and true protagonists in their own realities. Too long have others pleaded for them! It is time for them to plead their own cause.

Community involvement is already accepted as a contributing factor to multicultural education in the recommendations of a plethora of existing reports and studies (*Le comite sur l'ecole et les communautes culturelles*, 1985).

But let us examine the nature of that involvement. While policy makers and administrators have been anxious to tap the very considerable reservoir of talent and experience that is available in our respective communities, especially in response to projects initiated from within the established bureaucracy, they have shown no similar disposition to involve the same communities into the implementation of such projects (Organization for Caribbean Canadian Initiatives, 1984). Traditionally, more visible minorities are *not* plugged in at important decisionmaking levels. They do not have ready channels for ensuring qualitative input in policy planning and implementation. Their involvement has all too often been limited to predetermined roles for which the script has been already written:shallow tokenism, last-minute window-dressing, afterthought rubber-stamping and meaningless formalities. More visible minorities too frequently have been excluded from the boardrooms of power and authority on the basis of false assumptions, inane excuses, or the most touted fallacious pretext, that "more visible minorities cannot be trusted to be objective or impartial." And so, we carry on, business as usual, speculating, diagnosing, examining, studying, implementing and remedying, without once ever consulting the victims. To put it bluntly, we are virtually "doctoring" without ever having asked the patient: "What is the problem?"

More visible partnerships necessitates a break from the old practice of systematic exclusion and subordination. More visible partnerships means partnerships with more visible minorities on an equal footing. More visible partnerships means the sharing of power of appraisal, of opportunity and access, of responsibilities, of information, of resources, of perspectives, of feelings. More visible partnerships signifies sharing space – boardroom space, blueprint space, front page space, prime time space.

But, above all, more visible partnerships signifies a change in "mind-set," a refusal to defend automatically the way things are, a political will to come to grips with the necessary distinction between "racist," "non-racist" and "anti-racist." The concept implies taking positive action against majority racism, conscious or unconscious. It means exploring the meaning of being white in a white, racist society. For, as long as the majority fails to examine its motives in the area of race relations and of white privilege, the status quo will be maintained (National Education Association, 1973), cosmetic coverups will prevail and, in typical scapegoat syndrome fashion, non-whites will continue to be perceived as "the problem." Stamping racism out of our society "will require an examination and reorientation of our goals and priorities" (National Education Association, 1973).

Consequently, I am proposing that the majority in our society, whites, will have to develop a new self-concept that will allow them to affirm themselves without having to oppress people of another colour (National Education Association, 1973). The majority will have to come to acknowledge openly the discomfort often felt in race relations and to work to overcome it.This means that inquiries into racial disparities, too often using culturally loaded terms like "culturally disadvantaged," "economically underprivileged" and "socially depriv- ed" will have to be directed more and more towards individual and personal behaviour as well as towards traditional institutional educa- tional policies and practices (Moore, 1984).

While in theory we cherish an ideal of humaneness, our schools continue to perpetuate inhumane standards and norms: biased IQ tests, tracking systems, textbooks, counselling practices and low teacher expectations. There is a split between ideals and practices. To date, failure to eliminate racial discrimination has been the rule rather than the exception (National Education Association, 1973). More visible part- nerships, therefore, has very special implications in our schools.First and foremost, they imply a willingness to acknowledge the reality and legitimacy of non-white Canadians in order to reformulate approaches to problem-diagnosis and problem-solving (Cheek, 1977). *De facto* and *de jure* segregation, along with slavery, ridicule of skin colour, hair and facial features; rejection of ethnic culture; cultural genocide; and genocidal warfare, form the roots of the black and native experience in North America. To attempt to implement an anti-racist policy while ignoring these roots is tantamount to counselling a deaf mute without understanding sign language (Cheek, 1977).

More visible partnerships implies that prejudice and discrimination must be addressed as right versus wrong or legal versus illegal issues, or as situations of inequality remote from many people's experience (Buchignani, 1984). More visible partnerships will no longer permit policy approaches in schools to be given over to romanticizing the hardships of slavery or to sentimentalizing racism, poverty and injustice. These should not be unduly over-emphasized, but neither should they be played down to the point of extinction.

With more visible partnerships, helping agents or interveners will have to cease their allegiance to "traditional" approaches taught to them in white schools, by white teachers and based on theoretical assumptions standardized on white populations (Cheek, 1977). Multicultural education policies must present a clear challenge to assumptions of a white-dominated society, the false sense of superiority it provides to white youngsters and the self-hatred it encourages in non-white youngsters (Moore, 1979). In short, the flesh-coloured band-aid approach – that is, an absence of, or obliviousness to, interracial discussion – will have to resolutely be set aside (Cheek, 1977). It is very difficult to present a neutral teaching or analysis of race relations, to stress facts without directly challenging values. A discussion of race must be presented, not from an abstract sociological, historical or economic perspective, but from a psychological perspective that is meaningful to students and conducive to an eventual shifting of values (Buchignani, 1984). White teachers will be obliged to recognize that they are not competent, by themselves, to make these crucial decisions or carry out such initiatives on their own; but that they must enlist the aid and guidance of adult members of the communities in question (Buchignani, 1984). The fact remains that because most whites are miseducated or not educated at all about blacks and other non-white people, they end up filling in their lack of knowledge with impulsive guesses and intuitive assumptions. Strategies aimed at eliminating intolerance in majority group children, but which at the same time negatively affect the self-concept of visible minority children will have to be abandoned (Buchignani, 1984). Agents of change, well-intentioned do-gooders and self-proclaimed experts will also have to relinquish the false and popular belief that attitude changes should be promoted with deference to whites so that they will not be "turned off" by the whole thing (Thomas, 1984).

Confusing words make for confusing thoughts. In truly more visible partnerships, there will be no basis for convenient confusion between up-front exposure and window-dressing; participation and imposition; consultation and rubber-stamping; cooperation and exploitation; empathy and sympathy; speaking with and speaking for; listening to and telling; letting do and doing for.

Blacks, native peoples and others of non-white background will no longer have to watch powerlessly as people dismiss their efforts to change the rules of the social game by calling them impudent, impolite, arrogant, hostile, aggressive, abrasive or difficult to get along (Cheek, 1977). More concretely, more visible partnerships will ensure:

1) that multicultural education is not limited solely to a discussion of "cultural" or "ethnic" diversity;
2) that the "colour-blind" without reference to colour – is discarded as a fallacy, since colour is an essential part of every non-white person's experience;
3) that the good will and good intentions alone do not put anyone's actions beyond the pale of objective critique;
4) that no argument expounding the merits of a literary "classic" is strong enough to invalidate or justify its racist treatment of any person of colour;
5) that concern about the cultural content taught in our schools not be dismissed by groundless accusations of censorship;
6) that humour no longer be tolerated at the deliberate expense of ethnics;
7) that those who argue in favour of the harmlessness of such words as "nigger" should be made to realize that such racist epithets are offensive not only to blacks but also to whites;
8) that, just as we no longer teach that the world is flat, so should we no longer put focus on racist "anti-slavery" documents that speak of the evils of slavery. Rather, we should now be teaching children about race equality and social justice.

References

Banfield, B. (1981). Racism and sexism in teaching materials. Montreal: Report of the Education Conference of the Congress of Black Women of Canada.

Black Community Task Force on Education. (1978). *Final report on the aspirations and expectations of Quebec's black community in respect to education.* Montreal: Report submitted to the Superior Council of Education's Committee on Interconfessional and Intercultural Affairs.

Buchignani, N. (1984). Educational strategies to increase racial tolerance. In *Currents:*

Readings in race relations. Toronto: The Urban Alliance on Race Relations, 13-20.

Cheek, D.K. (1977). *Assertive black ... puzzled White. A black perspective on assertive behaviour*. San Luis Obispo, Calif.: Impact Publishers Inc.

Citron, A.F. (1977). *The "rightness" of "whiteness." The world of the white child in a separated society*. Detroit: Wayne State University, Office of Urban Education.

Clairmont, D.H. and Magill, D.W. (1974). *Africville: The life and death of a Canadian Black community*. Toronto: McClelland and Stewart.

Coleman, M. (Ed.) (1977). *Black children just keep on growing*. Alternative curriculum models for young black children. Washington: Black Child Development Institute.

Council on Interracial Books for Children. *Bulletin*. Published eight times yearly. 1841 Broadway, New York: Council on Interracial Books for Children.

Council on Interracial Books for Children. (1975). *From racism to pluralism*. (Script). New York: Foundation for Change Inc.

Council on Interraccial Books for Children. (1977). *Stereotypes, distortions and omissions in U.S. history textbooks*. New York.

Currents: Readings in Race Relations. Magazine published quarterly. Toronto: Urban Alliance on Race Relations.

Dixon, B. (1978). *Catching them young: 1. Sex, race and class in children's*. (Fiction). London: Phito Press Ltd.

Freire, P. (1981). *Education for critical consciousness*. New York: Continuum Publishing Company.

Freire, P. (1978). *Pedagogy in process. The letters to Guinea Bissau*. London: Writers and Readers Publishing Cooperative.

Freire, P. (1968). *Pedagogy of the oppressed*. New York: The Seabury Press.

Harding, V. (1981). *There is a river: The black struggle for freedom in America*. New York: Harcourt Brace Jovanovich.

Head, W.A. (1975). *The black presence in the Canadian mosaic. A study of perception and the practice of discrimination against blacks in Metropolitan Toronto*. Submitted to the Ontario Human Rights Commission by Wilson Head and Geri Lee. Toronto: Ontario Human Rights Commission.

Hill, D.G. (1977). *Human rights in Canada: A focus on racism*. Ottawa: Canadian Labour Congress.

Institutional racism in American society: A primer. (1970). Palo Alto, California.

Jeffcoate, R. (1979). *Positive image: Toward a multiracial curriculum*. London: Writers and Readers Cooperative in association with Chameleon Books.

Kehoe, J.W. (1984). *A handbook for enhancing the multicultural climate of the school*. Vancouver: Western Education Development Group, Faculty of Education, University of British Columbia.

King, E.W. (1980). *Teaching ethnic awareness. Methods and materials for the elementary school*.Santa Monica, Calif.: Goodyear Publishing.

Kirp, O.L. (1979). *Doing good by doing little: Race and schooling in Britain*. London: University of California Press.

Leinwand, G. (General Editor) (1972). *Problems of American society: Racism*. New York: Pocket Book.

Macmillan Publishing Company. (1975). *Guidelines for creating positive sexual and racial images in educational materials*. New York: Macmillan Publishing.

Marable, M. (1983). *How capitalism underdeveloped Black America*. Boston: South End Press.

294

Moore, R.B. (1979). *Racism in the English language. A lesson plan and study essay.* New York: Council on Interracial Books for Children.

Moore, R.B. (1984). School systems perpetuate racism and don't know it. Can we deal with it? In *Multiculturalism, racism and the school system.* Addresses given at a Canadian Education Association Seminar, Toronto: Canadian Education Association.

Morrison, L. (1976). *As they see it.* A Race Relations Study of Three Areas from a Black Viewpoint. London: Community Relations Commission.

National Education Association. (1973). *Education and racism.* An Action Manual. Washington, D.C.: National Education Association.

Organization for Caribbean Canadian Initiatives. (1984). Brief presented to the Special Committee on Visible Minorities. In *Currents, visible minorities: invisible.*

The Evaluation of Educational Provisions for Culturally Different Children: Some Issues

Ernest Cheng

Often, educators confuse the evaluation of educational provisions for culturally different children with the evaluation of educational programs designed for specific sub-groups of the culturally different. When asked *how* their school or district is meeting the needs of culturally different children, they often answer by pointing to *what* specific programs, past or present, were or are being offered.

It is by choice that this paper concerns not only the evaluation of educational programs which purport to be multicultural, but the evaluation of educational provisions of which programs are a part. The concept of program connotes a series of activities that tends to be formal and highly organized, narrow in focus, and has predetermined beginning and end points. Conventionally, program evaluation measures program outcomes and compares them to program objectives. To the extent that the outcomes represent some acceptable level of learning or change, the program is judged as successful. When programs, not educational provisions, are the objects of evaluation, important issues, such as the scope of the program, the stability of program effects over time and unplanned program effects, are seldom addressed. By choosing to focus on the evaluation of educational provision – that is, all methods, materials, programs, and curricula – one is forced to ask the broader, possibly more fundamental questions regarding the quality and quantity of educational provisions, the efficiency in program delivery, or, simply, whether or not the children concerned are being well served by their schools.

It is also by design that this paper concerns not any specific sub-group within the culturally different, such as ESL/D or immigrant children, but all "culturally different" children. In this paper, the term "culturally different children" is used loosely to represent all those students who share a unique set of needs that arise primarily as a result of their and/or their family's cultural transition. While these students share the general set of learning, social and emotional needs with their counterparts who have been socialized principally within the dominant culture (Beck, 1975), they possess an added, more specific set of needs that is clearly the result of cultural transition. It is in this sense that these students are "different." This broad concept of the culturally different child, then, encompasses at least the following categories of students:

– recent immigrants who, as a result of cultural transition, exhibit a specific set of learning needs (language deficits, basic concepts necessary for learning in Canadian schools) as well as social and emotional needs (to adjust to differences in social awareness, behaviour, appearance, values, concepts of time, work, child-adult relationships, literacy, competition, and so on);
– not so recent immigrants who have been in Canada for a period of time, but continue to exhibit a specific set of needs that has arisen out of their and/or their family's cultural transition;
– those born in Canada who were raised in homes whose values are quite different from the dominant Canadian culture, and who exhibit a specific set of needs arising out of their family's cultural transition.

Clearly, few multicultural school programs have all these categories of students as target groups. Therefore, it is unrealistic for anyone to expect the needs of culturally different children *as a group* to be met through formal multicultural school programs. Instead, one must look to the regular school curriculum and the everyday school experience, where much of the coping by these students takes place, and assess the extent to which their needs are addressed. The most that can be expected of multicultural school programs is that they augment whatever impetus the school curriculum has generated in providing a truly multicultural education. Evaluation of multicultural school programs is necessary because one needs to know which programs best complement the existing school curriculum and how effective they are, before committing large sums of money to their implementation (Kehoe, 1984). However, evaluating the success of a school in meeting the needs of their culturally different students must go *beyond* the evaluation of a few, mostly extra-curricular multicultural programs. As has been mentioned before, focus must also be directed on evaluating the educational provisions for multicultural education. The issues of scope of multicultural programs, of stability of their longterm effects and of unplanned program effects, which so often have not been raised, need to be addressed in any evaluation of educational provisions for the culturally different.

Scope of Multicultural Programs

The scope of an educational program is said to be narrow: 1) if the number of students who participate in it is only a small sample of the total number of students who could have benefitted from participation; 2) if the objectives of a program indicate that it is designed to meet only a small subset of needs of the target population; or 3) if the program is of very short duration, only minimally affecting the rest of the school year when the program is not being implemented.

Current multicultural programs in Canadian schools tend to be narrow in scope. Many of the cultural sharing and cultural appreciation programs, the so-called "song-and-dance routine," deal only with superficial phenomena. Many are "events" of short duration, such as caravans and international days. Programs designed to combat racism and discrimination or "problem oriented" multicultural programs, are typically short-term and intermittent (McLeod, 1984). Language acquisition and remediation programs, such as ESL/D, are singular in objective, that of language learning. Heritage Language Programs and Third Language Programs, available in only a small number of school districts, are designed for highly specific target groups.

The narrow focus of existing multicultural school programs is attributable to a number of reasons. First and foremost is the narrow definition schools have of their roles. Schools have traditionally viewed their primary responsibility as the teaching of basic skills and the inculcation of values that have been deemed by the dominant culture to be important for the maintenance of society. It is under this general rubric that most educational programs for the culturally dissimilar are conceived. Since these students do not yet possess the necessary language skills and values, schools see their task as that of bringing about linguistic and cultural assimilation. For this reason, educational provisions in Canada for culturally different children largely have been limited to remedial language instruction. Cultural sharing and cultural maintenance, while considered by a large segment of the educational community to be worthwhile goals, are thought best pursued outside the confines of the school (Day and Shapson, 1981; Livingstone and Hart, 1981).

A second reason for the narrowness of present multicultural programs is the tendency to define the needs of culturally different children very narrowly. Schools readily admit the adjustment needs of recent immigrants, particularly those from non-English, non-French backgrounds. But when these students show some success in their adjustment, especially in terms of language competency, they are soon "forgotten" as if their needs have suddenly been met. Graduates of ESL/D programs who have been mainstreamed are considered to be "just like the other children," even though ESL/D teachers know that, in fact, these children's needs have not simply disappeared but may have found expression in other forms. The problem may be that multicultural programs like most other programs in education, operate on a "deficit model." Inasmuch as the culturally different have reduced the gap in language and values, the programs are perceived to have accomplished their task.

Of course, the two reasons discussed above are really two sides of the same coin. Together, they reflect the continued dominance of the Anglo-conformity model as an operationalization of Canadian multiculturalism by schools (Young, 1979), and explain why resource allocation formulae often only reflect the surface statuses of these students; i.e., how many recent immigrants are in the school, how many new Canadians are below grade in reading comprehension, etc. While these considerations are salient and important, they leave unaddressed a host of other needs that are also present as a result of a student's cultural transition.

A third reason why school multicultural programs tend to be narrow in scope is because they also tend to be small in scale. Many programs receive no funding, and those fortunate to get some financial support have only "soft" monies to spend, without the benefit of building the necessary costs into the regular school budget.

Smallness in scale and narrowness in scope may also be a result of feelings of inadequacy of many school staffs in dealing with issues of multiculturalism. Despite the national policy since 1971 of multiculturalism within a bilingual framework, no mandatory teacher training in the area of multiculturalism has been initiated at either the pre-service or in-service levels. The fear of not receiving support from fellow teachers and administration; the perception by some that they are not qualified to lead multicultural school programs unless they themselves belong to an ethnic minority; the anxiety of venturing into an area that is potentially controversial – all these serve to discourage teachers and administrators from participation and commitment in multicultural school programs.

A fourth reason for the narrow scope of multicultural school programs might be the result of a tendency for culturally different students to concentrate in a few geographic pockets or areas in the school districts. Designing multicultural programs is perceived to be the responsibility of only a few schools rather than of the school board. In the absence of an explicit and clearly-stated school policy on multiculturalism, schools are often left on their own to grapple with issues arising out of their multicultural reality.However, the more these schools attempt to design special multicultural programs, the more likely they are to be identified as "multicultural schools," a label that is not entirely positive in connotation to so many. Uncomfortable with this image of their local school, families from the dominant culture in the local community may want to have their children transferred, resulting in greater ethnic and cultural segregation. That only these schools, with their ethnically pluralistic student population, should provide multicultural programs, and not others, becomes a widely held notion.

If most existing multicultural school programs are indeed narrow in scope, then one needs to consider, in addition to the question of program effectiveness, such questions as: How many students are being served by a particular program? How many students who could have benefitted from this program are not being served by it? What important needs are not being met by the program?

Stability of Long Term Program Effects

Often, multicultural school programs are implemented with a great deal of unproven optimism. While their effectiveness, in the short-term, can be and often is documented, their longterm effects are seldom evaluated. Kehoe, in discussing the evaluation of multicultural school programs, is correct in saying that "it would be very unusual for a program to have longterm effects and not have short-term effects that could be evaluated" (1984, p.145). However, one must also add that it is highly probable for a program to have short-term effects that could be evaluated, but *not* have any longterm effects. What program effects, if any, remain with the students over time? How reliable are the short-term effects? These are crucial questions because for multicultural school programs to be valuable, their effects should not reflect only temporary and superficial behavioural changes. Most programs should aim at developing important life skills or effecting changes to deep-seated attitudes and values.

It may be suggested that practical considerations render the evaluation of longterm program effects unfeasible. Few programs, some argue, are funded long enough to benefit from formative, systematic data collection. Typically, simple surveys are administered at the conclusion of a program to gauge program effectiveness before the axe of funding falls. In other words, the nature of funding for these programs demands immediate program results. One might argue, however, that if the only positive effects of a program are of a short-term nature, its demise may not be any great loss. Educators are only fooling themselves if they put so much faith into unproven programs.

There are other evaluation obstacles to overcome. Like any longitudinal study, there is the problem of tracking the students, not to mention controlling extraneous factors, particularly history and maturation (Campbell and Stanley, 1963). Follow-up programs, designed to reinforce initial learning, also tend to confound summative results.

The problems of measuring children and adolescent attitudes have been well documented in the social psychological literature. Attitude scales are often influenced too much by the ever-changing moods of young students to be reliable. There is the additional complexity of asking sometimes language-deficient children to verbalize their feelings. Questions can be misinterpreted; directions can easily mislead. Finally, demand characteristics may pose a problem to children who have come from educational backgrounds where teachers' expectations were always to be complied with.

However, neither short program duration nor evaluation problems should deter educators from finding out how stable longterm program effects are. If program effects are not stable, one may wish to direct one's school resources to other programs that have more lasting effects.

Unanticipated Program Effects

To state the objectives of a program is not to say that they will necessarily be attained . Similarly, to include a finite set of objectives is not to say that *only* these objectives will be fulfilled. Programs often effect important, unanticipated consequences than anticipated ones (Merton, 1968). When program developers are preoccupied with certain expected outcomes, other unexpected outcomes may be overlooked. For instance, programs designed to help socially inhibited immigrant students improve their relations with school peers may impart an added, though unintended, message regarding their personal worth. Language remediation programs may have the benevolent intention of changing a "non-standard dialect" while at the same time sending the students the subtle message that their dialect lacks sophistication. A staff training workshop in the area of multicultural education, when not handled carefully, may alienate teachers who are not attending the workshop (whether or not attendance is of their own choice). While the workshop may succeed in generating interest among the participants, the unforeseen antagonism of other staff members may prevent implementation of any new ideas. Unless the program evaluator is mindful of unanticipated consequences as well as anticipated ones, overall program effectiveness cannot be adequately assessed.

A multicultural school program may also succeed or fail because of a number of accompanying conditions. What prerequisite conditions must be present before the program can commence? What kinds of skills must program facilitators have? Is administrative support necessary? A program may fail, not because the program itself is problematic, but because of extraneous factors. Conversely, a program may succeed, not because it is intrinsically sound, but because of some hidden unforeseen factors.

Assessment of Educational Needs of the Culturally Different Child

Implicit in the recommendation to include all culturally different children into an evaluation of educational needs are two assumptions: that, due to cultural transition, a unique set of needs is commonly shared, and that these needs should be met by the school. Educational provisions for the culturally different should not be limited to a few "window dressing" multicultural school programs. Rather, an awareness of these needs must pervade the entire curriculum. Resource allocation formulae should not be based simply on the number of "new" immigrants in the school, newness being defined as an arbitrary number of years, say two or three. Policy-makers should not assume that children born in Canada from culturally different homes, or not-so-new immigrant students who have lived in Canada for a certain length of time, have the same needs as their counterparts who have been socialized principally within the dominant culture. Policy-makers should refrain from these assumptions, even though such assumptions are politically expedient in a period of restraint in educational spending.

Instead, educators must return to the more fundamental concern of student needs and determine to what extent these needs are being met. Educational provisions for the culturally different must be tied to a comprehensive needs assessment, taking into consideration general learning needs, not just needs of language acquisition; needs arising out of social and psychological adjustment, not just linguistic adjustment; needs to teach and contribute, not just to learn and receive. In short, educational provisions for the culturally different must take a developmental perspective; that is, to consider students learning, interacting and eventually contributing to an evolving Canadian culture. It is only then that Canadian education can truly be called multicultural.

Evaluating Educational Provisions

Unlike programs, which come in "neat packages," educational provisions are all-encompassing. They imply the sum total of methods, materials, programs and curricula. Therefore, evaluation takes on much greater complexity. However, educational implications in the evaluation of educational provisions for the culturally different differ within the levels of the educational hierarchy. At the school board level, implications tend to be of a policy nature; at the classroom level, they are mostly of a pedagogical nature.

Conclusion

Almost a decade ago, when the Toronto Board of Education's Work Group on Multiculturalism sampled the opinions of over a hundred educators, they found that "although there appears to be widespread *general* agreement about the need for multiculturalism....basic differences can be seen when people begin to talk about it specifically" (1976, p.90). The report described five conceptually distinguishable interpretations of multiculturalism whereby most of the differences in opinion could be classified.

One might suspect that a concensus on the exact meaning of multiculturalism is still lacking today. The work of Young (1978) has demonstrated very clearly that the many different conceptualizations of multiculturalism will remain, since they represent fundamentally different conceptualizations of what people consider normative in the social organization of an ethnically, racially and culturally heterogeneous society such as Canada. The diversity in the nature and purpose of multicultural school programs today reflects the continued different conceptions. On the one hand, those who want Anglo-conformity will exclusively advocate those school programs that lead to linguistic and cultural assimilation. On the other hand, those who hold dearly the promise of cultural pluralism will continue to support cultural maintenance programs. Without agreement as to what interpretation of multiculturalism is most functional to multicultural reality of Canada, educational provisions are often left to individual educators.

Program developers with different conceptions of multiculturalism will continue to design programs consistent with their conceptions. Since involvement in many of these programs is voluntary, the programs will tend to attract like-minded participants. In the absence of clear direction, those who stand to lose the most are the students.

This paper does not purport to be neutral with respect to the different conceptualizations of multiculturalism. On the contrary, the author's bias is clear. However, the main argument of this paper is that, regardless of one's value orientation and conceptualization of Canadian multiculturalism, the needs of the students must come first. The dilemma in multicultural education is the difficulty in ensuring equal educational opportunity for all, when the schooling establishment is one that was created to serve mainly the dominant culture. Equal educational opportunity exceeds equal schooling; it implies a commitment to maximize the personal potential of each child according to his or her needs. These needs include the cognitive, the affective and the physical. Implicit in this view is the acknowledgement that the psychological well-being of a child is a prerequisite to self-actualization. Tied to that psychological well-being is the preservation and cultivation of the child's ethnic, racial and cultural heritage.

This is not to say that a "pathological model" should operate in a school. The culturally different child is special, only because all children in the school are special. The resources, goods and services in the educational sector should be fairly distributed. Fairness, however, does not mean that each child receives the same or equal amount. Rather, it means that each is given an amount proportional to his or her needs. Once again, it must be stressed that the needs of the child is central to all educational provisions.

References

Bancroft, G. (1975). Teacher education for the multicultural reality. In A. Wolfgang

304

(Ed.), *Education of immigrant students: Issues and answers*. Toronto: Ontario Institute for Studies in Education.

Beck, C. (1975). Is immigrant education only for immigrants? In A. Wolfgang (Ed.), *Education of immigrant students: Issues and answers*. Toronto: Ontario Institute for Studies in Education.

Campbell, D. and Stanley, J. (1963). *Experimental and quasi-experimental designs for research*. Chicago: Rand McNally.

Day, E. and Shapson, S. (1981). *Multiculturalism: A survey of school districts in British Columbia*. Vancouver: Simon Fraser University, Faculty of Education (mimeo).

Gibson, M. (1976). Approaches to multicultural education in the U.S.: Some concepts and assumptions.*Anthropology and Education Quarterly*, 7(4), 7-18.

Kehoe, J. (1984). Achieving the goals of multicultural education in the classroom. In R. Samuda, J. Berry and M. Laferriere (Eds.), *Multiculturalism in Canada: Social and educational implications*. Toronto: Allyn and Bacon.

Livingstone, D. and Hart, D. (1981). *Public attitude toward education in Ontario, 1980*. Toronto: Ontario Institute for Studies in Education.

McLeod, K. (1984). Multiculturalism and multicultural education: Policy and practice. In R. Samuda, J. Berry and M. Laferriere (Eds.), *Multiculturalism in Canada: Social and educational implications*. Toronto: Allyn and Bacon.

Merton, R. (1968). *Social theory and social structure*. New York: Free Press.

National Study of School Evaluation. (1973). *Evaluation guidelines for multicultural/ multiracial education*. Arlington, Virginia: National Study of School Evaluation.

Wilson, J. (1984). Multicultural programmes in Canadian education. In R. Samuda, J. Berry and M. Laferriere (Eds.), *Multiculturalism in Canada: Social and educational implications*. Toronto: Allyn and Bacon.

Work Group on Multiculturalism. (1976). *We are all immigrants to this place*. Toronto: Toronto Board of Education.

Young, J. (1978). Education in a multicultural society: What sort of education? What sort of society? *Canadian Journal of* Education, 4(3), 5-21.